BRITISH ECONOMY
OF THE
NINETEENTH CENTURY

BRITISH ECONOMY
OF THE
NINETEENTH CENTURY

Essays by
W. W. ROSTOW

OXFORD
AT THE CLARENDON PRESS
1948

Oxford University Press, Amen House, London E.C. 4

EDINBURGH GLASGOW NEW YORK TORONTO MELBOURNE
WELLINGTON BOMBAY CALCUTTA MADRAS CAPE TOWN

Geoffrey Cumberlege, Publisher to the University

PRINTED IN GREAT BRITAIN
AT THE UNIVERSITY PRESS OXFORD
BY CHARLES BATEY PRINTER TO THE UNIVERSITY

PREFACE

THE investigations which these essays reflect had their origin in 1934, when I was an undergraduate at Yale. They were pursued there in 1938–9 as a graduate student, as well as at Oxford (1936–8) and as a Social Science Research Council Fellow in New York City (1939–40). Along this way many have helped. At Yale, Wallace Notestein, David Owen, Stanley Pargellis, Alvin Johnson, Charles Cole, and the late James Harvey Rogers; at Oxford, Humphrey Sumner, A. B. Rodger, W. M. Allen, and R. F. Bretherton, with memorable encouragement in the spring of 1938 from M. M. Postan and the late Eileen Power; and then, in New York, my collaborators A. D. Gayer, Isaiah Frank, and Anna Schwartz. In the excursion into politics, of Chapter VI, I hope to have profited from the friendly and occasionally sceptical observations of colleagues in the Faculty of Modern History at Oxford, and from the fellowship of the Stubbs Society.

Chapters III and IV, the former having been somewhat extended, and the latter elaborated in the Appendix, first appeared in the *Economic History Review*, the editors of which have kindly permitted their republication. The author is similarly indebted to the courtesy of the *Journal of Economic History*, where Chapter V was published; and to *Economic History*, for permission to reprint Chapter VII. Chapter VIII, here re-edited, formed part of the volume *The Economist 1843–1943*, published by the Oxford University Press in 1943. The substance of Chapters I, II, and VI was delivered before the London School of Economics in May 1947.

A special debt is owed to those who encouraged the pursuit of this field when its shape was only dimly perceived: R. M. Bissell, E. V. Rostow, and my mother.

W. W. R.

THE QUEEN'S COLLEGE,
OXFORD
May 1947

CONTENTS

INTRODUCTION

THESE essays are unified in two senses. They all concern the British economy over the period 1790–1914, and they represent aspects of an effort to combine the disciplines of economic theory and history. From the limited perspective of the author this is a collection of exercises in method, a fact reflected in the grouping of its chapters.

The period in British economic history from the end of the War of American Independence to the beginning of the First World War lends itself to unified study, in several respects. In the first place, data are available throughout which permit its treatment in fairly uniform analytic terms. The statistics improve as the century wears on, and the *Economist* is available after 1843. But before that date Tooke, Macpherson, and the *Annual Register*, as well as the parliamentary papers, make it possible to answer, in first approximation at least, many of the economist's questions. The data are sufficient to treat the years of the French wars with a degree of refinement not very much less than is possible for the decade before 1914. It seemed likely that this might be said, as well, of earlier periods in the eighteenth century; although the data have not yet been so fully mobilized.

Secondly, the period is unified by the fact that it contains the era of British industrialization. The seeds of the Industrial Revolution and of Britain's economic primacy can, of course, be traced several centuries behind 1790; but taking as the standard of demarcation not qualitative similarity of historical process, against which virtually no line of demarcation in history holds up, but, rather, the absolute and relative scale of the quantities involved, then the period around 1790 is a satisfactory point of departure for the study of modern industrial Britain.

Third, despite war and the often cataclysmic developments in various parts of the world which transformed the environment of the British economy, its institutional setting was reasonably constant. With occasional exceptions the principal economic decisions affecting transactions at home and abroad were made by individuals or by private institutions acting on the profit motive. Over this era Britain was a capitalist country, in a fairly whole-hearted way.

These considerations, which give a rough historical unity to the century and a quarter, commend themselves to the economist as well as to the historian. Here is a laboratory for the theorist concerned to test his hypotheses: spacious, varied, and, despite gaps in data, sufficiently documented for the filling, in first approximation at least, of many of the more interesting empty boxes. And the value of that laboratory is not likely to be diminished by the nature of the problems that will concern the economist over, let us say, the next decade in Great Britain or in the United States. It appears possible that the era of planning which confronts us will, in the end, attach a greater premium to the tools of classical economics, and their recent extensions, than the pathological inter-war years. We are back, and if we are reasonably forehanded we can stay, in a time when the assumption of full employment is legitimate, and scarcity is real. We are concerned with productivity, capital formation, and long-run rates of growth, as well as with the prevention of unemployment. To an understanding of the problems of our times a reconsideration of the British and the world economy of the nineteenth century may contribute.

In no sense do these essays constitute a complete history or analysis of the British economy over the years 1790–1914. At the minimum a satisfactory account, in the terms envisaged here, would include a full narrative of the kind illustrated by Chapter IX; a series of essays, like Chapters III and IV, covering each of the five trend periods; and a much expanded and refined consideration of the issues tentatively explored in Chapters I and II. In addition it might well contain an extension of the analysis pursued in Chapter V, to cover the years from 1850 to 1914; and a more systematic analysis of the course of political history than the speculative suggestions of Chapter VI.

The author has participated in the preparation of a detailed study of the early years of this era, 'The Growth and

Fluctuations of the British Economy, 1790–1850', directed by Dr. Arthur D. Gayer. It is hoped that this work will soon be published. It incorporates a narrative, similar in construction to Chapter IX, as well as detailed analytic essays, and a full treatment of available statistical data with the techniques developed at the National Bureau of Economic Research. Chapter V stems from this study, as well as portions of Chapters I and II. The author's unpublished doctoral thesis, 'British Trade Fluctuations, 1868–1896: A Chronicle and a Commentary' (Yale University Library), includes a narrative for the indicated years.[1] From that thesis Chapters III, IV, and IX derive. In 1935–6 a narrative of the period 1896–1914 was written (also unpublished), from which materials entering Chapters I, II, and the Appendix were drawn. These references should not be taken to imply the author's belief that adequate short-period narratives now exist for the British economy over the indicated years; nor is he anxious to stake a claim, as is the occasional custom of Introductions. It seems possible, merely, that knowledge of these manuscripts may be of use to those concerned with the field.

Whether the approach to the materials of history used here is of intrinsic interest is left to the exposition itself, rather than to an explicit excursion on method. From its beginnings in the nineteenth century the modern study of economic history has been accompanied by a virtually continuous counterpoint of methodological discussion and controversy; and in recent years its literature has been fortunately enriched by the inaugural lectures of the professors of economic history at Cambridge, Oxford, and the London School of Economics. It seems proper that this should be so, for the economic historian can evade less easily than his fellows the formal, the philosophical problem of the relation of theory to history. With all its imperfections, and its tendency to shift focus with each generation, economic theory is too useful a corpus of thought wholly to be ignored, either in setting up standards of relevance, for the organiza-

---

[1] An early version of this study, covering the years 1868–86, is deposited in the Bodleian.

tion of economic data, or in explaining the course of economic events. If theory is not used consciously and explicitly, it enters historical analysis implicitly. All this would now be widely agreed. The task of combining economic theory and history would be regarded as mainly technical rather than philosophical.

These essays represent four distinct applications of theory to history. First is the type of short-period narrative illustrated by Chapter IX. Any attempt to describe, in a co-ordinate way, the short-period movements of a whole economy is likely to prove clumsy. The economy consists of various related strands: the money market, the long-term capital market, the various industrial and commercial markets, the labour market, &c. If one is to examine each, some form of doubling back in time seems unavoidable. The not wholly satisfactory solution employed in Chapter IX is to take one phase of a general cyclical movement as the chapter unit; to divide the economy into four sectors; to describe successively the course of events within each; and to unite the whole with a general introductory section, and with liberal cross-references. This solution seems superior to a year by year chronicle. But the short-period history of an economy, whatever its virtues, is difficult to present with grace.

Within each section the story is told against a background of basic statistics. The aim of the narrative is to explain the major movements within those statistics, and such other developments of significance which they may fail to reflect. Sharp and occasionally arbitrary judgement is necessary to limit the scale of the narrative; and the aim must be the appropriate illustration, rather than the exhaustive presentation of the evidence.

Theory enters the narrative in several ways. It suggests the structure of narration most likely to yield a whole greater than the sum of its parts; and it supplies standards of relevance by which the evidence can be examined, and selection can be made. In addition, it enters into the explanation of events. But no effort is made to employ theory at a high level of abstraction. The purpose of the narrative is to mobilize the evidence in such a way as to make it capable of generalization, while presenting the movements within the economy as an essentially unique sequence of events. Such narrative can, by no means, answer in itself the more abstract and general questions which interest the economist; for example, those discussed in Chapters I and II. Nor does it supply an alternative to systematic statistical analyses of the data, such as those developed by the National Bureau of Economic Research. On the other hand it should give to the analyst a suggestive sense of the sequence of events by which the less likely hypotheses of causation can be quickly rejected; and for the statistical analyst such knowledge of the uniqueness of his data is necessary before he can judge the significance of formal measures of deviation from average behaviour. Like any other historical construction the narrative should impart to the investigator of higher abstractions a proper caution.

The section of this volume devoted to Analysis (Chapters I–IV) is written on two distinct levels. Chapters I and II examine trends and cycles over the whole period 1790–1914. The views advanced there are, for the most part, tentative. Much further statistical, historical, and even theoretical work must be done before the questions raised can be answered with any great confidence. It was thought of use, however, to set down in highly compressed form certain hypotheses which appear reasonable. The extreme compression of those chapters may have the advantage of revealing lesions in the data and in the analysis which a more spacious exposition might partially conceal. Chapters III and IV, dealing with the Great Depression period, permit greater detail, but they are addressed to a lesser range of issues.

While the level of theoretical abstraction employed is higher than that used in the narrative, it is usually simple, and occasionally crude. This stems from a conscious judgement; namely, that in historical analysis it is unwise to use theoretical concepts of greater refinement than the data which they are designed to inform. Data can be plentiful indeed, without being susceptible of grouping and refinement in such a way as to approximate the abstractions theory would suggest as relevant. The coat must be cut to the cloth; although it would by no means be suggested that the data of nineteenth-century Britain have here been mobilized around the issues raised in final and optimum form.

The two essays of Part III (Chapters VII and VIII) require little explanation. In both cases it was felt that an examination of theoretical concepts, in the context of their application to particular familiar events, was likely to illuminate the character of those concepts. Such a process tends to strip from comparative analysis of economic theories difficulties inherent in special definitions.

The concepts used in Chapter V are an outgrowth of various narrative efforts in short-period economic history, and especially of work on the study directed by Dr. Gayer. The larger and more speculative considerations of Chapter VI proceed from a somewhat wider experience. In 1946–7 the author was privileged to teach American history at Oxford. The structure of analysis set out in Chapter VI, though here applied to Britain, was elaborated in the course of lectures on American political life from 1763 to the present; and it seemed to illuminate the political behaviour, at home and abroad, of many nations in the post-war world, as viewed from the Department of State in 1945–6.

PART I

ANALYSIS

I

TRENDS IN THE BRITISH ECONOMY: 1790–1914

I

BRITISH industrial production, and the national income, did not expand continuously from 1790 to 1914, nor was the trend rate of increase constant. In some phases, further, the trends in commodity prices and interest rates were upward, in others they declined. The rate and the direction of the movement of real wages and the terms of trade varied as well. It is the view here that the diverse movements among the principal variables within the economy can be related to each other in a co-ordinate way, and to the whole character of economic development in Britain, and in the world economy.

In order to examine trend movements the era 1790–1914 is divided into five phases. The first runs from about 1790 to 1815; the second to the end of the forties; the third to 1873; the fourth to 1900; the fifth to 1914. No very special connotations attach to the particular years chosen as points of demarcation. They do roughly mark, however, moments when the direction or rate of movement of certain principal variables within the economy altered; and the periods they contain form useful analytic units for the examination of trends.

The accompanying table (I) sets out annual average percentage rates of change for a number of series which reflect, with greater or lesser accuracy, the movements of certain variables believed relevant to trend analysis. These variables are calculated between five-year averages, rather than between individual years, in order to avoid arbitrary bias due to short-run fluctuations; and the centre year is, in

Analysis

TABLE I

Trends in the British Economy: 1793–1912

The following table gives measurements for annual average percentage rate of change in the case of certain key economic variables within the British economy, on which reasonably accurate quantitative data exist for continuous periods. Except where indicated below the rates are averaged as between five-year intervals centred on the indicated year; e.g. figures for the period ending '1815' represent the rate of change between 1791–5 and 1813–17.

Annual Average Percentage Rate of Change
(plus, unless otherwise indicated)

For period ending	Population U.K.	Total industrial production	Consumers-goods production	Producers-goods production	Volume imports
	%	%	%	%	%
'1815'	1·4	2·1	1·9	2·3	2·6
'1847'	1·1	3·5	3·2	4·4	3·7
'1873'	0·7	3·2	2·6	4·1	4·4
'1900'	0·9	1·7	1·3	2·2	2·8
'1912'	0·9	1·5	1·0	1·9	1·2
'1793–1912'	1·0	2·6	2·2	3·2	3·1

For period ending	Volume exports	Gross barter terms of trade	Yield on Consols	Bank rate	General prices	Real wages		Output per capita employed
						Tucker	Wood	
	%	%	%	%	%	%	%	%
'1815'	4·1	1·6	0·8	..	1·8	−0·5	..	..
'1847'	2·8	−0·8	−1·1	−1·2	−1·4	0·7	..	(0·6)
'1873'	4·9	0·6	−0·05	0·3	0·6	0·6	1·1	1·1
'1900'	1·7	−1·0	−0·7	−0·1	−1·5	1·2	1·3	1·6
'1912'	2·7	1·5	1·5	0·7	1·5	−0·5	−0·5	0·6
'1793–1912'	3·3	..	..	..	..	..	..	..

NOTE: 1. The figures for U.K. population are affected by the rise in the population of Ireland, until the 1840's, and by its subsequent absolute decline. For these purposes the nearest census-year figures (e.g. 1801, 1811, &c.) have been taken. Population for 1791 is roughly calculated at 13·5 million.

2. The statistics for industrial production used are those of Walter Hoffmann, 'Ein Index der Industriellen Produktion', *Weltwirtschaftliches Archiv*, 1934.

3. The statistics for the volume of imports and exports are those of Werner Schlote, *Entwicklung und Strukturwandlungen des englischen Aussenhandels* (Jena), 1938. In the foreign trade calculations '1815' consists of the average figures for 1814–16.

4. The gross barter terms of trade represent the volume of exports over the volume of imports. A 'favourable' movement—that is, an increase in imports with respect to exports—is represented by a decline.

5. The general price indexes used are A. D. Gayer (unpublished) to 1815;

each instance, at or close to the peak year in the proximate major cycle.[1]

It will be noted that the turning-points employed here conform, generally, to those in price trends, which have for long been familiar. The rise in prices during the period of the French wars; the falling trend to the late forties; the rise to 1873; the fall to the late nineties; and the rise to the outbreak of the First World War have, for some time, been the subject of remark and speculation.[2] Although the trend periods chosen here conform to the long movements of prices, the analysis employed is not concerned exclusively, or even primarily, with the level of general prices.

Nor is any considerable attention given to the long-run forces determining the level of the real national income. Its rate of increase, like that of population, to which it closely relates, appears to be subject to laws of growth outside the

---

[1] The net effect of this procedure is to damp, in certain cases, the amplitude of the indicated trend movement; for, in effect, some years from the succeeding trend period are included within each turning-point averaged, except '1847' and '1912'. Since the analysis is primarily concerned with the direction of trend movements rather than their absolute amplitude or rate, this characteristic is not regarded as significant for present purposes. For a more refined analysis of trends the technique of overlapping averages employed by Arthur F. Burns, *Production Trends in the United States since 1870*, would have been more appropriate.

[2] See J. A. Schumpeter, *Business Cycles*, for the most extensive recent discussion of trend periods and their literature; also, N. D. Kondratieff, 'The Long Waves in Economic Life', *Review of Economic Statistics*, 1935, pp. 105–15, translated and digested by W. F. Stolper from 'Die langen Wellen der Konjunktur', *Archiv für Sozialwissenschaft und Sozialpolitik*, 1926, and G. Garvy, 'Kondratieff's Theory of Long Cycles', *Review of Economic Statistics*, 1943.

W. Layton and G. Crowther for the balance of the period (*An Introduction to the Study of Prices*, appendix A, table II).

6. Real wages are calculated from R. S. Tucker's figures representing London artisans only, 'Real Wages of Artisans in London, 1729–1935', *Journal of the American Statistical Association*, vol. xxxi; from 1850 the more general calculations of G. H. Wood (full work) are also presented (reproduced, W. Layton and G. Crowther, op. cit., appendix E, table I). '1847' consists of the average figures for 1850–2.

7. Output *per capita* figures are those of Colin Clark (*National Income and Outlay*, pp. 232 and 247); the rate for the period up to 1847 is limited in the time covered, and is particularly suspect, given the nature of available data. From '1815' to '1847' consists of the rate from 1830–9 to 1840–9; '1873' consists of 1870–6; '1900', of 1894–1903; '1912', of 1911–13.

scope of the present analysis.[1] The focus is, rather, the
complex of forces affecting the course of real wages; and in
exposing those forces emphasis is placed on the scale and
character of investment, the course of interest rates and
commodity prices, and the terms of trade.

Such an investigation would, of course, be much strengthened if adequate data on the national income were available: its real size, composition, and distribution; but the
national-income statistics, in their present form, are inadequate. There are, to be sure, occasional estimates of great
interest for particular years, as far back as the Reverend
Beeke and Patrick Colquhoun in the opening years of the
nineteenth century.[2] But unless national-income estimates
are continuous through time, uniform in construction, and
broken down to appropriate components they are not very
useful for important types of analysis.

II

At its core the theoretical framework employed in this
analysis of trends is exceedingly simple, however complex the
body of fact it is designed to inform. It might be described
as a dynamic version of the elementary theory of diminishing
returns.

In a closed community, with constant population, working
force, and money incomes, with full employment maintained
by private or communal action, with all expenditures except
those on consumption going into productive investment, and
with no changes in knowledge, we would expect prices to
fall, over a period of time, and real wages to rise. We would
also expect the yield on new investment to fall, as the
expected return on new investment fell towards the point

---

[1] The long-run growth-pattern for certain important British series is measured
in S. Kuznets, *Secular Movements in Production and Prices*. See also P. Douglas,
The Theory of Wages, especially chaps. xiii–xv.

[2] Rev. H. Beeke, *Observations on the Produce of the Income Tax*; P. Colquhoun,
Treatise on the Wealth, Power, and Resources of the British Empire, p. 65 for summary
table, pp. 89–101 for detailed calculations. See also R. Giffen, for a survey of
previous estimates to 1889, *The Growth of Capital*; A. L. Bowley, *Wages and
Income in the U.K. since 1860*; and Colin Clark, *National Income and Outlay*,
chap. x.

where known possibilities of new productive investment were exhausted or the return so small that leisure was preferred to further investment outlays.

If such a community were to divert the whole of its income, over and above consumption, to the prosecution of a civil war, or to the building of pyramids or churches, we would expect prices to cease their decline. And if such enterprise were expanded to a scale larger than the previous allocation to new productive investment, we would expect prices to rise and real wages to fall.

Assume that the closed community is an island, devoted exclusively to the production and consumption of wheat, which has been devoting a fixed amount of its labour and other resources to the clearing and planting of additional inferior wheat land, on the island. The land brought into cultivation is progressively less productive; but, nevertheless, the productivity of labour, and the total wheat supply is increasing each year. The wheat price is falling, if at a diminishing rate, so long as the fixed labour supply is not spread so thin that additional increments of land fail to yield some positive increase in production.

Assume, further, that another island is discovered nearby, with virgin soil, of distinctly higher potential productivity. It is found that two years' work by the whole normal investment force is required to clear the first plot on the island, and another year will pass before the first harvest is in. Over the period when the new island is being prepared and planted, the fall in the wheat price and rise in total consumption would cease; and it would be resumed, at an accelerated rate, when the crop from the new island was, at last, harvested. If, excited by the vista, the islanders were to devote an increased proportion of their total effort to clearing the new island, the wheat price would rise over the shortened period of development.

The data are not sufficient, of course, progressively and systematically to relax the assumptions governing this primitive parable to a point closely approximating the turbulent developments of the British economy in the nineteenth century. It is evident that the British economy was not closed;

that the population and working force and money incomes were not constant; that full employment was not continuously maintained;[1] that the proportion of the national income spent for purposes other than consumption varied;[2] and that the state of knowledge was almost constantly enlarged. The parable has been cited, however, because it is central to the subsequent analysis that outlays for purposes other than consumption be distinguished with respect to their being productive or non-productive; and that attention be focused on the relative productivity of the productive outlays, and the quantity of resources and time periods required before they yielded their productive results. It is the view here that the main trends in the British economy, over the period 1790–1914, are best understood in terms of the shifting balance between productive and unproductive outlays; and among types of productive outlays with differing yields and differing periods of gestation.

This approach to the British economy, or to virtually any other economy in modern times, has what is perhaps an important implication for the study of economic history. Much of Britain's investment was foreign investment, related to developments on distant continents, in which Britain participated, but which British initiative did not wholly determine. And the course of events at home, in other respects as well, derived in part from forces generated

---

[1] Chapter II (pp. 46–50), below, examines evidence on the average level of employment in the various trend periods. Significant differences in the level of employment would affect the validity of an analysis which put primary emphasis on the character of investment rather than its volume. No significant distinctions on existing evidence are found.

[2] It seems quite possible that the conclusions set out below may, in the future, be modified somewhat, by the extension and refinement of knowledge concerning the proportion of the national income invested. Adequate data do not now exist for any of the trend periods examined. The most promising calculations available cover the period from the sixties to 1914: for the national income, C. Clark, *National Income and Outlay*; for new investment, P. Douglas, 'An Estimate of the Growth of Capital in the U.K., 1865–1909', *Journal of Economic and Business History*, 1930. Clark speculates briefly about their relationship, op. cit., pp. 272–3. Douglas's interesting calculations do not appear satisfactory for these purposes, however, because they exclude building, and because the procedures followed for capitalizing and deflating the income from capital may well result in bias, as between periods of rising and falling prices and profit margins.

abroad. The fluctuations and trends in Britain were shared, with variations, by most other areas in the world. It is likely that the optimum unit for the study of economic history is not the nation, but the whole inter-related trading area; certainly that is the frame within which many of the most important national, regional, or even industrial problems must be placed, if they are fully to be understood.[1]

III

The trend movements that must be explained, over the period from about 1790 to 1815, are the following: a rapid rise in production, within both industry and agriculture; a substantially greater increase in exports than in imports; a rise in interest rates and prices; a falling tendency in real wages.

The central economic characteristic of these years is that it was a period of war. From that fact the following four consequences may be traced:

1. The establishment of British men regularly in service was raised well over 500,000, perhaps 400,000 more than the peace-time establishment.[2] Depending on the population base taken, the mobilized force constituted

---

[1] An interesting and suggestive study, in terms of the world economy from 1870, is *Industrialization and Foreign Trade* (League of Nations), mainly the work of Folke Hilgerdt.

[2] Colquhoun, op. cit., p. 47, gives the following figures for men in arms in the British Empire in 1814:

		East India Company	
British Army	. 301,000		
Local Militia	. 196,446	British Troops .	20,000
Volunteers, G.B. .	88,000	Native Troops .	140,000
Ireland . .	80,000	Marines . .	913
Colonies .	25,000		160,913
Foreign Troops .	30,741		
	721,187	GRAND TOTAL	1,062,020
Navy . .	147,252		
Marines . .	32,668		
	179,920		

A substantial part of the force based on U.K. was not steadily withdrawn from the labour force. Colquhoun estimated (p. 66) that in 1811 640,500 military men were being fed, in addition to the working population and their families. This would include foreign troops, but exclude that portion of forces overseas subsisting on the land they occupied.

between 3 per cent. and 5 per cent. of the total population and, of course, a much larger proportion of the total working force.

2. The real cost of certain basic commodities rose: imports, because of the circuitous and often dangerous routes followed, the necessity for convoys, and the consequently very large increases in freight rates; foodstuffs, because of the obstruction of imports from the Baltic, and the necessity for diverting resources into expansion of British agriculture caused by this factor in conjunction with a rapidly rising population. The rise in the prices of foodstuffs was accentuated by chronically bad harvests over the war years.

3. Large resources were diverted into ship-building, to replace war losses and to support an artificially expanded foreign trade; into the expansion of dock facilities; into armament manufacture, and to other manufactures consumed by British and Allied armies.

4. Substantial general resources were diverted abroad, by means of loans and subsidies to allies on the Continent.

The British foreign balance was kept in equilibrium, without large bullion movements, by an extraordinary increase in British exports and especially in re-exports.[1]

[1] The extent and significance of the rise in re-exports may be seen from the fact that, whereas the volume of British goods exported, from 1793 to 1815, rose at an annual percentage rate of 3·8 per cent. per annum, total exports, including re-exports, rose at an annual rate of 4·1 per cent. Colquhoun, explaining the failure of this rise, which was at a greater rate than for imports, in value as well as in volume, to yield an influx of bullion, wrote (p. 85): 'On a minute investigation of the British commerce it will be found, that the exports are more valuable than the public documents make them, while the imports are less; and hence the balance is greater in favour of the country than is generally supposed; but in a war so extensive, and with colonies, dependencies, and navies and armies in every quarter of the world, this balance has for the last twenty years been swallowed up by the enormous drafts upon the British treasury for subsidies to foreign princes, for the expenses of the army, navy, and ordnance abroad,—the allowance to British governors and courts of justice, fortifications, and expensive barrack establishments,—the salaries of various officers in the revenue and other civil departments, ramifying in all directions, and amounting to many millions yearly, independently of the payment of the dividends on the public debt due to foreigners. The balance of trade, therefore, is not remitted in bullion in this country in the present state of things, but is actually paid out of the revenues of the country.'

Britain enjoyed a virtual monopoly in West Indian products which, for the most part, were sold through the various entrepot ports: at first Hamburg, and then the arc of peripheral ports, from Scandinavia to the Ionian islands. The profits in this trade, coupled with those in the export of British manufactures, largely financed the war-time outlays abroad. There was, indeed, a great boom in trade; but the resources needed to sustain it, in ships, manpower, and newly constructed docks served simply to meet the deficit in the foreign balance caused by the extent and character of the war effort. They did not generate an equivalent rise in imports for the British economy. Thus exports increase more than imports; that is, the gross barter terms of trade turn unfavourable.

And, on the whole, the behaviour of the variables in the economy follows closely that which one would expect from a shift in investment to what are called, above, unproductive outlays, or to outlays which did not yield fully their productive results within the trend period. The course of the British economy during the French wars conforms well to what textbooks in international trade would call 'a case in capital exports'; or to the pattern of lend-lease.

There was, of course, a very substantial increase in total production, related to and required by the great population increase of this period. These were the years when the effects of abundant American cotton, released by the invention of the cotton gin, in combination with the new textile machinery and the steam engine, began to transform the cotton industry. The volume of exports of British cotton goods rose at an annual rate of 10·6 per cent., from 1793 to 1815. Iron output, freed of its dependence on Swedish ore, also increased rapidly. But on balance the wastes of the war years, and the diversion of resources to uses less productive than those of peace, were so great that the level of real wages could not be fully maintained; and there are evidences, as well, that various types of investment at home languished, under competition from more profitable adventures in agriculture, foreign trade, and the limited portion of industry directly affected by war contracts. H. A. Shannon's index of brick production shows no trend increase over this period, despite the substantial general growth in the economy.[1]

It is easy, in the examination of trends, to lapse into a vocabulary which appears to imply that the movements within the economy were smooth, and at constant rates. This is an incorrect conception for all the trend periods. In the French wars the decade from 1793 to 1803 is dominated by large outlays abroad, and a concomitant boom in foreign trade, based largely on Hamburg.[2] Then there is an interval, to about 1808, when outlays abroad are on a modest scale, trade is inhibited, and a revealing passage occurs, in 1807, when frustrated investors turned briefly to the flotation of joint stock companies at home. Two cycles follow, with peaks in 1810 and 1815, against a background of steadily increasing outlays abroad: the first looking to Latin America, as a means of evading Napoleon's briefly effective warfare against the British balance of payments; the second, to American and continental markets, in successive years (1814, 1815) on the coming of peace. The bulk of the price rise occurred swiftly, in the period up to 1803; and the trend over the next decade was relatively steady. And within the general price-index the cost-reducing processes of the Industrial Revolution were already beginning to bring down the prices of cotton textiles and iron from about the turn of the century.

[1] Average annual brick production for the years 1791–5 and 1813–17 are virtually identical, being, on Shannon's figures, 751 million bricks and 751·2, respectively (*Economica*, 1934, 'Bricks—A Trade Index'). Shannon quotes Mrs. Dorothy George, *London Life in the Eighteenth Century*, p. 79, for evidence that not only the French wars but also previous eighteenth-century wars had limited construction: 'Each war is said to have checked building operations in London; builders' labourers joined the army or navy and materials became dearer, while peace brought a renewed outburst of building.' In 1816 brick production was 673 million; in 1819, exhibiting a typical lag at the cyclical peak (1818), the figure was a new high level of 1,101·6 million, a remarkable post-war 'outburst'.

[2] Short-term movements of the economy during the war years are summarized in 'Adjustments and Maladjustments after the Napoleonic Wars', *American Economic Review*, Supplement, March 1942, by the author. See also 'Trade Cycle Index', pp. 124–5 below.

IV

Perhaps the most suggestive commentary on the trends of the economy during the French wars is their course in the three decades that followed. Without exception higher rates of increase in industrial production prevail than during the war years; and real wages, which actually fell to 1815, rise substantially. Brick production, stagnant in the previous quarter century, leaps forward, at an annual rate of 2·8 per cent., and with it a wide range of domestic investment. As can be seen in Table I, this was the period when the rates of increase in industrial production were at a maximum for the whole era to 1914. These were truly years of Industrial Revolution.

The period between 1815 and 1847 was one of uninterrupted peace for Britain; and there were only minor wars elsewhere. Investment outlays were thus almost wholly productive. Investment was, for Britain, heavily concentrated, too, in enterprises which yielded their cost-reducing results within a fairly short period. The installation of machinery in cotton textiles; the enlargement and improvement of metallurgical plant; the introduction of Nielson's hot blast; the building of bridges, roads, and even of the British railways—all these brought lower real costs; and the period of gestation for such investment was relatively short. It was natural that the price trend should be downward. As a writer in the *Edinburgh Review* asked, in reply to contemporary arguments for national policies of inflation and protection, 'What but the facilitating of production, or, in other words, the reduction of price, is the object of inventions and discoveries of the arts?'[1] And the natural downward trend was strengthened by the tariff reformers, from the twenties onward.

The course of prices was not, of course, downward continuously, or at a constant rate. There was a period of rapid

---

[1] Vol. lv, July 1832, p. 425. The evidence before the Committee on Manufactures (1833) contains substantial data on the decline in real costs over the previous two decades, strikingly similar to that before the Commission on Depression (1885); and in a much wider sense the periods after 1815 and after 1873 are analogous.

decline, beginning in the latter years of war and extending into the twenties; a slower trend decline in the thirties and forties. Each of the major trade cycle expansions yielded, for a part of their duration, upward breaks in the powerful downward trend: in 1818, during the brief post-war boom; in 1825, at the peak of the long expansion of the early twenties; then most notably in the thirties. The great British railway boom of the forties caused only a very slight rise in prices, until bad harvests and the continued American boom, which affected the quantity and prices of British exports, brought prices up in 1847, well after the British cyclical turning point in 1845.[1]

It is significant that the thirties saw the most substantial and sustained rise in prices of this whole trend period. For in that decade a larger proportion of British investment was directed abroad than in any other between the war years and the fifties. This was not, to be sure, the first British adventure in foreign securities in the nineteenth century. Immediately after 1815, with the Government removed as a borrower from the capital markets, greatly developed by the experience of meeting the large requirements for war finance, London had granted loans to various continental countries; and there had been the considerable Latin American flotations of 1824–5. In the thirties, however, a great and protracted wave of 'internal improvements', sponsored by the not wholly reliable American state governments, caught the eye of British promoters and of the broadened investment public.[2] The balance of investment outlays shifted somewhat from home to abroad; and from projects which would yield their cost-reducing results in a relatively short period, to the relatively longer period involved in the opening up of new territories, the building of its canals and roads, and the clearing of its rivers. Thus, for a time, prices rose.

[1] See below, p. 38, n. 3, for the possibility of defining a second cycle in the forties, with a peak in 1847.

[2] For the scale and direction of the land sales, in these years, see W. B. Smith and A. H. Cole, *Fluctuations in American Business, 1790–1860*, pp. 55–8. In terms of the analysis used here it is the whole complex of investment involved in the opening and improving of the new territories which is relevant; not, simply, the portion of that investment financed from London.

But over the period as a whole, not only prices in their downward trend, but the course of interest rates, real wages, and the terms of trade conform roughly to the stylized conception of these three post-1815 decades as a period of intensive domestic development. Interest rates fall; real wages rise; and the terms of trade shift favourably to Britain.

These years, however, have a bad name in economic history. In part that repute stems from factors which do not belong within the scope of this analysis; namely, the conditions of housing and of health in portions of the new industrial cities. In part it stems from intervals of severe unemployment, bad harvests, and high food prices.[1] In part it stems from the unhappy position of portions of the agricultural community, readjusting to the unfavourable position in post-war grain markets. In part, it stems from the pressure on industrial prices and profit margins, imposed by rapidly expanding industrial capacity, exploiting successively more efficient methods, in a régime of relatively free competition. Here, however, the focus of analysis is the rate of change in industrial production, the volume of imports and exports, and the level of real wages. And in terms of these related criteria the period emerges as one of extraordinary development, perhaps the most rapid rate of development of domestic resources throughout the whole of Britain's economic history.

Lower duties on grain imports would, surely, have meant a higher level of real wages; nevertheless, despite a number of difficult years, real wages rose for a rapidly expanding population. This took the form of a relatively lesser decline in money wages than in retail prices. The inflated money wages of the war years, which had inadequately compensated the working classes for the rise in living costs, did fall away, especially in the period of adjustment, immediately following upon the end of war. Costs of living, however, fell to a greater extent. And the calculated rise in Tucker's index for London artisans is supported by a wider range of evidence.[2]

---

[1] See below, Chapter V.
[2] The average annual percentage rate of change for tea consumption was upwards, at the rate of 1·3 per cent., between 1793 and 1815; 2·1 per cent. from

V

The third trend period embraces what is usually referred to, with some considerable ambiguity, as the great mid-Victorian boom, running from about 1850 to the crisis of 1873. As Table I indicates, the rates of growth in production were only slightly less than for the previous trend period. In the other variables we find a worsening in the gross barter terms of trade and a rise in general prices. The interest rates of which continuous record exists exhibit no clear-cut trend movement: the Bank rate, and the open market rate on good three months' bills, in net, rise very slightly; the yield on Consols falls very slightly. All that can be said firmly, from these rough measures, is that the previous downward trend in interest rates was arrested. And, from the sixties, at least, real wages rose.

As a first approximation, the period may certainly be characterized as one in which an increased proportion of the investment outlays, of the world community, went into unproductive ventures, or to ventures which yielded their results only over a long period of time. For Britain this was a notable period of capital exports, concentrated particularly in the fifties and the early seventies.

Taking the world economy as a whole three factors can usefully be distinguished. First, there were wars: principally, the Crimean War; the American Civil War; and the sequence of Prussian campaigns that ended with the French defeat in 1870. By present severe standards these wars—excepting the American Civil War—were minor affairs. They undoubtedly wasted, however, a significant portion of the resources normally available for productive investment, in the years over which they took place, and within the countries directly affected; and these effects were transmitted, through the international markets, to the rest of the world.[1]

1815 to 1847, measurements in each case being between five-year averages centred on the indicated year. For wine consumption the trend figure is minus 2·1 per cent. for the first period, due in part to war-time obstructions in supply, plus 0·9 per cent. for the second. See also J. H. Clapham, *An Economic History of Modern Britain*, vol. i, pp. 560–2; and G. D. H. Cole, *A Short History of the British Working Class Movement*, vol. i, pp. 177–88.

[1] If, in fact, reductions in consumption and in average unemployment com-

Second, there was gold-mining. The economic effects of gold-mining over this era have by no means been fully or satisfactorily explored.[1] In general, however, its consequences are clear. Gold, for those who mined it, was a useful product, capable of exchange for goods and services, including imports. The United States financed a part of its trade deficit and capital imports by mining and exporting gold, as did Australia. India, which absorbed large quantities of the new-mined gold, surrendered for it exports of goods. The real effort required by Australia and the United States in mining gold was quite probably less than that necessary to purchase an equivalent volume of imports by growing and exporting, say, additional wheat or wool or cotton; although there were significant wastes of manpower and resources among the prospectors who did not strike it rich. On the whole, however, it is likely to prove the case, on close investigation, that in terms of the mining area the production of gold was a thoroughly reasonable enterprise, in the nineteenth century.

For the world as a whole, however, gold-mining constituted, in part, a tax on resources, capricious in its incidence, for the maintenance of the gold standard. Leaving aside, for the moment, the requirements of the banking systems for new gold, and its effects on the supply and terms of credit, it is evident that, except in its limited ornamental or industrial uses, gold supplied no service to the world: neither food, shelter, nor clothing. In this limited perspective the pursuit of gold absorbed resources without producing an enlargement or cheapening in supply of commodities or of services. To the extent, of course, that India wanted gold, and was satisfied to surrender other resources for it, and to the extent

pensated fully for the outlay of resources on war and for the destruction of capital caused, then no effect on the course of trends would be expected except for real wages. But this seems very doubtful.

[1] William Newmarch's analysis, in vol. vi, pt. vii, of Tooke and Newmarch, *History of Prices*, remains still the best consideration of this question. See also W. Layton and G. Crowther, *An Introduction to the Study of Prices*, pp. 67–70 (1938 ed.); the excellent discussions in the *Economist*, 1849, pp. 4–5, 320–1; 1850, pp. 1010–11, 1317–18, 1373–4; 1851, p. 1425, 1852, pp. 1, 6–7, 557–8, 1061–2; 1853, pp. 1934, 221–2, 642–3, 985; 1855, pp. 977–9.

that gold elsewhere was used for ornamental or industrial purposes this stricture does not apply.

The issue, then, narrows to the question of whether the banking systems of the nineteenth century required gold on the scale in which it was mined, in order to avoid the imposition, for technical reasons, of deflationary policies. This, too, is a question which deserves further exploration; but the evidence strongly suggests that men in the past have, on the whole, and over a period of time, been sensible enough to adjust their monetary institutions to their requirements.[1] Over the era under consideration here, it seems very doubtful if mankind was crucified on a cross of gold, except, perhaps, that too large a proportion of resources was expended in pursuing and mining it.

Even if one assumes that the new gold was, in fact, required for the successful working of the banking systems of the world, mining would still constitute a tax; a drain on resources from alternative uses. And in this aspect, like a war, or the building of a pyramid, gold was a price-raising factor, quite apart from any possible effects it might have had on central bank reserves, the rates of interest, and the willingness of banking systems to lend.

Nor is there satisfactory evidence that the effect of the new gold on bank lending was of any considerable significance. In this trend period, for example, one cannot trace an effect from the gold influx on short-term interest rates, through bank reserves, prolonging or accelerating cyclical expansions, beyond the point to which they would otherwise have proceeded, or shortening the periods of cyclical depression. Gold-mining in California and Australia, and the concurrent development of those territories in other directions, certainly constituted, at the time, a significant and attractive form of investment; and it was a form of investment tending to raise world prices, both because gold-mining was involved, and because of the considerable period of gestation involved in the opening up of new territories. On the other hand, the strictly monetary effects of the new gold, operating through

---

[1] See especially J. T. Phinney, 'Gold Production and the Price Level', *Quarterly Journal of Economics*, 1933.

central bank reserves and interest rates, do not appear to have been important.

The third great new factor in this trend period was, of course, railway building. Some 21,000 miles of railway-line were laid in the United States in the fifties, firmly binding the north-west to the north-east, on the eve of Civil War: a fact of political and military, as well as economic significance. At the time of the crisis in 1857 it was estimated that fully £80 million in American railway securities were held in Britain. This was also the period when Thomas Brassey crossed the Channel, and with British funds and even some British labour, began laying track on the Continent. In 1852 Brassey held contracts for 264 miles of French line; and later in the decade there was at least one British director on the board of nineteen Continental railway companies.

It is suggested, then, that the upward trend in prices, as well as the trend of the other variables, in the quarter century before 1873 was due mainly to a shift, essentially on a world-wide scale, towards unproductive outlays in war, and in a limited sense, in gold-mining; and to extensive investment, serving to lay railways and to open new territories, which yielded their consequences for the position of supply curves, in individual markets, more fully in the period after 1873 than in the quarter century which preceded it.

As in the other trend periods, the variables did not move continuously. Prices, for example, rise very rapidly from 1852 to 1854; but the trend, from that time until the final stages of the boom of the early seventies, some two decades later, is steady. The pattern of the sixties, like the first decade of the century and the thirties, constitutes in many ways an exception to the main trends of the period within which it lies. The glamorous external developments of the fifties and the early seventies were lacking, inhibited in part by war in the United States, and the various enterprises of Prussia on the Continent. Britain turned, for the time, to homely domestic tasks. There was an expansion in ship-building which doubled the tonnage of steam vessels in British registry between 1860 and 1868. Another 5,000 miles of British railways were laid. And a wide variety of domestic

developments were centred in a company floatation boom,
which crashed in 1866. Whereas the crisis of 1866 was largely
a British phenomenon, those of 1857 and 1873 were world-
wide; and, in this, each conforms to the character of the
expansion which preceded it. It was in this decade, significantly, that real wages resumed their rise. Over the fifties
they had, in net, been stagnant.[1]

The great cyclical expansion, from 1868 to 1873, in many
ways repeated the phenomena of the fifties, with developments external to Britain commanding the stage, especially
in the latter stages of the boom (1871–3). There is, however,
an important exception to this parallelism. The powerful
forces set in motion earlier, to open new grain lands, were
already operative; and in the United States they were
released from the obstructive influence of war. Food prices
rose less than money wages, in the course of the expansion,
and real wages continued the upward course of the early
sixties. But prices in general rose, and exports increased
more rapidly than imports.

[1] The net rise in real wages, over this trend period, breaks the symmetry of the
analysis, in a sense, and constitutes an apparent exception; that is, real wages in
Britain appear to fall during the other two secular periods characterized by war
and extensive or unproductive investment: 1793–1815, and 1900–12. In fact the
analysis used here does not call for an absolute fall in real wages, upon a shifting
in the balance of investment away from productive types of short period of
gestation, but simply for pressure in that direction. In the quarter century
before 1873, in net, such pressure was overcome: in part, for Britain, due to
further tariff reductions; in part due to the partial effects within the trend period
of the opening up of new areas; in part due to the productivity of other types of
investment which were taking place, for example, the new British ships of the
sixties, which lowered the real cost of imports. Nevertheless the pressures on
real wages were sufficient to prevent their rise, in the fifties. The following
table indicates the extent to which the rise in real wages indicated in Table I,
above, was concentrated in the latter years of the trend period, and in the two
years of the subsequent trend period, following the crisis of 1873:

					Real Wages	
					(Wood)	(Tucker)
1850	.	.	.	.	100	100
1855	.	.	.	.	95	93
1860	.	.	.	.	103	96
1865	.	.	.	.	117	100
1868	.	.	.	.	110	102
1870	.	.	.	.	118	113
1873	.	.	.	.	128	116
1875	.	.	.	.	135	128

VI

The fourth of the trend periods runs from 1873 to the eve of the Boer War, in 1898. It is more usual practice to date the ending of this phase with the middle nineties. On close examination, however, the character of the expansion running from 1894 through 1898 belongs, in the character of its investment and the behaviour of the principal variables, rather with the Great Depression period, than with the phase of war and capital exports, which give a distinctive character to the fifteen years preceding the outbreak of the First World War.

The phenomena to be explained here are essentially the same as those which dominated the period from 1815 to the end of the forties: a favourable shift in the terms of trade; a fall in interest rates and commodity prices; a maintained rise in real wages.[1] In terms of the primitive model set forth earlier there is no doubt that Britain, over these years, turned on the whole to internal developments, yielding their results over a relatively short period. These were the years of steel, the iron and steel freighter, and the machine tool; of the telephone and the electricity company; and, in the nineties, of the bicycle. Gradually, in the eighties, South Africa and other parts of the Empire began to claim an increasing proportion of British enterprise; and in the late eighties, briefly, the trend movements were broken by the Argentine boom, which left the house of Baring tottering in its wake. But the evidence for a net shift towards intensive investment at home is undeniable; and, moreover, these were not only years of peace, but the world was spared until the nineties, any substantial new diversion of enterprise to the pursuit of gold. Falling prices and rising real wages are to be expected.

Nor was this simply a characteristic of British enterprise. The United States, recovered from Civil War, devoted itself to the exploitation of the great Western Empire. Grain prices fell almost steadily, which aided the working classes throughout the world, but turned the American farmer, for

---

[1] For a more complete analysis of this period see Chapters III and IV. The course of events in the years 1874–9 are described in some detail in Chapter IX.

three decades, into something of a political radical. In the East great new industries, their foundations laid or strengthened during the Civil War, grew rapidly. And in Germany a similar process of domestic development and exploitation took place.

The rate of rise of total industrial production in Britain fell off sharply in this period; but it rose in output *per capita* and in real wages. The rate of increase of both imports and exports declined; but the gross barter terms of trade moved favourably to Britain. For these years there is available, as well, the net barter terms of trade; that is, the relation between import and export prices.[1] These show, as would be expected, a greater fall in import than in export prices. The whole behaviour of Britain's foreign balance conforms to what one would, theoretically, expect of a shift in the character of its investment flows from foreign to domestic enterprise, and to what one would expect in a world consolidating and exploiting, on the whole, its previously opened resources, rather than breaking new ground.

VII

The fifth trend period covers the interval from the outbreak of the Boer War to the First World War. Here there is a clean reversal in the trends of interest rates, prices, the terms of trade, and even in real wages.

The character of new enterprise reveals the same three elements that characterized the mid-Victorian quarter century. Again there are wars: the Boer War, the Spanish American War, the Russo-Japanese War, and the Balkan wars. In addition, military budgets claimed an increasing amount of the national expenditure throughout the world. Second, there was gold, not only from South Africa, but also an increased flow from the other producing areas, as more efficient techniques of mining were introduced. Third, there was another world-wide wave of extensive investment, involving Africa, South America, Canada, Australia, and India.

The capital market had no sooner freed itself of the brief but real burden of financing the Boer War when, roughly in

[1] See below, pp. 102–3.

1905, foreign governments, railways, and mining enterprises came to London on a large scale, with attractive prospects. Interest rates rose, and British investors were, in part, driven from the capital market. Industrial floatations at home continued through the boom to 1907, on a small scale; but floatations by home railways, gas works, and water companies fell off very sharply, to reappear in the slump of 1908, when their modest but solid appeal again seemed attractive to the briefly disillusioned investor. Although the expansion which ran from 1908 to 1913 saw some increase in domestic investment, there is no doubt that the diversion of funds abroad was at some real short-run cost to the development of the British economy. G. T. Jones, tracing the course of the Lancashire cotton industry and the building industry in London, found a cessation in the decline of real costs at about the turn of the century.[1] And unemployment in the building trades, which had been down to less than 1 per cent. in 1898, perhaps the last authentic year of the Great Depression, was never less than 3 per cent. from 1901 to 1914; and it averaged almost 7·5 per cent. throughout the general business expansion, from 1904 to 1907.[2]

On the other hand, the export branches of British trade enjoyed very great prosperity, and the rate of increase in the volume of exports was considerably greater than in the previous trend period. The increase in imports, however, was at a lesser rate. Both the gross barter and the net terms of trade turned unfavourably to Britain; and real wages, in net, declined.[3] This decline, although mitigated by a shortening

---

[1] *Increasing Return*, pts. ii and iii.

[2] The components of the trades' union figure for average unemployment are reproduced accessibly in A. C. Pigou, *Industrial Fluctuations*, appendix, table i, pp. 381–2. While the number of workers in the mining, engineering, and textile industries rose substantially between 1901 and 1911, those in the building trades fell from 1,124,387 to 1,037,080 (Page, op. cit., vol. i, p. 3).

[3] The course of world trade, for the period from the mid-seventies to 1911–13, broken into primary products and manufactured articles, reveals the Great Depression as an interval of more rapid increase of trade in primary products than in manufactured articles, the years after the turn of the century showing the more rapid increase in manufactured articles (*Industrialization and Foreign Trade* (League of Nations), especially pp. 14–20). This evidence is consistent with that relating to the British economy alone; and it is consistent with the analysis presented here of the causal forces operative in the two trend periods.

of work hours, increased social services, and a more equitable tax structure was real; and it can be seen in the figures
for *per capita* consumption of sugar, meat, and beer, as well
as in calculated indexes of real wages.

Whether Britain, in some sense, exported too much capital
in the decade preceding 1914 is a matter for judgement. In
any such calculus, however, the long-run effects of those
investments, in strengthening the economies within the
Empire, in opening new sources of supply for British imports,
and in increasing the national holdings of negotiable international wealth would have to be taken fully into account.
It is clear, however, that in the context of the development
of the world economy as a whole, the rate of growth of capital
within Britain, and the real wages of the British working
classes, were adversely affected in this period.[1]

VIII

Taking the century and a quarter as a whole, from 1790
to 1914, one can trace in population and total industrial
production a long-term movement, reaching its peak rate of
increase, for population, during the second decade of the
nineteenth century, and for production, in the three decades
after 1815; and from that time forward one observes, in
general, expansion at a declining rate of increase. Throughout this era the British economy was an important, and perhaps the decisive segment, of a world economy, to which the
rate and character of its development is related.

Within this majestic framework of growth five trend
periods can be distinguished: analytically by the character of
investment outlays, and statistically by trends in real wages,
the terms of trade, and the rates of interest. The parallelisms
between the first, third, and fifth of these trend periods, and
between the second and the fourth are interesting and even
striking.

Professor Schumpeter, in his study, *Business Cycles*, has
raised the question of whether the whole of this trend

[1] See below, pp. 103–7, for Bowley's calculations of the unfavourable shift
for labour, in the distribution of the national income between 1900 and 1913.

sequence should not be regarded as part of a series of long cycles, each somewhat more than fifty years in length. In that case, the era examined here would comprise about two and a half cycles.

There are a number of objections to Schumpeter's system and to his formulation of it, among which are these:

First, there are grave ambiguities as to just what fluctuates in the course of the long cycle: employment, real wages, interest rates, the rate of increase in production, prices?[1]

Second, he adduces no intrinsic reasons for a recurrent cycle of this length, or for that cycle to have a relatively constant periodicity;

Third, the scale and consequences of innovations, in the technical sense in which Schumpeter uses the term, are demonstrably inadequate to explain the central phenomena of several of the trend periods, if they are examined in detail; e.g. the innovations of the Industrial Revolution, during the French wars, and the role of electricity and the automobile in the fifteen years before 1914.

Fourth, if the concept of innovations is broadened until it approximates to what are called here outlays for purposes other than consumption, or investment outlays, the theory would have to be broadened to include the timing and character of wars, as well as other more or less adventitious events, without which a satisfactory historical explanation of these years is impossible.

It is possible that Schumpeter, while recognizing the force of some of these strictures, would insist that they are irrelevant to his purpose of presenting a stylized but unified and

---

[1] Historically the conception of the long cycle begins with trend movements in prices; although Schumpeter's system is designed to account for a much wider range of evidence. The ambiguity which attaches to the concept of the long cycle is dramatized in *Business Cycles*, vol. i, p. 213, in a chart in which the three types of cycles which Schumpeter adduces, are, in abstract form, superimposed. The short and medium cycles (Kitchins and Juglars) are superimposed on the long wave (Kondratieff), yielding a composite curve. The short and medium cycles are conventional cycles in employment and production. The long cycle, as described by Schumpeter, is not, essentially, a cycle in either. What meaning, then, attaches to the composite curve?

suggestive view of the course of economic development. Whether the long cycle sequence, as a formal structure for modern economic history, illuminates more than it conceals, is a matter of judgement. At the least Schumpeter's formulation raises questions to which the historian and the economist have thus far given inadequate answers.

II

CYCLES IN THE BRITISH ECONOMY:
1790–1914

I

THE previous chapter sought to outline the broad pattern of growth to which the British economy conforms, over the century and a quarter from about 1790 to 1914. Within the framework set by the expansion of population and total production, an attempt was made to establish and briefly to explore five periods during which the nature of new enterprise, in Britain and throughout the world, is judged to have given a distinctive cast to the movements of real wages, commodity prices, interest rates, and the terms of trade. The present chapter seeks to move an approximation closer to the pattern of economic events as they actually unfolded, by examining short-period fluctuations in total industrial output and employment.

A reading of the evidence, statistical and qualitative, on the movements within the British economy in modern times, taken year by year, month by month, or week by week, leaves two enduring impressions. First, one is impressed with the uniqueness and variety of the story of economic life. The combinations of forces within the moving economy are, like those in political life, in an important sense always new and fresh. No year is quite like another year; and after a time one gets to know them like old friends. Contrast the lively impression to be derived from Tooke and Macpherson and the *Annual Register*, in the early days, and later the *Economist* and *Bankers Magazine*, with the story presented in conventional texts, or the view from the statistics alone. Second, one is impressed with the solid reality of the cyclical pattern which steadily recurs, in Britain, and then gradually widening, throughout the world from the end of the American Revolution to the outbreak of the First World War. No two cycles, of course, are quite the same; and one can trace, as well, certain long period changes in the character of cycles. But it is evident that the whole evolution of modern society in the West occurred in a rhythmic pattern, which had consequences for social and political as well as for economic events.

II

Table II sets out annual dates for the turning-points in British trade fluctuations from 1788 to 1914. For the whole of this era it is possible, on evidence available, to set down monthly turning-points, of reasonable accuracy, although that refinement is unnecessary for the level of analysis pursued here.[1] The annual dates do not necessarily define the year within which recovery or depression began.[2] The years are taken as analytic and statistical units, and are weighed as a whole. For example, it is likely that recovery, after the decline from 1792, began at about June 1794; on the whole, however, 1794 was a year of greater prosperity than 1793; and so the latter is marked as a trough year.

It should be emphasized that the year designated in this table is, in many cases, a matter for judgement. The pro-

[1] A. F. Burns and W. C. Mitchell, *Measuring Business Cycles*, p. 79, present turning-points in British trade cycles annually from 1792, quarterly and monthly from 1854–5. Monthly turning-points were established from 1790 to 1850 in the course of the forthcoming study directed by A. D. Gayer, *The Growth and Fluctuations of the British Economy, 1790–1850*. In the annual dates presented in Table II, the author has deferred to the Homeric researches of Burns, Mitchell, and their staff in several instances where his earlier calculations diverged from theirs. The setting of these dates is a matter of judgement; and little would be gained by opening this specialist sport to public controversy. Something, in fact, would be lost; for in the technique of measurement developed by the National Bureau of Economic Research these dates serve as the framework against which other statistical data are measured. Alterations in the framework involve laborious new calculations which are most unlikely to yield results of analytic significance. Unless new data are adduced, it is likely to prove useful and proper to accept the National Bureau dates as standard. The author, however, has retained the decline in 1801 as a cycle; and he has not judged the movement from 1901 to 1903 as, in net, an expansion. The most serious error that might arise from the use of turning-point tables would be the assumption that, analytically, the cycles were of the same order, or represented necessarily comparable phenomena. As the National Bureau has been careful to emphasize, the definition of turning-points constitutes merely a preliminary working stage in the process of analysing cyclical phenomena.

[2] For an authoritative discussion of the problems involved in the setting of turning-points the reader should consult Burns and Mitchell, op. cit., especially chap. iv.

cesses involved in the cyclical turning-points are complex; and they are woven in each case into unique historical circumstances. Perhaps more important, there are no accurate, continuous, and sensitive indexes of production, national

TABLE II

Annual Turning-points, British Trade Cycles, 1788–1914

Trough	Peak	Trough	Peak
1788	*1792	1842	*1845
1793	1796	1848	*1854
1797	1800	1855	1857
1801	*1802	1858	1860
1803	1806	1862	*1866
1808	*1810	1868	*1873
1811	1815	1879	*1883
1816	*1818	1886	*1890
1819	*1825	1894	*1900
1826	1828	1904	1907
1829	1831	1908	*1913
1832	*1836	1914	..
1837	1839	..	..

NOTE. An asterisk (*) indicates that the cyclical expansion thus marked was characterized by substantial long-term investment, at home and/or abroad; and that conditions of virtually full employment were reached. Of these, the most ambiguous case is that of 1907, where capital exports occurred, during expansion, on a considerable scale, but home investment was not sufficient to create conditions of full employment. In the case of most other cycles not marked by an asterisk (e.g. 1796, 1806, 1810, &c.) the primary impulse towards expansion lay in foreign trade. The cycle marked by a peak in 1800, a trough in 1801, is to be regarded as an interruption in the expansion from 1797 to 1802, rather than as a minor cycle confined to foreign trade. Similarly, the setback of 1861–2 is to be regarded rather as an interruption in a major cycle expansion than as a minor cycle contraction, being affected by the outbreak of the American Civil War.

income, or employment which might singly, or in some aggregate, be regarded as definitive of general trade movements, throughout these years. Hoffmann's indexes of production, and Beveridge's, until 1850, however valuable they may be, are, because of their constitution and weighting, dubious instruments for turning-point analysis.[1] And the

[1] Lord Beveridge's index, to 1850 (*Full Employment in a Free Society*, Appendix A; also *The Trade Cycle in Britain before 1850*, and a subsequent emendation, *Oxford Economic Papers, 1940*), invites two basic criticisms, both of which stem

invaluable statistics for unemployment within the trades'
unions, available from 1850, represent for much of the
period so partial a sample of the total working force as to

from the role of the brick production and ship-building figures in his calculations. First, because of their large amplitude of movement, they tend to dominate the general movements of his index as a whole. Second, because they
represent capital investment, of considerable period of gestation, they lag what
are regarded here as the general movements of the economy, at both troughs
and peaks, as follows:

Turning-points, Table II		Turning-points, Beveridge Index	
Trough	Peak	Trough	Peak
1793		1795	
	1802		1803
1803		1804	
	1806		1805
1811		1812	
	1815		1813
1819		1821	
	1828		1827*
	1839		1838–40
1842		1843	
	1845		1846

* In the case of 1828 the fall in the indexes of capital goods' production used
  by Beveridge outweigh the rise in the volume of exports; on the judgement
  here the latter movement was the more significant. A decline in indexes of
  investment in the course of a minor cycle expansion is not inconsistent with
  our definition of a minor cycle.

These criticisms imply the view that the Beveridge index under-estimates the
role of the volume of exports, in cyclical fluctuations of the first half of the
century, and over-estimates the significance, for the economy as a whole, of
brick production and ship-building, as well as certain other series reflecting
capital construction. Hoffmann's index of production is subject to similar
criticism. Both indexes, and any possible formal index constructed on the
basis of known statistical data alone, for this period, suffer from the poverty
of consistent quantitative evidence on production. For the eighteenth century,
as well, and for earlier periods, it is likely to prove more satisfactory to exploit
the quantitative evidence fully, whether in continuous series or covering a
limited number of years, and to muster in addition all relevant forms of
qualitative evidence, in the setting of turning-points.

. It should be pointed out, however, that Beveridge's central purpose was
amply served by his index; namely, to indicate the existence of a persistent
trade cycle in Great Britain from the close of the eighteenth century. The
result of its deficiencies, however, is to obscure the existence of minor cycles,
to 1850, as well as to distort somewhat the timing and shape of the major
cycles.

require cautious use.[1] The years given here are derived
from an examination of a wide body of both statistical and
qualitative evidence; but no absolute validity attaches to
them. One might conduct fairly even-balanced, if not very
fruitful, debate as to whether 1794 rather than 1793 was a
trough year, or 1809 rather than 1810 a peak, and so on.

Leaving aside the technical problem of establishing turning-
point years, or months, there is a prior issue of conception.
How big a movement, in what indicators of production and
employment, justifies the marking off of a formal trade cycle?
The criterion employed here is that the movement be one
which is evidenced by a significant change in direction of
overall indexes of industrial production and employment,
or such other reflections of those variables, covering particular segments of the economy, as are available. There are
occasions, such as 1823, when the volume of exports declined;
and in the twenties the volume of exports must be regarded
as an extremely important element in the trade cycle. On
the other hand, the evidence relating to total employment
and production suggests that, in net, they increased in 1823.
The mild downward impulse imparted from the export
markets was overwhelmed in stronger domestic forces making
for expansion; and thus no cycle is recorded between 1819
and 1825. An obverse case is that of the decline from 1800
to 1801, where the movements indicated in the various forms
of data available are diverse, some indicating expansion,
some contraction. On the whole, however, it has been
thought proper to mark off a down-turn in that year, with

[1] The extent to which the pre-1914 trades' union unemployment figure may
be regarded as representative was raised before the Royal Statistical Society
in February 1923 (*J.R.S.S.*, 1923, pp. 154–205) by J. Hilton, in the course of
an examination of the unemployment statistics derived from the Unemployment
Insurance Acts. See especially pp. 154–5, 181–7, 197–8 (Pethick Lawrence),
200–3 (Ramsbottom). On the basis of comparative behaviour in the period of
overlap between the trades' union figures and the more modern official
compilation of insured workers unemployed, Hilton concluded that the trades'
union figure appeared to be representative of general unemployment in years
of low unemployment, but over-estimated unemployment in years of severe
depression due to the heavy weighting of the engineering, ship-building, and
other cyclically sensitive industries. See also A. L. Bowley, 'The Measurement
of Employment: An Experiment', *J.R.S.S.*, July 1912; and Colin Clark, op. cit.,
p. 232.

recovery following in 1802, during the brief Peace of Amiens. The analyst of cycles, like other historians, cannot be relieved of the burden of making arbitrary judgement, no matter how large or superficially comforting the mass of statistics with which he is able to surround himself.

III

Table II distinguishes twenty-four cycles, over the period of 126 years. Both the initial and terminal dates are untidy points of demarcation. The year 1788 marks a mild trough in a long sequence of expansion begun after the end of the American War of Independence. There was a brief post-war slump; then revival started in foreign trade, gathered momentum from the middle of the decade, but was set back briefly in 1788; recovery then moved on to a considerable and general boom, reaching its peak in 1792. On the other hand, 1914 was the first year in a cyclical decline which would have continued, almost certainly, for several further years had war not intervened. The average duration of these 24 cycles, taken as a whole, and thus regarded implicitly as comparable units, is about 5·25 years.

The average figure for the duration of all cycles distinguished is not particularly meaningful, since these cycles differed significantly in character among themselves. The most important of these differences has been indicated in the accompanying table by distinguishing fourteen of the cycles with an asterisk, and designating them major cycles. A major cycle is defined by two related criteria: first, that, at its peak, conditions of relatively full employment were attained; second, that in its latter stages at least, persons and institutions proved willing to enter into long-term investment commitments, at home and/or abroad, on a large scale. In most cases an application of these criteria to the evidence clearly and satisfactorily distinguishes the major cycles.

Some problem is raised, however, by the cases of major cycles before 1825. On the whole, long-term investment played a lesser part in the economy in the earlier than in the later years of the era; and in addition, as noted in Chapter I, the economic requirements of war, to 1815, diverted resources abnormally into foreign trade and agriculture. Nevertheless, the behaviour of brick production, as well as other indicators of long-term investment, justify the distinction of cycles reaching their peaks in 1792, 1802, and 1810. The not very impressive, but nevertheless real, post-war cycle, reaching its peak in 1818, also falls in this category of lesser major cycles.

Perhaps the most ambiguous of the cycles, however, lies not in the early years, but is that which reached its peak in 1907. Average unemployment in Britain in the peak year was almost 4 per cent., a considerably higher figure than for any of the other major cycle peaks after 1850; and, looked at closely, it is evident that domestic long-term investment was on a depressed scale throughout the upswing from 1904 to 1907.[1]

The minor cycles were characterized by limited general expansion which, for various reasons, gave way to depression before conditions of relatively full employment were reached. In most cases the primary impulse sustaining expansion, in the minor cycles, was confined to foreign trade; and although multiplier effects undoubtedly operated to spread the increase in production and employment, the economic system failed to move continuously upward to full employment. In some cases the downward movement can be traced, in part, at least, to an external event; e.g. the coming of Civil War in 1861. In other cases (e.g. 1828), the timing of decline appears in large part to proceed from a virtually autonomous short rhythm in foreign trade itself; although some of the minor cycles were supported by the completion of acts of investment, with long periods of gestation, undertaken in the peak years of the previous major cycle, and their end was accompanied by the final collapse of these waves of long-term investment.

In general, this dual distinction among cycles appears useful so long as the individual cycles are so well understood that their abstraction into categories is not compounded to advanced abstract conclusions which the raw historical evidence does not support.

[1] See above, p. 27.

Taking the major cycles apart, we find a consistent duration of about nine years;[1] and this duration does not vary
significantly through time. From 1792 to 1900 the major
cycles may be associated in 4 successive groups, of 3 each.[2]
Although the individual cycles vary in length, the average
for each of the 3 groups is remarkably similar: 8·7 years for
the period up to 1818; 9·0 years to 1845; 9·3 years to 1873;
and 9·0 years to 1900. The author can adduce no simple
and persuasive reason why the rhythm of fluctuations in
long-term investment should have remained so stable, at
about 9 years, through the nineteenth century; but there
seems little doubt concerning the reality of the phenomenon.

The minor cycles, of which ten are distinguished over
these years, are consistently about four years in length; and
these too exhibit no very significant change in their average
duration over the century. It will be noted in Table II,
however, that the minor cycles tend, virtually, to disappear
from the array of trade cycles after 1860, excepting, of course,
the special case of 1907. This characteristic of cyclical
behaviour proceeds from the nature of the two types of
cycles, as they have been defined, and from the character of
the basic changes in the British economy over the century
and a quarter: four minor cycles are in the first trend period,
to 1816; three are in the second;[3] two in the third; none in

---

[1] The average duration of major cycles varies with the form of measurement.
Measured from peak to peak (1792–1913) their average duration is 9·4 years;
measured from trough to trough (1788–1914) their average duration is 9·0 years.
The consistency of the duration is indicated, in the latter case, by an average
deviation of 1·29 years.

[2] Measurement is here taken from 1792 to 1900, dropping, in effect, the
first and last major cycles, because the major cycle trough preceding 1792 is
not established; and because the final trend period, 1900–14, includes by our
definition only one major cycle, that reaching its peak in 1913. Economically,
as noted above (p. 36), the trough in 1914 is almost certainly artificial. The
major cycle trough preceding 1792 probably falls in 1784–5; and the expansion to 1787 and the decline to 1788 would be accounted a minor cycle movement.

[3] A secondary cycle, after the peak in 1845, can be detected in the monthly
data, running from a trough in Sept. 1846 to a peak in Apr. 1847. Analytically
it shares some of the characteristics of the secondary peak (after 1836) in
1839, involving stimulus from both the completion of railway projects, earlier
initiated, and from the export trade; but it is too slight a movement to justify
inclusion among the annual dates. Such inconclusive secondary movements,

the fourth; and one in the fifth. The euthanasia of the minor cycle presents, in fact, no great analytic mystery.

IV

The minor cycles are distinguished here by the fact that they involved increases in production and employment arising preponderantly, but not exclusively, from increases in exports. In the first half of the nineteenth century textiles and other consumers' goods constituted the dominant element in British exports. Against the background of a rising world population and real income, and cheapened real costs of production, the amounts capable of being sold in world markets increased steadily, year after year: the demand curve for British exports shifted steadily to the right, and the supply curve as well. The markets through which British exports were sold abroad, however, were speculative in the sense that more or less was sent abroad, by individual merchants, depending on their information and judgements concerning stocks and prices in foreign markets at future times. In addition, because time lags were involved at various stages in the process of trade, current and expected conditions with respect to the price and the availability of credit entered the calculation.

Acting, in fact, on similar or identical intelligence, British merchants tended, roughly, to behave in the same manner. When inventories fell off, and prices rose abroad, word was received from overseas agents and fully circulated; and more goods were shipped from Britain. Such actions, individually taken, tended to reverse the conditions in foreign markets which justified the increased shipments, in the first instance; and the reversal could not be reported instantaneously, nor the production decisions which stemmed from it instantaneously reversed within Britain. And so the curve of British exports did not rise smoothly, in continuous accord with market conditions abroad. It moved upward, with occasional

among others, can also be detected in the course of the downswing of the seventies, the upswing of the later nineties, and the downswing following 1900, the latter movement having attained the dignity of a separate cycle in the calculations of the National Bureau.

set-backs, fluctuating about the imaginary line which, at any moment of time, would have represented the equilibrium volume of exports. There was, undoubtedly, a tendency for British foreign trade to fluctuate cyclically, in what we might call an inventory cycle.[1]

The rhythm of that cycle was, of its nature, relatively short; and, in times of peace and normal market relationships, the amplitude of its movement relatively mild. There are several reasons why this should have been so:

First, while there was undoubtedly an element of judgement about future markets, and future costs involved in the export trade, the period of time between a change in market conditions and the receipt of intelligence in London was not very great, even before the introduction of the cables.

Second, the flow of exports could be altered quickly and sensitively, with changed knowledge and judgement about future market conditions; a commitment to build a railway is binding over a number of years; commitments to manufacture and to ship textiles were capable of review and alteration in a matter of weeks or months.[2]

[1] Thomas Tooke's *History of Prices* is the best source of data on the course and the mechanics of short cycles in foreign trade, his account deriving vitality and authority from a long merchant's experience. The institutional arrangements, with their time lags, credit arrangements, and dependence on expectations, are described by N. S. Buck, *Anglo-American Trade, 1800–1850*: for the system of credit advances on consignments, and the 'interlacing of credits' and speculation with foreign trade operations see especially pp. 12–14, 23, and 39; for reference to the inventory nature of the foreign trade crises of 1816 and 1831 see pp. 138–9. For a recent analysis of the nature and possible causes of inventory fluctuations, partially relevant to this problem, despite its application to a closed economy, see L. A. Metzler, 'The Nature and Stability of Inventory Cycles', *Review of Economic Statistics*, 1941, and 1947, 'Factors Governing the Length of Inventory Cycles'.

[2] Buck, op. cit., p. 102, notes: 'As it generally took from a month to six weeks to manufacture the goods and prepare them for shipment, merchants, who purchased from the manufacturers, were required to place their orders for goods fairly early'. To establish what Metzler, in his articles cited above, calls 'the planning period' one would, presumably, have to take into account the length of time from the placing of the order by the merchant to the receipt of the manufactured goods. This would include the period from transmission to receipt of orders, from overseas, as well as the period for shipment and delivery of the finished British products. In fact, shipments from Britain to the United

Finally, the demand for consumers' goods from peoples abroad was under fairly steady impulse to enlargement; the purchases of foreign merchants were, of course, sensitive to changes in British prices, and to general movements of demand within their own market regions; but behind them were enlarging populations, with increasing real incomes; and they were trading in consumers' goods.[1]

Together these forces made for a relatively short cycle, of mild amplitude, in the basic British exports of the first half of the century. And it is this type of inventory cycle which one could, almost certainly, trace back into the eighteenth century; and perhaps even back to medieval times. Its character stems from the nature of the merchant's trade.

From the late 1780's at least, however, this rhythm is woven into the longer and deeper rhythm of fluctuations in long-term investment. In the latter stages of the boom reaching its peak in 1792, for example, there was an expansion in canal- and road-building, agricultural inclosures, and an increased building of ships, houses, and factories. This element of long-term investment grew relatively as the economy became increasingly industrialized; and it grew notably after the ending of the French wars had lifted the burdens and removed the distorting pressures which war had imposed. Until the sixties, however, the short cycle can not only be detected but, on the judgements which entered the compilation of Table II, it had sufficient power

States tended to be concentrated in two periods of the year: 'There were the spring shipments, from the middle of January until the middle of April, and the fall shipments, during the months of July and August (idem).' It is not unlikely that 'the planning period', fully analysed in this trade, would work out to something close to six months.

[1] The economies to which Britain sold its exports were themselves subject to cyclical fluctuations, as well as to secular growth: fluctuations in harvests, in their income from exports, and in their domestic industry. These fluctuations undoubtedly affected the demand for British exports; and they were both affected by, and influenced the course of, British cycles. Probably the optimum form in which to analyse these foreign trade fluctuations would be as an aspect of inter-regional trade, within a single economy moving to the rhythm of fully interrelated, if not synchronous, cyclical forces. What is essential to the argument here, however, is that, until about the fifties, the principal British exports were consumers' rather than capital goods.

to produce distinguishable general movements in total production and employment.

As industrialization progressed, however, and the metal-lurgical and engineering industries began to play an increased proportional role in the economy, the long-term investment cycle became increasingly dominant. This was the trend not only for Britain, but for certain key British markets on the Continent and in the United States; and thus the longer rhythm—the nine-year average—infected not only British domestic activities, but foreign trade as well. In 1808 to 1810, when Britain enjoyed a boom focused on Latin America, freed for trade by the Spanish Revolution of 1808, the goods sent out, as recorded in the famous quotation from McCulloch, were: textiles, cut glass, chinaware, ham-mers, and the inevitable skates for Rio de Janeiro.[1] From the fifties onward not only did railway-iron and other capital equipment go abroad, but the further industrial develop-ment of certain of the importing economies probably made their demand for British consumers' goods more sensitive to cyclical fluctuations than had been the case in earlier, more pastoral times.

The net effect of the British and world-wide transition towards capital development and industrialization was to overwhelm, in a sense, the minor cycle as an independent cyclical phenomenon. Its rhythm, however, can still be detected in the export figures for British textiles. Whereas, between 1848 and 1914, ten trade cycles can be marked off, there are some fifteen cycles which can be detected in the value of exports of cotton goods and yarn, with an average duration of somewhat over four years. In the early decades of the century the movement of textile exports might have been decisive to the contour of fluctuations in the economy as a whole; in the latter year it was simply one determinant of general fluctuations, and by no means the most powerful. But the short rhythm of its movement persists.

Thus, the statistical conclusion that the average duration of trade cycles increased after 1860 is to be understood in general as the shifting from a secondary to a primary posi-

[1] Quoted, Tooke, op. cit., vol. i, pp. 276–7.

tion of the rhythm of long-term investment;[1] and a reduction in relative status within the world economy of the shorter rhythm which, for Britain, took the form notably of textile exports. From the beginning to the end of the era, however, the two rhythms are detectable in the evidence.

The two types of fluctuations did not pursue their course in separate and discrete channels. They were linked in at least four ways:

First, both partially depended, in their timing, on the state of the capital market; and their course related to conditions in the interwoven complex of credit markets in London and the provinces.

Second, and more broadly, the consumers' goods industries and capital goods industries competed for labour and raw materials in common markets; cost calculations which affected decisions in both stemmed from, partially, identical data.

Third, a part of British exports depended on the export of capital; and in most cases waves of capital exports occurred at the same time, and under the same general impulses that lead to long-term domestic investment.

Fourth, a source of the confidence and the funds for long-term investment were the increases in profits and in general income derived directly and indirectly from prior increases in the export trade.

For these reasons, among others, fluctuations within the British economy must be examined and understood as a whole, no matter how useful or illuminating the abstraction of elements within them may be for special purposes.

The shift in the balance and structure of the British and world economies, and thus the changed character of cyclical fluctuations, had consequences for the relative impact of the trade cycle on the economy and the society as a whole. At

---

[1] 1860 in no sense constitutes a sharp analytic line of demarcation with respect to the relative role of the two types of cycles. The coming of the railway on a very large scale in Britain in the forties affords a sharper conceptual breaking-point. Indeed, the minor cycle of the late forties is so slight a manifestation that it is not recorded in the annual turning-points; and that of the fifties (peak 1857) would, perhaps, not have stood out so strongly, but for the distortions imposed on the pattern of the decade by the Crimean War.

the beginning of the era Britain was, in agriculture, virtually self-sufficient, with only minor capital industries, and a foreign trade mainly in consumers' goods. By the end of the era Britain was heavily deficit in agriculture, with its industries closely tied, in both their domestic and foreign markets, to long-term capital development. Undoubtedly a larger proportion of the population felt the impact of the trade cycle on their lives and fortunes in 1910 than in 1790.

There is, further, good evidence for concluding that the amplitude of trade cycles, in both their expansion and contraction phases, increased after the French wars. From 1819 to 1848, however, covering the three great major cycles of the twenties, thirties, and forties, there appears to be no clear trend increase in the amplitude of cyclical movements.[1] From 1850 there is available the trades' union unemployment figures, which cover a gradually larger proportion of the labour force. It is difficult to judge whether the changing constitution of that index gives it a bias towards greater or lesser average unemployment, over time, and greater or lesser amplitude of fluctuation. The greater coverage in terms of industries which are less sensitive to cyclical move-

---

[1] In the course of the study *The Growth and Fluctuations of the British Economy, 1790–1850*, directed by A. D. Gayer, an index of trade fluctuations was constructed which, while not fully satisfactory for the definition of turning-points, is judged reasonably to reflect the amplitude of the cyclical movements. It exhibits the following behaviour from 1797 to 1848, for major cycles:

Trough to Peak		Peak to Trough	
	%	%	
1797–1802	15·1	4·2	1802–3
1808–10	12·7	10·8	1810–11
1816–18	24·6	11·3	1818–19
1819–25	45·7	39·7	1825–6
1832–6	41·8	29·0	1836–7
1842–5	49·3	50·0	1845–8

Unfortunately, data available to the author do not permit the extension of this index at the present time. Regarded analytically, the measurements from peak to trough for the last three major cycles are not comparable. Due to the lag at the peak, the waves of long-term investment took some time to subside. After 1825 and 1836, only one year of decline, measured by turning-points, occurred; after 1845, on the other hand, the trough is measured to 1848.

ments may well be compensated for by its greater coverage of, and the weighting given to, industries with a high sensitivity to cycles.[1] If one regards the unemployment figures as a uniformly representative sample, one is lead to the conclusion that, while the trade cycle undoubtedly affected an increasing proportion of the population, the relative amplitude of cyclical movements in employment did not change in a systematic and significant way from 1850 to 1914.[2]

Unfortunately, the data are not now in such a form that the important gap from the forties to the fifties can be bridged by a continuous and satisfactory general index of cyclical fluctuations; nor have the measurements of particular series made by the National Bureau of Economic Research yet been fully mobilized on this problem. Tentatively, however, it would appear that the percentage movements in total employment and production do not exhibit a significant long-term trend variation, paralleling the growing industrialization of the British economy from, roughly, the 1820's to 1914.

A separate but related question concerns the possible relationship between the character of trade cycles and the trend periods, explored in Chapter I. It has long been believed that the trend periods after 1815 and 1873 were, in some sense, more depressed than the other three, whether that depression was associated with trends in the price-level or the more complex inner rationale of Schumpeter's Kondratieff process.[3]

---

[1] See above, p. 35, n.

[2] This is not to imply, of course, that all cycles, or even all major cycles, were of similar amplitude. The cycles varied among themselves in intensity; and there is, from the seventies to 1914, an apparent trend towards a diminished amplitude of cyclical movement in the unemployment index, which can be seen in the successive figures for peak unemployment in the various cycles: 1879, 11·4 per cent.; 1886, 10·2 per cent.; 1893, 7·5 per cent.; 1908, 7·8 per cent. Leaving aside the margins of error and biases that may exist within the unemployment series, it seems preferable to analyse these cases in terms of their particular environment than in terms of an indicated trend change in the nature of the trade cycle. See below, pp. 47–50.

[3] See Schumpeter, op. cit., pp. 161 ff.; also J. Viner, *Studies in the Theory of International Trade*, p. 218; and W. C. Mitchell, *Business Cycles* (1927), pp. 407–12. For a recent interesting but inconclusive and partial test of this hypothesis see Burns and Mitchell, op. cit., chap. ii, especially pp. 431–40.

There are many possible tests of this hypothesis of which two appear tractable within the limits of present data:

(*a*) the dubious test, of comparing the proportion of years of increasing prosperity to years of increasing depression for cycles within the trend periods;

(*b*) a superior test, where possible, of comparing the average level of unemployment for cycles within the trend periods.

The first test is of doubtful value because, if applied directly to this issue, it implies that all cycles designated by turning-points were comparable analytic units, of similar amplitude, and similar rates of expansion and contraction. In particular, the gradual disappearance of the minor cycle influences the measurements over this era in a manner such as to diminish the proportion of prosperous to depressed years.

This phenomenon occurs because the characteristic pattern of the minor cycle, based on the course of foreign trade, was one of a preponderance of years of prosperity to years of depression. The trend was strongly upward, and a single year of setback was usually sufficient to bring down inventories sufficiently to permit the resumption of an upward movement: e.g. 1819, 1826, 1829, 1832, &c. As this element loses its power to affect what are judged to be general movements of employment and production, the rhythm of long-term investment, more evenly balanced between expansion and contraction phases, stands forth, and the proportion of years of prosperity to years of depression tends to fall. This factor does not affect comparative measurements significantly as between the first two trend periods, to the mid-century. After that time, however, it becomes significant.

From 1793 to 1816 inclusive, 67 per cent. of the years are years of rising prosperity; from 1816 to 1848, 64 per cent.[1]

---

[1] In all such measurements a problem exists of establishing periods which both fall within the trend intervals being compared, and which represent an equitable balance of cyclical phases. The years chosen here are regarded as representing a fair comparison, although the fact that the trough years are counted at the beginning and the end of each period somewhat under-estimates the 'proportion of prosperity' in each case.

The impropriety of drawing any distinction between the two periods on the basis of this calculation is indicated by the fact that if, for example, the single year 1847 is regarded as one of rising prosperity, as the monthly data suggest might well be done,[1] the prosperity proportions become identical, as between the two trend periods.

Applied to the period after 1848, however, the measure yields a less steady result, as follows:

Period	Prosperity Proportion
	%
1848–68	67
1848–79	59
1879–94	50
1879–1904	54
1904–14	73

From these overlapping measures one might firmly draw the conclusion that in the seventies the relative periods of prosperity fell away, and rose again after the middle nineties. The evidence appears unambiguous, and the orders of magnitude substantial. And, indeed, such is the result one obtains if the cycles are regarded as analytically comparable units over the period 1848–1914.[2]

These measures of the 'prosperity proportion' should be contrasted with measures of the average level of business activity and of unemployment. For the period up to 1850 an index of general business activity has been constructed, on the basis of all available evidence, in which each year is rated from 0, a year of deep depression, to 5, a year of virtually full employment.[3] The average standing of years within each trend period was then calculated. The fairest measure, analytically, runs from 1793 to 1816; and from 1816 to 1848, all years of demarcation being cyclical troughs. The average standing of years in the first period is then 2·10, in the second, 1·95. Given the nature of the data, any very firm conclusions do not appear justified from this distinction in average standings.

[1] See above, p. 38, n. 3.
[2] This is the conclusion drawn, in more generalized form, by Burns and Mitchell, op. cit., pp. 437–40, from Table 167; although they regard their results as preliminary and tentative.
[3] This index is reproduced in the Appendix to Chapter VI below, pp. 124–5.

An examination of the unemployment data from 1850 yields a similar inconclusive result. The most satisfactory measuring periods, analytically, are the following: 1855–73; 1874–1900; 1901–13.[1] For the first, the mid-Victorian period, average unemployment is 4·8 per cent.; for the second, the Great Depression, it is 4·9 per cent.; for the third, the pre-1914 period, it is 4·5 per cent. These figures, or any other reasonable analysis of the unemployment data, do not appear to justify the view that the Great Depression period was marked by significantly higher unemployment than the average from the mid-century to the outbreak of war in 1914.

The traditional conception, which associates falling-price trends with high secular unemployment, probably stems from a quantitatively inaccurate picture in our minds of the cyclical depression of the seventies and of the expansion of the early eighties, so far as the Great Depression is concerned; and, for the three decades after the French wars, from the

---

[1] These periods are taken because 1850 comes after the beginning of revival, in 1848; and 1914 is the first year of what would, almost certainly, have been a more protracted depression. The lack of any very great distinction between unemployment in the Great Depression period, as opposed to the trend periods which lie on either side, is indicated in the following supplementary calculations:

Average Unemployment by Decades

	%
1850–9	5·03
1860–9	5·16
1870–9	3·83
1880–9	5·61
1890–9	4·35
1900–9	4·83

Average Unemployment by Cycles

	%	
1850–5	4·0	(1849, year of depression, lacking)
1856–8	7·5	
1859–62	4·8	
1863–8	4·9	
1869–79	4·1	
1880–6	5·9	
1887–94	5·1	
1895–1904	3·8	
1905–8	5·3	
1909–14	4·1	(downswing interrupted by war)

The overall average for unemployment, 1850–1914, is 4·69 per cent.

imprint of the falling price-curves of Peterloo, the Irish
famine, the Chartists, and Engels on the forties.

In the seventies a surprisingly high level of activity was
sustained from the beginnings of the downswing in 1873 to
1878–9. From 1874 through 1877, all regarded as years of
'depression' in the earlier measurement, average unemployment was only 3·1 per cent., as opposed to the 1850–1914
general average of 4·7 per cent.; and the behaviour of statistics of production, and other evidence, support this view of
the period.[1] Prices, to be sure, were falling, and interest
rates and profits as well; but the impact of depression, for
Britain after 1873, like the preceding prosperity, came largely
from abroad; and the country turned promptly, after 1873,
to housing, ship-building, and other domestic enterprise
of low expected yield; while the quantity of sales abroad,
at lower but still profitable prices, was surprisingly maintained.

The years from 1879 to 1883 are regarded, usually, as a
minor upward movement in a period of general depression.
But the expansion in production was very real indeed; and
unemployment was down close to 2 per cent. in 1882 and
1883. This expansion did not move, in its latter stages, into
a phase of new adventurous investment. A floatation boom in
electricity companies was about the best it could summon;
and the economic system was not pushed, as in the special
circumstances of the early seventies, to a phase of almost
absolute full employment and rapidly rising prices. Moreover, in its muted character the expansion of the early
eighties is related to what we have defined as the central
quality of the Great Depression period, namely, the lack of
high yield outlets for new investment. The years 1884–7
were probably the worst continuous sequence, from the point
of view of unemployment, of any throughout this era. The
expected yield on new investment was not as high as it had
been in the seventies, or the fifties, although the position was
in many ways similar to that in the sixties. The volume of
investment was, however, sufficiently high over the Great
Depression period as a whole to avoid a significantly greater

[1] See below, Chapter IX.

average level of unemployment than in the trend periods which preceded or followed.

This judgement, based on materials and an analysis that are patently subject to later refinement, is advanced not only because of its intrinsic interest in cyclical history, but also because it relates to an important implicit assumption that runs through much of the discussion of trends in Chapter I. If it is possible to assume, roughly, that resources were about equally employed, on the average, in the various trend periods, then the emphasis on the importance of the different types of investment outlay, as the decisive factor determining the trend course of the principal variables, is thereby the more legitimate.

V

It is impossible, within the compass of the present volume, to examine systematically the typical cyclical behaviour of the major elements within the economy, and to explore the sort of trade cycle theory which appears best to account for their course. It may be useful, however, to present some interim observations on the cyclical behaviour of the British harvests, commodity prices, long-term investment, and the Bank of England.

For the period to 1850, clearly, and probably to the seventies, the domestic harvests played a significant part in British trade fluctuations. Theoretically, a good harvest, with a consequent fall in the price of bread, could be assumed to increase real wages, and thus to increase the demand for commodities other than bread; or, less likely, and mixed in its effects, it might reduce the resistance to a decline in money wages, making possible lowered marginal costs for entrepreneurs. On the other hand, an abundant harvest might be regarded as reducing the money incomes of the agricultural community, and thus decreasing its demand for non-agricultural commodities; for the demand for grain was highly inelastic, over this period. Undoubtedly fluctuations in the yield of the harvests did shift the demand curves for non-agricultural commodities within the community, although it is impossible on present evidence to trace those shifts in detail. One emerges, simply, with the impression that an abundant harvest was a good thing for the non-agricultural community; a very mixed blessing for agriculture; and, in net, clearly a good thing for the country taken as a whole.

There is, however, a more solid approach to the effects of harvests in these years, and a more clearly definable set of effects, namely, those which operated through the foreign balance and the money market. A good harvest reduced the requirements for imports of grain; a bad harvest increased those requirements. The orders of magnitude of the outlays in a poor harvest year, as opposed to those in a time of domestic abundance, were very considerable. And an increase in grain imports served to put pressure on the money markets, to raise interest rates, and thus to discourage other forms of foreign trade, domestic commerce, and long-term investment. In addition, it set in motion strong forces in the labour market making for higher wages. A good harvest, on the other hand, tended to reduce the pressure on the foreign balance, to ease the money markets, to lower interest rates, and to free funds for other purposes.

The good harvests of 1797–8, 1820–3, 1832–5, 1843–4, and 1850–2 undoubtedly helped foster the major cycle expansions which were set in motion in those years; conversely, the high wheat prices and increased imports of 1795–6, 1800–1, 1810, 1817–18, 1824–5, 1836–7, and 1846–7 undoubtedly contributed to the pressure on the money market in those years of strain or crisis. The evidence is not such, however, as to justify the conception of a trade cycle detonated into its upward phase by a good harvest, operating through the foreign balance and the monetary mechanism, and brought to its close by an inadequate harvest and monetary stringency. Nevertheless, the harvests must be accounted, to the seventies, a significant permissive and contributory factor, which affected the timing of recovery, and which counted among the various strains within the economy which helped bring on the downswing. As Britain's harvest came to contribute a decreasing proportion of the total food supply, however, and foodstuffs were drawn from an increasingly large number of sources, this factor appears to diminish in importance within the trade cycle.

It is a potent heritage of the quantity theory of money, in its less sophisticated applications, that commodity prices are believed to move in close conformance with trade cycles.[1] There is no very good theoretical reason why this conformity should have been assumed. The quantity theory provides that an increase in MV can result in an increase in T, the volume of trade, as well as in P, the level of prices. In fact, the early stages of most trade cycles in Britain in this era were accompanied by stagnant or falling prices: the early twenties, thirties, forties; the periods from 1848 to 1852, 1868 to 1871, and so on. Later in the era the conformity somewhat improves; but prices are, in general, a very inadequate index of British trade cycles before 1914.

The periods of falling or stagnant prices were, normally, the intervals when the largest increases in production occurred, and the greatest declines in unemployment. From 1868 to 1871, for example, an index of total production (1900 equals 100) rises from 52 to 60; while unemployment falls from 7·9 per cent. to 1·6 per cent. Prices, however, rise from 132 to 133, the rise being confined to the last quarter of 1871, to which point prices had, in net, fallen from 1868. From 1871 to 1873 production rises from only 60 to 64; unemployment falls only from 1·6 per cent. to 1·2 per cent.; but prices rise from 133 to 148. Thus, in the first phase, to 1871, a rise of production of eight points was accompanied by a one-point rise in prices; in the final years of expansion a rise of four points in production was accompanied by a price rise of fifteen points. And for the nineteenth century in Britain this relationship of prices to production and employment, in the course of cyclical upswings, is not exceptional.

The principal explanation for this phenomenon is, of course, that the early stages of expansion represent a condition of partially unemployed resources; and the latter stages represent more nearly full employment. But it is also worth emphasizing that, while it is often useful in business cycle

---

[1] For a late example of this view see Beveridge, op. cit., appendix A, pp. 286–7.

theory to assume Marshallian short-period conditions and to ignore changes in fixed factors, the historian concerned with actual events, as they occur in time, cannot permit himself the luxury of that abstraction. The late Lord Keynes, in one of the stories on which we are now all brought up, is reported to have remarked that in the long run we are all dead. It is, however, a clear lesson of economic history, including the recent history of war economies, that the long period, in the Marshallian sense, can be very short indeed. Thus, in studying the movements of prices, even over relatively short periods in time, it is necessary to look at the changes in productive capacity and technique, and the productivity of labour, as well as at the supply of money, the state of effective demand, and the extent of unemployed resources. Changes in real costs undoubtedly served to restrain the tendency of prices to rise in the early stages of cyclical expansion.

One of the most consistent cyclical phenomena, throughout this era, is the tendency for long-term investment decisions to concentrate in the latter stages of the upswing of the major cycles. This appears to be true, not only of formal floatations in the capital markets, but to a considerable extent, also, of other forms of investment. From 1790 to 1850, over which period a great many statistical series have been subjected to analysis, with respect to their cyclical behaviour, brick production exhibits a significant average rise only in the latter stages of expansion of major cycles.[1] The cyclical behaviour of ship-building is similar, except that there were, on the average, declines in ship-building during the early

---

[1] These measures will be presented in the forthcoming study directed by A. D. Gayer, referred to earlier. For brick production, the measures are as follows. Stage I–III constitutes the early phase of expansion; III–V the late phase of expansion; V–VII the early phase of contraction; VII–IX the late phase of contraction.

Averages and average deviations of per month rate of movement in the reference cycle stages of major and minor trade cycles

		I–III	III–V	V–VII	VII–IX
Production of bricks	Major	+0·1 (0·2)	+1·6 (0·4)	0·0 (1·6)	−0·5 (1·8)
	Minor	−0·7 (0·7)	0·0 (0·4)	−0·6 (0·5)	−0·7 (0·4)

stages of both major and minor cycles; and as befits the tie between minor cycles and foreign trade, there was a substantial rise in ship-building during the latter stages of minor cycles, although a lesser rise than in the latter stages of major cycles.

With respect to the expansion of industrial plant, the evidence available is less systematic and must be pieced together industry by industry, cycle by cycle, from diverse forms of evidence. On the whole, the impression one receives is that the Industrial Revolution, regarded as a process of plant expansion and the installation of new industrial methods and techniques, lurched forward in a highly discontinuous way, with a high concentration of decisions to expand, or to improve technique, occurring in the latter stages of the major cycles.[1]

There are, of course, exceptions to this general pattern, some of considerable importance. The modern iron industry in Scotland, for example, based on Nielson's hot-blast, was founded in 1828 and grew steadily, for a considerable time, with apparently little relevance to the trade cycle.[2] Moreover, in several instances the result of the withdrawal from the capital market of the high-yield new investment, which had dominated the latter stages of expansion, and which had been discredited in the course of the turning-point and crisis, was to bring promptly into the market the low-yield type of investment which had been, as it were, starved out in the course of expansion.

It was the decision to undertake long-term investment,

---

[1] An interesting but extremely limited example of this pattern can be derived from figures given by E. Baines, *History of Cotton Manufacture*, p. 395. Baines gives the number of cotton mills in the Manchester district at three-year intervals between 1820 and 1832 as follows:

1820	. 66 factories
1823	. 72 ,,
1826	. 92 ,,
1829	. 95 ,,
1832	. 96 ,,

The greatest increase occurred in the latter stages of the major cycle expansion reaching its peak in 1825 (1823–5). Increase in the two subsequent minor cycle expansions (1826–8, 1829–31) was negligible.

[2] H. Hamilton, *The Industrial Revolution in Scotland*, pp. 179–83.

rather than the consummation of these acts, which has been noted as a particular but not exclusive characteristic of the latter stages of major cycle expansions. In fact, the period of gestation of many types of investment was such that projects undertaken in the boom were not completed until some time after the turning-point. And, as a result, the impact of depression, in its early stages, was cushioned by the necessity for completing projects earlier begun. A notable, but by no means unique, instance of this was the period 1845 to 1847. The mileage of new railway lines actually opened reached its peak in 1848, although the cyclical downturn came, clearly, in 1845. As noted earlier, this element of lag at the peak is quite generally typical of brick production and of ship-building.

In general, the nature of the trade cycle would suggest the likelihood that decisions to undertake long-term investment be concentrated disproportionately in the latter stages of expansion, rather than spread evenly throughout its course. One would expect a gradual growth in confidence concerning the future, as incomes rose, and a willingness to make commitments over increasingly long future periods. The first impact of recovery, for Britain, came normally through an increased demand for exports, especially of consumers' goods. This involved only short-term financing, usually from London, and thus relatively minor hostages to fortune. Then, gradually, one can trace the growth of daring, often leading to a concentration of interest in a particular line of new investment, at home or abroad, in the final stage of expansion. Mr. Hicks's elasticity of expectation increases.[1] The process is real, and can be quite sharply, if not quantitatively, delineated, stage by stage, in the evidence of cyclical expansions.

We turn, finally, to the behaviour of the monetary system in the course of cyclical fluctuations, and especially to the position of the Bank of England. The early stages of revival were normally marked by easy money conditions, and by falling rates of interest, short and long, inside and outside the Bank. To this tendency, as noted earlier, abundant

[1] J. R. Hicks, *Value and Capital*, p. 205.

British harvests contributed in several important instances. Credit advanced in all forms outside the Bank, for which evidence is poor, probably increased mildly in most such early stages; but the falling tendency of prices made it possible to finance an increased volume of transactions with a given supply of money. Within the Bank, bullion increased, bills and notes discounted decreased, and the Bank rate fell, or remained steady at a low level.

In the latter stages of expansion there was a gradual tightening in the market, and a tendency first for the market and then for the Bank rate to rise. Credit advanced outside the Bank rose sharply, and an increased amount of business came to the Bank as well, as other credit resources became more fully employed.

After the peak, interest rates continued to rise, but credit advances outside the Bank fell off. The Bank's discounts rose, often rapidly, as it fulfilled more or less adequately its role as *dernier resort*. Up to the turning-point the Bank had been gradually coming to share a proportion of the burden of financing expansion; after the turning-point it was meeting a crisis in confidence, an increase in liquidity preferences. The great financial crises of this era occur, almost without exception, after the downturn of the cycle; and in fact they result, largely, from the change in expectations which can be taken, analytically, if not statistically, to define the beginnings of the downturn. The nature of financial crisis, with its hasty liquidations and spreading of panic, accelerated the course of the decline in production and employment. It would, however, be incorrect to regard the financial crises of the nineteenth century as the mechanism by which prosperity was turned to depression.

The question still remains, nevertheless, as to whether the gradual tightening of the money markets, and the rise in interest rates, in the latter stages of expansion, well before financial crisis, played a decisive part in causing a changed view of the future, and the downturn. A full exploration of the mechanics of the upper turning-point is outside our present scope. The evidence suggests, however, that rising interest rates, like rising prices, symbolized an approach to an unstable position of full employment, in the major cycles. They made cost conditions different from those which had been expected when various commitments were undertaken, and they carried psychological overtones as well; and the situation was also being altered by the completion of acts of investment, previously undertaken. From these basic alterations in the complex of forces determining the volume of investment, rather than from a short-term credit shortage, the turning-point appears to occur.[1] Like the supply of labour, or commodities, or fixed capacity, the short-term money supply set a limit to the extent to which expansion could proceed. But that limit was elastic, so far as money was concerned, more elastic, certainly, than for other factors of production. So long as confidence prevailed the money supply for domestic purposes appears to have been ample. In no cycle, over this period, does inelasticity in the supply of money appear to have been the decisive factor in determining the moment of the downturn.

It is, indeed, possible that the powers held by the Bank of England, in different hands, with different conceptions of central banking function, might have been so manipulated as to alter somewhat the timing and intensity of general cyclical fluctuations. In fact, however, playing a consistently passive role, the Bank more or less adequately fulfilled its function as protector of the reserve and as *dernier resort*; but in meeting the 'legitimate demands of trade', as conceived at different points in the cycle, the Bank, and the monetary system as a whole, would appear to have been an essentially negative element in the British trade cycles of this era.

[1] For a discussion of the upper turning-point in Britain in 1920, in terms similar to these, see A. C. Pigou, *Aspects of British Economic History, 1918–1925*, pp. 188–97.

INVESTMENT AND THE GREAT DEPRESSION

'I am never weary of preaching in the wilderness "the only very important thing to be said about currency is that it is not nearly as important as it looks".'—ALFRED MARSHALL.[1]

I

THE period from 1873 to about 1896 has been known in economic history as the Great Depression. Although the trade cycle ebbed and flowed through these years, they were characterized by a set of persistent secular trends. Among these were a fall in industrial profit margins and in the rate of interest as measured by the yield on fixed-interest securities, by the yield on industrial equities, by the rate at which new floatations were made. Industry and finance were conducted in an atmosphere unsatisfactory to entrepreneurs and to many of Lombard Street's operators. 'The classes who have the most ample opportunities of proclaiming their grievances' felt 'a great social distress'.[2] Royal commissions on the depression and on gold and silver sought the causes and possible remedies for the situation. The almost continuous fall in prices, a proximate cause of reduced profit margins, was widely analysed and prescribed for by politicians, economists, men of business and finance.

It was immediately recognized, however, that the Great Depression was not an extended cyclical contraction. Output and real wages continued to move upwards at impressive rates. Marshall, the *Economist*'s editors, Giffen, both sets of royal commissioners, and most other serious commentators were aware of the limited meaning that could be attached to the word 'depression' in this context. Nevertheless the appellation has stuck. Historians are aware that output rose, and that real wages advanced rapidly, but the aura of discontent remains.

Mr. H. L. Beales, in the *Economic History Review* of October

---

[1] *Memorials to Alfred Marshall*, 1925, p. 375, in a letter to James Bonar.
[2] R. Giffen, *Essays in Finance*, 'The Liquidations of 1873–6', 1882, p. 119.

1934, did much to dispel some of the haze which still over-hangs the period.[1] He emphasized once again its highly progressive character and the extent to which the term Great Depression is a misnomer by standards of output and real wages. There is no further need to pursue the unhappy phrase, or to give the lie to the melancholy entrepreneurs and bimetallists of the eighties. The Great Depression was not a depression. But what was it?

A reading of the *Economist*, the *Bankers' Magazine*, and the evidence and reports of the royal commissions reveals a set of secular trends affecting every section of the economic system: a widening gap between the Bank and money-market rates, a fall in all rates of interest, a fall in equity prices, a shift in the direction of long-term investment away from foreign towards home channels, a fall in profit margins and prices, an increase in output and real wages. These are the facts the economist-historian must attempt to relate and explain. They dominate the years from 1873 to 1898. But they are all evident by 1886. The data in the following account will be drawn mainly from the period 1873–86.

Explanations of the Great Depression have been deter-mined by competing analyses of prices:[2] the monetary analy-sis and the approach through supply and demand. From the first, causal emphasis has depended on the method employed. The monetary perspective viewed prices as a fraction relating 'money' and 'commodities'. The fall from 1873 to 1886 was explained as an increase in 'commodities' with the amount of 'money' stagnant.[3] Money theorists pointed to a failure of the gold stock to increase at its previous rate and to the large new gold demands that accompanied the widespread movement to a single standard. They never investigated in detail the process whereby a gold shortage might have affected individual prices: they never ascertained whether bank deposits, the most important part of the circulating

---

[1] 'The "Great Depression" in Industry and Trade', pp. 65–75.

[2] For a more detailed discussion of explanations of the Great Depression, see below, Chapter VII.

[3] For a diagrammatic representation of this view, Sir R. Giffen, *Economic Inquiries and Studies*, 1904, vol. i, p. 214, 'Recent Changes in Prices and Incomes Compared'.

medium, showed the assumed contraction.[1] Occasionally
they would be forced to admit that the mechanism of the
money market and the interest rate must have been called
into play if a gold shortage were to reduce prices.[2] But they
remained, whenever possible, on the level of quantity theory
homilies. Analyses of this type usually emerged with causal
emphasis on the gold question and bias towards bi-metallist
remedy.

The approach through supply and demand was an extension to general prices of the conventional analysis of an
individual market. Its advocates mustered enormous evidence attesting to new methods and machines, cheapened
transport costs, new raw material sources, and increased
competition. They tended to deprecate the alleged monetary forces. They insisted, in short, that individual cost
curves had fallen far and shifted to the right: that the average
cost of producing a given output had decreased, and that
diminishing returns—rising marginal costs—set in at a further point, requiring a higher level of demand to yield rising
prices. They found in the case of each market no residual
movement to be explained after its unique conditions were
examined.[3] No monetary factor was required. Their motto
might have been Marshall's: 'Gold has behaved very well.'[4]

Since the eighties there has been little advance in the
analytic literature relating to this problem. The accepted
view, if it can be defined, is one which combines but does not

[1] J. T. Phinney, after examining the influence of gold on prices through the
banking system as assumed in the arguments of Hawtrey, Kitchen, Cassel, and
Layton, concludes: 'Between variations in gold production and variations in
the rate of growth of the most important part of the circulating medium, there
seems to be almost no correlation that is assumed by all studies of the problem
of price trends that deal in terms of gold and prices alone' ('Gold Production
and the Price Level', *Quarterly Journal of Economics*, 1933, p. 677).

[2] P. B. Whale has pointed out that the two 'crucial' assumptions underlying
the classical view of bullion movements were that general changes in incomes
and prices only occur as a result of changes in the volume of circulation; and
that such changes are brought about by changes in discount rates and thus
changes in the process of saving and investing in particular countries. ('The
Working of the Pre-War Gold Standard', *Economica*, 1937, pp. 18–19.)

[3] The account of D. Wells (*Recent Economic Changes*, 1889) was of this type.
See also N. Pierson, *Principles of Economics*, 1912, vol. i, pp. 384–94, for an
analysis of Wells's method and application of it to the silver question.

[4] *Memorials*, p. 68.

relate the two explanations given above: prices fell because of cheapened costs and foreign competition, but there was a 'monetary factor'. The accounts of Lord Layton and Mr. Crowther, of Prof. Clapham, of Prof. Cole, of Mr. Beales fall into this category.[1] These are directly in the line of the *Economist* and Marshall. Both stressed the increased productivity of industry as the primary cause, but added that the gold shortage was 'felt a little in the Bank parlour'.[2] Marshall gave a slightly larger place to gold than the *Economist*, which attacked any explanation which assigned to it more than a slight frictional importance.

An examination of the weekly reports reveals that the money market was well insulated from such pressure as foreign demands for bullion might have exerted on the Bank rate, and that the movements of long-term capital supply and demand can be explained without reference to forces emanating from the short-term market. None of the major characteristics of the Great Depression can be traced to a restricted response from the banking system. The prevailing tendencies in the short-term capital market, on the contrary, were towards abundant supply, with rates insensitive to changing demand conditions, and a restricted demand in several important branches—notably inland bills and Stock Exchange speculation. This fact, and a variety of institutional developments, seem to account for the gap between Bank and market rates. Neither the bullion shortage thesis nor more explicit propositions about the supply of loanable funds can be employed effectively to explain the secular fall in commodity prices, interest rates, and equity prices; nor can they account for the peculiarly depressed outlook of entrepreneurs, their complaints of over-production, or the failure of prosperity in the early eighties to attain as high a level of employment as that a decade earlier.

The bias of economic theory until the development of general income analysis, in the late 1930's, had focused

[1] W. Layton and G. Crowther, *An Introduction to the Study of Prices*, 1935, chap. viii, pp. 81–102; J. H. Clapham, *An Economic History of Modern Britain*, vol. ii, pp. 338–9; G. D. H. Cole, *British Trade and Industry, Past and Future*, 1932, chap. v, pp. 77–97; H. L. Beales, op. cit., especially pp. 74–5.
[2] *Official Papers of Alfred Marshall*, 1926, p. 128; *Economist*, 1885, p. 687.

attention on the price problem as something apart. Current analyses of output as a whole tend to distribute emphasis differently. Price movements are considered as a result of logically more profound changes in the system. General theories promise an explanation that relates the capital markets to the commodity markets. They give access to price and production problems 'without finding ourselves sometimes on one side of the moon and sometimes the other'.[1] The framework of general theories seems to resolve the dilemma of the dual approach to prices which has persistently harassed commentators on the Great Depression.

Keynes set forth the conditions of supply under which the quantity theory would hold in the short run, as follows:[2]

. . . assume (1) that all unemployed resources are homogeneous and interchangeable in their efficiency to produce what is wanted, and (2) that the factors of production entering into marginal cost are content with the same money-wage so long as there is a surplus of them unemployed. In this case we have constant returns and a rigid wage-unit, so long as there is any unemployment. It follows that an increase in the quantity of money will have no effect whatsoever on prices, so long as there is any unemployment, and that employment will increase in exact proportion to any increase in effective demand brought about by the increase in the quantity of money . . . the Quantity Theory of Money can be enunciated as follows: 'So long as there is unemployment, employment will change in the same proportion as the quantity of money, and when there is full employment, prices will change in the same proportion as the quantity of money.'

He then modifies the formal assumptions under which this would hold with a series of observations about actual markets, concluding:

. . . the increase in effective demand will, generally speaking, spend itself partly in increasing the quantity of employment and partly in raising the level of prices . . . we have in fact a condition of prices rising gradually as employment increases.

[1] J. M. Keynes, *The General Theory of Employment Interest and Money*, p. 292. See Chapter I for an extended discussion of the relation between the cast of various modern theories and explanations of the Great Depression.
[2] Ibid., pp. 295–6.

This structure links the monetary and supply-demand analyses of prices. The shape of short-run supply curves forces modification in the concept of a price rise proportional to the monetary increase. Keynes indicated the complexity of the problem by tracing in detail the price consequences of increased monetary demand under alternative conditions. The importance of the elasticity of supply (i.e. the extent to which increased output necessitates higher prices) emerges from this argument, as it does from the later exposition of Mr. Haberler.[1] But movements in the cost unit are not simple, nor do they lend themselves to general dogmatic statement.

The Keynes theory of prices proceeded under the assumption of a fixed state of equipment and technique. A purely short-period view, however, is not appropriate to historical analysis. It is of the essence of investment that it change the state of resources, equipment, and technique. The construction of new equipment is indeed time-consuming. The inauguration of a piece of investment does not coincide with its amalgamation into the capital stock of the system, and this has obvious importance. It is, nevertheless, unsatisfactory to assume that the period of gestation is always longer than the cycle, or even half the cycle: that the investment of one cycle or expansion only effects supply curves in its successor. 'If we assume a sufficient interval for the quantity of equipment itself to change, the elasticities of supply will be decidedly greater eventually';[2] 'eventually', that is, the Marshallian long period, certainly falls within the range of the time period under discussion.[3]

In the present investigation of the relation between investment and prices, supply and demand conditions in the markets where particular prices are determined will be observed. In so far as possible the sources and shifts in demand will be investigated, and related, where feasible, to the direction of new investment; the state of supply (i.e. the shape, position, and movement of particular supply curves) will be similarly related to previous investment, whether

---

[1] G. von Haberler, *Prosperity and Depression*, 1937, pp. 186, 209, 255–6, 267, 282–3.

[2] Keynes, op. cit., p. 300.   [3] See above, Chapter II, pp. 52–3.

within the same cycle or its predecessor. A satisfactory account of the Great Depression demands a focusing on the relation between the character of investment and prices. Changes in costs, demand, and investment have received much discrete historical attention. Any claim advancing the discussion must arise from a study of their interconnexion.

An increase in investment affects costs in two ways. First, even in the relatively short period, the increase in the effective quantity of money tends to bring into play inelasticities of supply. The considerations enumerated by Keynes may make for rising prices almost from the outset of recovery, and certainly in its later stages. In cyclical analysis the fact of rising prices at some stage in the course of most periods of expansion has caused great attention to be given to the effects of new investment on demand. Second, in the long period—'eventually'—investment tends to lower costs. If a strong secular downward movement in prices seems to run through cyclical fluctuation in employment and output, if one cannot establish the existence of chronic depression, a prima facie case exists for the long-run influence of investment on costs and prices.

In general, the extent to which prices rise in any period of expansion depends on the relation between the rates at which supply and demand schedules shift and change their shape—the extent to which resources and fixed capital equipment have been expanded and are being expanded and the monetary demand increased. Factors affecting both supply and demand may be influenced by the character of the new investment supporting expansion. For Britain in the latter half of the nineteenth century a world-wide railway boom was likely to produce a greater rise in prices than a boom depending on more widely spread channels of internal enterprise. On the side of demand large-scale rail-iron orders created almost immediately rising prices in that industry. They also placed great pressure on the iron and coal-mining trades, where output was subject to severely decreased returns as full employment of labour and immediately workable mineral deposits approached. Capital goods' prices and the general level moved up rapidly as the peak came close.

On the side of supply new railroads did little in the course of expansion to reduce costs, although when built they helped substantially to reduce the element of transport cost in the price of British imports.[1] Other types of cost-reducing investment might be pursued in a boom thus inspired, but their effects would almost certainly be countered by the heavy pressure on inelastic supplies of capital goods.

In a boom less singly inaugurated, in which new investment followed several directions, involving some reduction of costs in the relatively short period, different price results might be expected. The spreading of initial demand through a large number of channels would tend somewhat to put off the appearance of 'bottle-necks', or at least those inelasticities associated with a sudden and large-scale increase of orders in a single branch of trade. The fact that individual units of new investment would be smaller and capable of being postponed would probably make for more elastic demand schedules, and a less easy road to higher prices. A rise in price was more likely to lose customers if they consisted of a dozen joint stock companies and local corporations in Britain, than a single optimistic railway contractor operating in the United States or Russia. Railway builders are at the mercy of their original decision to construct. A very great change in prices or expectations is required to persuade them to halt. But when capital goods' demand arises in small orders, for smaller units of investment, the total demand will almost certainly be more sensitive to upward price revisions. Finally, the fact that the average period of gestation of new investment would be shorter would make it more difficult to maintain the phase of optimism before expectations were belied.[2] It would tend as well to lower costs even within the compass of the expansion period.

This analysis is by no means a complete explanation of the disparity of price movements in the two booms, 1868–73 and 1879–83. It provides, however, a rough framework for more detailed inquiry.

[1] See Layton and Crowther, op. cit., pp. 89–90, on the manner in which American railway building affected the price of wheat.
[2] A. C. Pigou, *Industrial Fluctuations*, 1929, pp. 90–2 and 230.

Assuming constant tastes and money incomes, an end to wars, a stable population, and no new lands to be developed, one would expect to find an economic system in which prices fell steadily in response to intensive cost-reducing investment. An assumption of this kind underlies Mr. Durbin's conception of equilibrium.[1] It is reasonable that the placid community garner the rewards of its abstinence (ignoring the effects on saving of a fall in its price) in a rising state of welfare achieved through ever lower prices.

Entrepreneurs and financiers in this community, however, could be counted on to complain bitterly of their position. The expected yield on new investment would fall, dividends would drop, and Stock Exchange operators might find it difficult to arouse interest in speculation. Fixed capital would be re-valued downward. One might expect also an appearance of the bogey of over-production. Optimum output would be at a constantly further point. The amount of output produced under decreasing costs would increase. Should this relative growth in the proportion of fixed capital be world-wide, the atmosphere of over-production would be accentuated, trade restrictions encouraged. The elasticity of demand curves for home products would increase with the efficiency of foreign competitors: the British producer would have over him constantly the threat of orders transferred abroad if prices were raised. Barring monopoly tactics competition within the country would also become more severe. If output continued to fluctuate cyclically the long-term tendency to falling prices might dominate periods of expansion as well as contraction. Normal inelasticities of supply and expectations of them would operate against forces which might, in net, yield stagnant or even falling prices in a boom.

These cryptically stated hypotheses will be tested against the data of the Great Depression. Corroboration will proceed

---

[1] *What Everyone Wants to Know about Money* (edited by G. D. H. Cole), chap. vii, pp. 253–79 ('Money and Prices'). See also Keynes, op. cit., pp. 306–9. The assumption that the rate of interest will necessarily fall in a stationary state has been in recent years a subject of much controversy. The proposition has been by no means universally accepted. It conforms, however, to the view taken here of the Great Depression; and has been therefore employed as a background for the historical exposition.

along two lines. The extent to which new British capital investment shifted from foreign to home channels will be examined, and its partial analogue in the reduction of costs in various of the principal industries. These sections will not give a consecutive historical account, but will attempt to evaluate the net changes in the first decade of the period. The relation between investment and prices will then be traced through the cyclical phases from 1868 to 1886.

II

Statistics of new capital issues and of joint stock enterprise supply by no means complete data of new investment. Capital goods' production indexes are perhaps the best indicators for cyclical analysis. Total capital estimates, such as Mr. Paul Douglas's compilation,[1] are useful in judging long-term movements. The figures for new issues and company floatations do, however, usefully suggest the direction investment is taking, as well as its relative increase and decrease. The years 1870–5 and 1880–5, 1873 and 1883 are approximately comparable phases of cyclical movement. The relative amounts of new British enterprise at home and abroad are roughly revealed by the following figures:[2]

(Statistical abstract) *Average annual number new joint stock companies registered*		(1900 = 100) (Beveridge) *Average annual capital per head new joint stock companies registered*		(Hobson) *Average annual capital issues in U.K.*	
1870–5	1880–5	1870–5	1880–5	1870–5	1880–5
21·6	31·2	55·9	92·6	18·7	23·6

(Hobson) *Average annual capital export*		(Douglas) *Relative total capital invested overseas*		(Douglas) *Estimated total capital in U.K.*	
1870–5	1880–5	1875	1883	1873	1883
176·5	82·1	55·4	62·7	58·9	76·6

[1] 'An Estimate of the Growth of Capital in U.K., 1865–1909', *American Journal of Economic and Business History*, Aug. 1930.

[2] All figures have been reduced to 1900 = 100. Sir William Beveridge, *Unemployment*, 1930, pp. 42–3, col. 6. C. K. Hobson, *The Export of Capital*, 1920, p. 223. P. Douglas, op. cit., pp. 679–80.

However inaccurate these statistics may be, however limited the area of new investment they may cover, however dubious any quantitative statements drawn from them, they do attest to a shift away from capital export towards new investment at home.

The changed direction of investment was, quite consistently, accompanied by a fall in rates of interest. Labour-saving machinery is not generally expected to yield as high a return as railroads or gold mines. This is indicated by the following figures:[1]

	Rate on bankers' best three months' bills	Yield on Consols per cent.	Index of fixed-interest securities prices (1900 = 100)	Index of industrial securities prices
1873	4·70	3·24	81·5	84·3
1879	2·14	3·08	85·5	58·0
1883	3·22	2·96	91·5	61·8
1886	2·33	2·97	93·0	58·7

The money rate showed some cyclical fluctuation; the Consol rate was influenced from 1883–6 by special factors affecting government credit; the advantages of a fixed yield increased steadily; industrial dividends, actual and expected, fell with important interruption only in the short-lived speculation of 1879–80. Generally the evidence attests overwhelmingly to a fall in the abstraction called the rate of interest.

Giffen had said in the seventies: 'In the course of time, if the taste for foreign investment does not revive, the capital and labour employed in making articles for export will be turned to the production of articles for consumption and investment at home.'[2] The changed direction of investment was in fact accompanied by a rapid refinement in the capital structure of British industry; while the rail makers, who had benefited so largely from the capital exports, were forced to

[1] The rate on three months' bills is from A. C. Pigou, op. cit., p. 399; the yield on Consols is calculated from the annual average price; the securities' indices, with the base year shifted, are those of K. C. Smith and G. F. Horne, 'An Index Number of Securities, 1867–1914', Memorandum No. 47 of the Royal Economic Society, June 1934.

[2] Op. cit., p. 121. Although exports continued to rise the balance of trade was immediately sensitive to the decrease in capital export, fulfilling the true sense of Giffen's prophecy.

look to other lines. New machinery, methods, and supplies
of raw materials created a virtual revolution. The pressure
of falling prices, the increase in foreign competition, the
abundance and cheapness of funds should all have tended to
encourage capital export. But the failures of the middle
seventies had eliminated many of the most important borrowers, while lenders grew cautious. The market for high-
risk foreign issues all but disappeared. A graphic, though
extremely crude, indicator of the direction which new capital
investment was taking are the *Economist* advertisements. The
last pages of each issue were devoted to the seduction of the
investor. In 1873, bonds for the Turkish Government, water-
works for St. Petersburg, railroads for Montevideo, banks
for Mexico, gold mines for Peru were in order. By the
eighties new steam-engines, three-furrow ploughs, insurance
companies, Appleby's cranes and engines, Bush's concentrated fruit essences, Smith and Coventry's labour-saving
machine tools, and Galloway's boilers command the stage.

The secular development of savings institutions and habits,
aided by the rise in real incomes, helped the home investor.
Funds were easily available for safe ventures. The daring of
investors varied, of course, with the stage of the cycle, but
the experiences of 1873–7 seem to have chilled issuing-houses
and private lenders to the exciting types of foreign securities
which had dominated 1870–3. Such new foreign issues as
appeared were for more stable governments (there was a
decided shift towards colonial investment, especially in
Australasia) at steadily falling interest rates. The character
and means of investment were described by Goschen in
1885:[1]

Those gentlemen (the bimetallist inflationists) have their wish
now in a certain sense. They have capital at two per cent. There
seems to be no dearth of capital. . . . With regard to cheap
money . . . it appears to me it is not only the traders and the
manufacturers who are complaining (because of falling prices and
profit margins), but that other capitalists find it exceedingly
difficult to find a good return for their capital. The colonies are
borrowing at four per cent. and less whereas they used to be

---

[1] *Addresses on Economic Questions*, 1905, pp. 198–200, 'The Prospects of Trade'.

borrowing at six per cent. Corporations are borrowing more cheaply than they were ever able to borrow before. The borrowers, steady borrowers, sober borrowers, have an extremely good time of it, and what is the meaning of this cheapness of capital? I think it means that the savings of the country have gone on increasing, while there has been more prudence in selecting the securities into which they were put. Foreign loans used to carry off a large portion of our savings, but the Income Tax returns show that the profits derived from foreign securities have scarcely increased during the last few years. Savings are being used in another way. Never before has there been so keen a desire on the part of the whole community to invest every reserve shilling they may have in some remunerative manner. There is a competition between men who have a few tens of pounds and a few hundreds of pounds to put them into business, and into business they are put. Joint-stock enterprise has swept up all these available resources. Like a gigantic system of irrigation it first collects and then pours them through innumerable conduit pipes right over the face of the country, making capital accessible in every form at every point.

The fact that investment showed a tendency to turn inward during the Great Depression might be expected to have ramifications on the supply-demand conditions of specific markets. On both sides, it will appear, there were forces making for lower prices: cost curves shifted down and to the right, demand curves for particular firms and British industries became more elastic. A given output could be more cheaply produced, home and foreign competition became increasingly severe. Two sets of questions will be asked of the data. First, over a period of years, did the expected secular trends exhibit themselves in specific markets? Can those trends be associated with the shift in the direction of investment which has already been established? Second, can the characteristics of the cyclical phases 1868–73, 1874–9, 1880–3, 1884–6 be similarly related to the type of new investment pursued and to the effects on industry of this investment, previously investigated over a longer period?

It is unnecessary to recount at length the technical development in British industries during the seventies and eighties. Economic historians have told its story fully as an institu-

tional development. It is important here to select evidence
from the more important industries to illustrate the character
of the process. To that end the iron, coal, and cotton trades
will now be examined.

Changes in the demand for British iron and steel in the
decade following 1873 may be summarized as follows:

1. A decreased demand for rail-iron and rail machinery,
   except from the colonies and South America.
2. An increased demand for the building of machinery and
   ships.
3. A moderate net increase in foreign demand for iron and
   steel generally.
4. An enormous increase in the demand for steel.

It was Clapham's opinion that 'the remarkable maintenance of the output of puddled iron during the decade
1873–83, in face of competition from the continent and the
open hearths, and in spite of the abandonment of iron railway
by all great companies before 1879, was due principally to a
great expansion of the demand for iron plates and angles in
ship-building'.[1] This development is illustrated by the production figures from a group of malleable-iron producers in
the north-east:[2]

(*In thousand tons*)			Plates	Angles	Bars	Rails	Total
1873	.	.	166	44	79	324	613
1876	.	.	172	53	88	108	421
1878	.	.	234	88	78	22	422
1880	.	.	317	93	71	27	508
1883	.	.	440	134	81	3	658

Total railway-iron and steel production did not fall everywhere to this disastrous extent. Although the intervening
years were dark indeed, there was an increase in railway
metal produced from one cyclical peak to the next, from
897 thousand tons in 1873 to 1,051 in 1882.[3] Since the price

---

[1] Op. cit., p. 61. See also Sir Lowthian Bell, Statement Relating to the Iron
Trade, *Second Report, Commission on Depression*, appendix A, p. 330 (pamphlet,
p. 42). Bell's statement appeared originally as a pamphlet. Page-numbers of the
pamphlet are given in the minutes, enabling more precise reference.

[2] Bell, op. cit., p. 18.

[3] Ibid., p. 27.

of iron fell 60 per cent. in this decade, money earnings from the production of rail-iron were much decreased.[1]

The growing importance of machinery to the iron trade is shown by these figures of the comparative value of machinery production:[2]

(In £ millions)

				%
1873	.	.	.	10·0
1879	.	.	.	7·3
1883	.	.	.	13·4

If a rough price corrective is applied (Sauerbeck minerals index, 1900 = 1·00), they become:

				%
1873	.	.	.	7·6
1879	.	.	.	10·8
1883	.	.	.	19·8

Bell commented that 'these figures justify the assertion that the engine and machine builders are very important customers of our iron works . . . and that the use of iron is extending into those requirements of life which are, it may be expected, less liable to those excessive fluctuations which have marked the progress of railways'.[3]

Total British export of iron and steel (including machinery reduced to terms of pig bars) was 3·9 million tons in 1873, 5·6 in 1882.[4] At the bottom of depression, in 1878, the total was 3·0. Of this amount there was a general evenly spread increase of about 0·4 million tons in the sale of iron and steel pig-iron bars to industrial nations. In the purchase of manufactured iron (railroad, bar, angle, bolt, and rod) a remarkable shift occurred in which the colonies, South America, and other semi-developed areas superseded Germany, France, Belgium, Russia, and the United States as Britain's most important customers.[5]

---

[1] The prices of iron fell as follows:

	Cleveland pig	Haematite
1873	109s. 2d.	156s.
1883	43s. 5d.	56s. 7d.

[2] Bell, op. cit., p. 27. These figures include machinery produced for export as well as home consumption.

[3] Ibid., pp. 22 and 155.   [4] Ibid., p. 28.

[5] Foreign trade supplements of *Economist*, January of each year.

From 1878 on, steel became increasingly important in the shipbuilding industry.[1] At the same time steel was superseding iron as rail material.[2] The substitution of steel for iron had, among others, these two effects on demand: steel competed successfully in many uses with malleable iron; the longer life of steel rails made, over a period of time, for a relative fall in rail replacement orders.[2] The production of steel by the basic process rose from 20 tons in 1878 to 179,000 tons in 1884; while the difference between Cleveland and imported haematite iron prices fell from 21*s*. 5*d*. to 7*s*. 11*d*.[3] The consumer of steel owed much to Messrs. Gilchrist and Thomas. Steel rails, which had been sold for £12. 1*s*. in 1874, were marketed for £4. 5*s*. ten years later.

In the iron industry, as elsewhere, there were also numerous economies through the use of new methods and machines. Bell concluded that 'the improvements which have been applied to production are such that it is difficult to compare costs with those of former times. To produce a ton of pig something like 20*s*. only is expended in wages':[4] and wage rates rose or were maintained. I. T. Smith estimated that 'the labour on a ton of rails is not half what it was when we first began to make rails'.[5] In finished as well as intermediate iron products this trend is evident. In the manufacture of steel files, for example, cutting machines were introduced, requiring two skilled operators, throwing out of employment six to eight men, who, 'instead of working as skilled artisans, became labourers'.[6]

While this revolution in the techniques of production proceeded in Britain, world output was expanding rapidly. The relative fall in British foreign lending did not check the growth of capital-goods industries elsewhere. The United States, Germany, Belgium, and France all tended to free themselves from dependence on the British semi-monopoly of the early seventies. In 1873 Britain produced 44·7 per cent.

[1] Bell, op. cit., pp. 20–4.
[2] Idem.
[3] Ibid., pp. 17 and 24.
[4] *Second Report, Commission on Depression*, 1955–9.
[5] Ibid., 3648.
[6] Ibid., 1156–81, 1198–1204, 1274–82 (S. Uttley), and 1448 (J. Dixon).

of the world's pig-iron, in 1883, 40·5 per cent.; British production for 1873 (1870 = 100) was 110·1, 154·9 for the world—in 1883, 143·0, 239·1 for all other countries.[1] Although British iron exports continued to rise in quantity, although Bell could proclaim England 'still without peer as a producer of iron and steel',[2] the semi-monopoly days of 1871–3 were over, and the profit margins that had accompanied them. The threat of foreign competition, and the occasional appearance in Britain of German cutlery or German girders, was sufficient to warn producers that costs must be cut and prices kept low if their share of world production were to be maintained.[3]

More generally the significance of the world extension of facilities lay in the resultant increased elasticity of supply. The boom of 1871–3 had stimulated the opening and extension of iron works. This 'undue extension', wrote Bell, 'justified, perhaps, at the moment, over a term of years, was more than the world required'.[4] Full employment of resources became harder to attain. Price-cutting resulted wherever price-fixing did not.[5]

Although wage-rates in the iron industry actually rose in this decade,[6] iron producers were relieved by the steady fall in the price of coal. Sauerbeck's index number for the price of coal was 145 in 1873, 82 in 1883.[7] A third of the coal output was consumed in iron production. The latter industry was extremely sensitive to price movements in coal.[8] A 44 per cent. drop in its price facilitated the difficult transition

---

[1] Bell, op. cit., p. 58.

[2] *Second Report*, 2371 and 2373.

[3] Bell, op. cit., pp. 62–4, and *Second Report*, 2369 (I. T. Smith).

[4] Bell, op. cit., pp. 165–6. Speaking of excess capacity, T. E. Vickers said (*Second Report*, 3533–4), 'the duty in the past has fostered the building of these works, these works are there, and must be kept going. 3533. At a profit? At a profit or no profit, they must be kept going.'

[5] For classic testimony on the factors making for monopoly see I. T. Smith's statements on the international rail ring, *Second Report*, 2271–89. The impulse arose in this case from the existence of excess capacity and cutthroat competition after the short American railway boom of the early eighties had ended.

[6] See Bell's testimony, *Second Report*, 3648.

[7] *The Course of Average Prices*, 1908, p. 65.

[8] For discussion of this relationship, see *Economist*, 1873, p. 187.

to new methods and new demand conditions in the iron and steel markets.

Foreign competition did not constitute a problem to the coal industry.[1] Even in neutral markets there was little perceptible opposition. Competition among British producers, however, was severe. Between 1871 and 1875, 1,401 new pits were sunk: 'The cause of depression, I think,' answered John Ellis,[2] 'is the large number of pits which were sunk immediately after that excitement' (1871–3). The element depriving coal-operators of their profit was 'a demand not so great or nearly so great as the supply in our district, and therefore the selling price is lower',[3] or, as one producer agreed, 'a competition between our coal producers to get rid of their surplus stock'.[4] The demand for coal increased steadily as the process of world industrialization proceeded. The rise in British coal production was only slightly interrupted even in the years of worst depression.

The expansion of iron and coal resources and improved techniques and labour efficiency applied helped to produce a fall in prices throughout the capital-goods industries. In each branch of trade this reduction was accentuated by its own technical developments. In many places machine tools superseded the skilled artisan. Machinery was sought as a means of escaping the tyranny of money wages that could not be reduced. Everywhere 'the growing depression stimulated invention of labour-saving devices'.[5]

The British cotton industry also underwent great technical improvement and expansion, yielding price-reducing competition and falling dividends.[6] Output of yarn rose (1900 = 100) from 76·7 in 1873 to 82·3 in 1883, piece-goods' exports from 69·2 to 90·2; the Sauerbeck textile index (1900 = 100) fell from 156·1 to 106·1 in the same years. As in the case of iron the rate of increase was slower than on the Continent

---

[1] *Second Report*, 3025–6 (J. D. Ellis).
[2] Ellis was chairman of John Brown & Co., and also chairman of the South Yorkshire Coal Association, ibid., 3002–16.
[3] Ibid., 3083.
[4] *Third Report*, 12, 310 (J. B. Simpson).
[5] Bell, *Second Report*, 2689. See also D. Wells, op. cit., pp. 364–70.
[6] For good general statement, Wells, op. cit., p. 184.

and in the United States. The proportion of cotton consumed
is given by the following figures:[1]

	Great Britain	Continent	United States
1871–5 . .	47·2	32·9	19·9
1881–3 . .	39·9	35·9	24·2

Within Britain, as well as abroad, capital was pouring into
new ventures. Three hundred and seventy-three new cotton
companies, with a nominal capital of £20·4 million, were
floated between 1873 and 1883.[2] The many mills erected
in the early eighties were built at a cost of from 20 to 30 per
cent. less than those of 1874–5,[2] and thus competed more
easily in home and foreign markets. New machinery and
methods were widely introduced, to which (in the case of
Oldham) Ellison ascribes entirely the reduction of costs and
the possibility of profitable production at lower prices.[3]
G. T. Jones estimated that money costs in the Lancashire
cotton industry fell from 114·8 in 1873 to 84·6 in 1883, real
costs from 108 to 106.[4] If a ten-year moving average is taken
of real costs, the downward trend is more apparent than in
the annual figures. In the decade 1870–80 Jones estimated
that real costs fell at the rate of ½ per cent. per annum.[5]

In statements before the Royal Commissioners, cotton
representatives universally attested to a chronic 'over-production'.[6] That output could only be sold at a falling price
was the witnesses' chief complaint when pressed for definition.
A consequent falling yield on fixed capital was accepted 'for
the simple reason that it might have cost them (the operators)
more to have stopped the works than it cost them to keep
them going'.[7] There is little doubt that the supply curves of
the British cotton industry conform to the general pattern.

[1] T. Ellison, *The Cotton Trade of Great Britain*, 1886, p. 100. In 1882–3, however, Britain was still far ahead of any other nation in *per capita* cotton spun
with 41·8 lb. per head; next was the U.S.A. with 18·7, and Switzerland with
17·30 (ibid., p. 147).

[2] Ibid., p. 135.

[3] Ibid., p. 139.

[4] *Increasing Returns*, 1933, p. 115.   [5] Ibid., p. 199.

[6] *Second Report*, see especially 4294–6, 4419–33, 4478–85 (S. Andrew and
S. Taylor) and 5127–30, 5215–46, 5257–8 (J. Mawdsley) and 5314–15 (G. Lord).

[7] Ibid., 5229 (J. Mawdsley).

On the side of demand, the secular growth of real income produced steady increase. When the quantity of cotton exports were examined contemporaries found little of which to complain.[1] Severe competition was felt only in the case of the Indian mills.[2] American and German tariff barriers were a hindrance, and a growth of cotton industries within them. But in 1886, writing of sales abroad, Ellison was able to proclaim:[3]

There is scarcely a nook or a corner in the habitable globe where the products of the spindle and looms of Lancashire do not find a market, although in some of the more civilised countries special efforts have been made to hinder, or altogether prevent, the import of British yarns and piece goods. The industry and ingenuity of our spinners and manufacturers, and the ability and enterprise of our merchants, have enabled them, more or less successfully, to compete with their rivals abroad, even where the latter have had the protection of exorbitant import duties; while in respect of the business done with the open markets of the world, Manchester almost monopolises the trade in cotton goods.

The answer to the dilemma of over-production lay, it was felt, in the opening up of China, Asia, and Africa, which, Ellison believed, might be 'a second India to Lancashire'.

This relative over-development of fixed resources can be traced to almost every large British industry—shipping,[4] paper, chemical, and textiles other than cotton.[5] Evidence before the 1886 Commission affirmed an increased amount of capital invested, a decreased net return, an increased volume of trade, a stagnant or proportionally lesser increase in the gross value of trade.[6]

[1] See, for example, Ellison, op. cit., pp. 149–62.

[2] For a more depressed picture of cotton in 1886, see *Second Report*, appendix A (6), pp. 368–9, in which T. Stuttard condemns the 'unscrupulous and barbaric' competition of Indian mills.

[3] Op. cit., p. 150.

[4] *Third Report*, 10, 065–9 (W. R. Price) and *Final Report*, p. ix. The fall in freight rates had, of course, important influence on the prices of all imports.

[5] See ibid., p. ix, for summary statement on paper, chemicals, and textiles.

[6] Ibid., pp. 123–9, where the evidence given before the Commission is summarized.

III

No attempt has been made to present here a complete historical account of British industries in the first decade of the Great Depression. It has been sufficient to indicate the extent to which developments in specific industrial markets are consistent with the general framework relating investment and prices. The chronicle of cost-reducing investment is far from complete; but it will have been sufficient here to show the shift to the right and lowering of supply curves: the shift to the right, but growing elasticity of demand curves facing particular firms and British industries. These meant, simply, falling prices and profit margins, despite rising output; and the rigours of severe competition.

Questions of monopoly tactics and the net effect of trade barriers have not been developed. They may be regarded, from this limited perspective, as an effect of economic developments, not a cause; although they did have significant consequences in several markets. But measured against the sweep of forces developing from 1873, they are of minor importance. They heralded, however, the beginning of the crystallization of British capitalism.

At the risk of some repetition the relation between investment, output, and prices will now be traced through short periods, in an attempt to answer the second set of questions addressed to the data. This analysis, including within it the pre-1873 boom, should give some insight into the essential differences between the periods of rising and falling prices. It may permit also a further isolation of the separate effects of investment on supply and demand schedules.

(Note: all statistics 1900 = 100, unless otherwise indicated.[1])

---

[1] The following material is drawn from a more detailed chronicle of events, constructed largely from the *Economist* and the *Bankers' Magazine* of which Chap. ix constitutes a portion. The price statistics are Sauerbeck's; the capital-goods, consumers' goods, and general-production statistics are from W. Hoffmann. 'Ein Index der industriellen Produktion für Grossbritanien seit der 18. Jahrhundert', *Weltwirtschaftliches Archiv*, Sept. 1934, pp. 383–98; coal, iron, and textile production and export figures are from the Statistical Abstract for U.K. given in W. Page, *Commerce and Industry*, 1919, vol. ii; money and real wages are from Layton and Crowther, pp. 265–6; the unemployment figures are derived from Beveridge, op. cit., 883–98, pp. 42–3, col. 3.

From 1868 to 1871 output rose from 43 to 51, unemployment fell from 6·25 to 1·75 per cent.; but the general price index rose only from 132 to 133. Within the general index a tendency for the prices of minerals and other raw materials to rise is tempered somewhat by a fall in the food and textile indexes; nevertheless, until the second half of 1871 business widely reported large but unremunerative production. Recovery up to that point had encountered no serious inelasticities in supply and therefore produced no important price advances. Even the mineral index (weighted heavily with coal and iron) rose only from 79 to 86, despite a rise in iron and steel exports from 59 to 92, of pig-iron production from 56 to 74, of coal production from 46 to 52.

With the settlement of European peace a world-wide boom was launched. Orders poured into British works from every direction, at home and abroad. An almost classic case of full employment was reached in 1872–3. Bottlenecks appeared, especially in the markets for labour and coal. Unemployment was 1·65 per cent. in 1871, 1·15 per cent. in 1873, yet money wages had risen from 77 to 89; general production rose only from 51 to 55, while the general price index rocketed from 133 to 148. The mineral price index moved from 86 to 131, coal output, however, increased only from 52 to 56, pig-iron output was 74 in both years.

The rapid increase in demand (i.e. a shifting of demand curves to the right, curves which for British capital industries were highly inelastic) brought not only a rise in costs and prices, but also a reduction in productivity. In the crucially important coal industry new men were inefficient, and labour in general quite willing to abstract a part of its reward in increased leisure. There was, in addition, some tendency for work to become less efficient, even among experienced hands. This may account in part for the failure of output further to expand. Essentially, however, the large blocks of new investment, undertaken under independent but common impulse at the close of the war, were simply too much for British fixed capital facilities to bear.

Rising labour and raw material costs began to cut into the profitability of trade, both within the areas of industry directly affected by the export boom and outside. Textiles, British railways, gas-works—outside the primary area—complained of narrowing profit margins, while only the temporary inelasticity of the export demand permitted the capital-goods industries to carry on (through higher prices) in the face of rising marginal costs. Early in 1873, before either of the great financial crises of the year, the turning-point in iron had appeared. In January, 'prices are rising for the present, but as new business is not active, the stronger tendency is due rather to a deficient supply than to increased demand'.[1] Puddling furnaces in the north and in south Wales were blown out in January and February; the demand for finished iron was 'not as good as expected' in April.[2] Export orders for finished goods were being held off in the hope of a fall in prices:[3] 'lower prices are still looked for and concessions continue to be slowly made. . . .' By the end of the year the demand for railway iron had fallen off sharply, the pressure on coal supplies had relaxed.

Reports from the capital industries during 1872–3 show that the inelasticity of coal-supply was, along with that in various labour markets, by far the most serious. Its effects were especially pervasive because of the iron industry's central position in the boom. The high prices of the latter stages of expansion, however, induced an enormous opening of new pits as well as an extension of operations to less productive coal veins. The danger of coal famine was removed for a quarter of a century. Expansion of plant in other branches paralleled on a smaller scale that in coal. Although foreign issues offered severe competition in the existing state of confidence, joint-stock floatations in 1871–3 were on a high level. The maintenance of internal prosperity, the immediate fall in the long-term rate, the incomes amassed in the previous boom all encouraged wide plant expansion in 1874–5. The great extension and technical improvement in cotton and metals came after 1873 rather than before.

The general price index fell from 148 to 110 between 1873 and 1879, general production from 62 to 60; unemployment

---

[1] *Economist*, 1873, p. 106. [2] Ibid., pp. 74, 106, 204, 235.
[3] Ibid., pp. 726 and 788.

rose from 1·2 to 10·7 per cent. The increased productivity
represented by these figures came in part from the greater
efficiency of labour. Entrepreneurs did everything in their
power to eliminate the laxity encouraged in the easy days
of 1872–3. In part it arose from the extension and improvement of plant that boom expectations had helped stimulate.
By 1879 many new cotton mills were in operation, new coal
pits were producing, and despite a strong tendency for unit
output to rise, the number of blast furnaces had increased
(1900 = 100) from 147·6 (1873) to 153·0.[1] The boom had
also brought with it new methods and machinery. The
period of relative recession served only to accentuate the
advantages of such labour-saving devices. These years clearly
show a downward and outward shift of supply curves in the
major British industries. The presence of excess capacity in
the existing state of demand aided the movement to lower
prices and lower returns on fixed capital. Increased output
did not bring increased marginal costs.

The enormous orders of 1872–3, which had forced the
system to full employment and virtually pure inflation, had
come from abroad and had centred on the rail-iron trade.
From 1873–9 that source of demand fell off heavily. Until
the latter half of 1877 the engineering and shipbuilding trades
helped maintain output. A building boom, instigated by a
combination of large boom profits, a falling interest rate,
and a profound distrust of new issues in the London market,
gave secondary sustenance. The demand for engineering
iron was strengthened by the building of new factories and a
variety of local government projects. The index of capital-
goods production actually rose from 55·3 in 1873 to 61·4 in
1877. The export demand in the latter stages of expansion
had been accompanied by a relatively small increase in
output. Ignoring, for the moment, changes in supply conditions, it would not have been startling if a relaxation of that
demand brought only a minor reduction in output.

In 1877–8 a variety of factors caused a cessation of home
as well as foreign investment. Output and employment

[1] The change in unit output is illustrated by the fact that in 1873 pig-iron
production was 74·1 with 169·5 blast furnaces in blast, 67·4 in 1879 with 123·1.

descended into severe depression. The building boom had ended. The capital market was wracked by falling dividends, doubts about the banking system, uncertainty over the state of international politics, and high money rates. Expectations could not have been worse. There was no incentive even to maintain stocks. Business was executed on immediate order, materials purchased for hand-to-mouth production. And yet so considerable were the secular forces making for increased output that capital-goods production fell less than 8 per cent. from the peak of 1877 to 1879.

Mr. Colin Clark maintains that periods of increased productivity tend to be associated with heavy average unemployment.[1] There is some evidence in this recession of technological unemployment, and of considerable short-time. But on the whole the years 1873–7 were remarkable for the high level at which employment was maintained. Only in 1877 was unemployment over 4 per cent. The descent after 1877 is explicable on quite other grounds than the frictions which accompany increased productivity. In the first six years of the Great Depression it is more probable that the net effect of investment increasing productivity was towards greater than 'normal' employment.[2]

It has been assumed throughout that supply and demand conditions depended not only on judgement of current conditions, but on expectations as well. In the years after the crisis especially, expectations of a further fall in prices tended to make purchasers keep stocks low, and drive hard bargains. This willingness to postpone purchase produced increased competition among sellers, increasingly elastic demand curves facing the individual firm at a moment of time. Entrepreneurs, sensing that the price future would be even more black than the present, were willing to accept a falling return on fixed capital, attempting to improve their net position by

[1] *National Income and Outlay*, 1937, pp. 269–73. Clark seems to hold that the cyclical peak in the seventies was 1876, that from 1870–6 unemployment was low and (because?) productivity stagnant, that from 1877–85 average unemployment was higher and (because?) productivity rose rapidly.

[2] Layton and Crowther conclude that, 'looking at the whole period (1873–96) there seems to be no evidence that employment was less regular than in preceding periods' (op. cit., p. 95). See also Chapter II, above, pp. 47–50.

expanding output and introducing cost-reducing machinery. The growth of competition among sellers is almost as common a complaint as over-production.

Price movements in the expansion of 1880–3 came in two phases: a rise from late 1879 through the first quarter of 1880; an irregular decline in most markets to 1883. Prices were 110 in 1879, 117 in 1880, and 109 in 1883. Production in those years was, respectively, 60, 71, and 78. The large American rail orders in the last quarter of 1879 stimulated a rapid speculative rise in output. Stocks were replenished in expectation of a recurrence of 1871–3 boom conditions. But the increase in American purchases was not maintained, the expected inelasticities did not appear, and prices stagnated or fell.

Recovery in its first phase was based on rail-iron orders. In its second phase it derived from a British ship-building boom, from joint-stock development in Britain, and, to a lesser extent, from widespread export increases. Previous and current investment so extended fixed plant that increased output was accompanied by stagnant or falling prices. So great were the facilities for iron production that even the enormous boom in ship-building caused increased output, but no important rise in price. The first reversal of the upward output trend came in 1882, with a fall in exports, after the continental crises; the second, in 1883, when the fall in freight rates, and a realization of the extent to which ship-building had been overdone, cut short new orders there. Over-optimism on the Clyde was soon corrected and the capital-goods industries were immediately sensitive.

The failure of prices to rise in the latter three years of expansion, the continued narrowing of profit margins, the chronic Stock Exchange slump never yielded a general over-optimism. In ship-building alone can one trace that reconsideration of expectations associated with the normal crisis. Many reports show no realization that output and employment were pursuing a cyclical pattern.

When the speculations of 1879–80 came to an early halt, the business and financial communities settled into passive gloom. The joint-stock boom of these years, involving still further plant expansion, was not calculated to raise fears of shortage. The investor was, moreover, meeting constant disappointment when he tried to escape the régime of falling interest rates in more speculative ventures. Nor was this disappointment long postponed. Booms in Indian and Cornish mines and the electric light industry flickered and were quickly extinguished within the expansion years.

After three years of such recovery in the previous boom large capital exports and export demands for capital goods had intervened. The impetus which had produced full employment and rising prices in 1871–3 was no longer available. The character of investment had changed, and British industry could not again revel in the illusion of indefinitely rising prices and profits: in particular markets demand curves neither shifted far enough to the right nor became sufficiently inelastic to achieve that happy condition. Excess capacity and severe competition (but not abnormal unemployment) still dominated the industrial position.

Investment at home had supported a substantial part of general recovery in 1880–3. Such investment, ship-building aside, suffered little from false expectations. New issues had been abnormally low in 1883, and the capital market actually revived somewhat in 1884, declining in 1885, reviving sharply in 1886. There was no steep descent to pessimism. Two primary deflationary forces operated on industry: a decrease in exports and a decline in ship-building. Production and prices fell off generally: the former (from 1883–6) by 8 per cent., the latter by 12.

The nature of the previous boom, if anything, shortened the length of the recession. The first signs of returning confidence came late in 1885. There were, generally, no heavy capital losses to liquidate. Even the shipbuilding industry felt ready to revive after a two-year decline. The revival in capital export which had begun in 1879 was interrupted only in 1885. The figures for 1884 and 1886 were considerably higher than for any years in the previous decade. The enticements of the Argentine and the Rand were soon to appear. Towards the close of 1886 even prices showed some tendency to rise, bringing a breath of optimism to trade reports.

IV

The analysis has thus far concerned itself with Great Depression phenomena as they exhibited themselves in the years 1873 to 1886. The subsequent period which falls within the Great Depression has been omitted largely for purposes of analytic convenience; but the behaviour of the British economy virtually to the eve of the Boer War may be regarded as dominated by the secular forces of the Great Depression.

The cyclical expansion from 1886 to 1890 constitutes a break in the trend pattern; but a meaningful break. The downward movement of prices, from 1873 to 1886, was traced to a relative cessation of foreign lending: their rise to 1890 is closely connected with a revival of foreign lending. In its initial stage a revived export demand from both North and South America contributed to the expansion. In the latter stage (1888–90) South America was the dominant feature in both the long-term capital market and in the expansion of commodity exports. It was activity in this direction which distinguishes the boom of 1886–90 from that of 1879–83; for, aside from the South American adventures, the other bases of revival were much as they had previously been: a variety of internal developments, associated with joint-stock formation and ship-building. Reports from the engineering, iron, and steel trades indicate the extent to which the margin of prosperity which lead to rising prices was dependent, over the final years of expansion, on the export trade to the developing South American areas. The role of exports in the boom of the late eighties, as compared with the early years of the decade, is indicated in the following figures for the value of exports:

Value of Exports
(1900 = 100)
1880: 80·8
1883: 86·2
1887: 79·4
1890: 92·6

With the home market strong, and with the added impetus of expanding exports, the heavy industries reached a position of nearly full employment in 1889–90. The coal industry, for the first time since the early seventies, approached a stage where fairly serious inelasticities in supply appeared. The coal boom was not on the extraordinary scale of 1871–3, but it was sufficient to colour cost-price relations throughout the capital-goods industries.

That prices rose as little as they did during these years (from 92 to 96, 1886–90, as compared with 132 to 148, 1868–73) can be attributed in substantial part to the persistence of the cost-reducing investment which had dominated the scene since 1873. The net result of the shifting of supply and demand curves in each market was, broadly, in the direction of higher prices, in the late eighties. But there was no cessation of the technological development which had distinguished the previous fifteen years. The engineering reports still contain an impressive series of cost-reducing innovations. At the same time expansion in scale was proceeding, both within Britain, and in foreign countries. Although much of the joint-stock floatation which took place at this time involved merely a conversion from private to corporate ownership, the actual construction of new plant was on a scale to be counted an important stimulus to production in the capital-goods industries. The consequences of these shifts in long-period supply conditions were quickly evident when the various lines of new investment, at home and abroad, weakened in 1890, and expectations altered.

The Great Depression was back again strongly from 1890 to 1894. Prices fell, and the existence of some unemployed resources lead to bitter competition, at home and abroad. Affected groups again clamoured for redress, by monopoly arrangement and tariffs. The colonies again loomed as a saving possibility. But the underlying forces making for industrial advance were so strong that production fell off but slightly. Testimony to the technological advance of the previous and concurrent years are the following figures, which compare 1890 with 1895, the first year of cyclical revival:

	Unemployment per cent.	Total production (1900 = 100)	General prices
1890 . .	2·10	85·8	96
1895 . .	6·00	87·7	83

In each market the inverse or disproportionate movement of production on the one hand, and prices and employment on the other, can be traced to changes in cost and supply conditions. A significant change on the side of demand, the increased severity of international competition, was also a product of these expansionary forces. In the nineties there were at least three major industrial powers; Britain did not face a monopolist's demand curves for capital goods. That did not mean a fall in British output; for the world economy was expanding. It did mean, however, increasingly severe competition, and, in cyclical depression, rapidly falling prices.

The relatively high level of output maintained can be traced, as in other cyclically depressed years in the Great Depression, to the maintenance of a considerable volume of home investment. Ship-building, despite the tremendous expansion of 1888–90, did not lapse fully into the expected depression. New and special types of steamers were needed, and regarded as profitable, for the growing Atlantic passenger trade, and for the carrying of fruit and meat. These were the years when Manchester rapidly carried forward the building of the ship canal. Builders, too, remained abnormally active, with average unemployment well below the general average:

	Unemployment per cent.	
	General average	Carpenters and joiners
1890 . .	2·1	2·2
1891 . .	3·5	1·9
1892 . .	6·3	3·1
1893 . .	7·5	3·1
1894 . .	6·9	4·3

At no time did the engineers, despite the loss of South American orders, suffer more than a relatively mild recession. In this they were aided by one type of foreign investment, which had continued on an important scale: mining, in South Africa and Western Australia.

Gold-mining had been, of course, a significant but minor

feature of the expansion reaching its peak in 1890; and gold
was pouring into the central banks of the world. Whatever
factors produced the Great Depression phenomena of the
nineties it was not a lack of gold, inhibiting the supply of
short-term loanable funds. Cheap money, as in other stages
of this secular period, did, however, encourage various
modest types of home investment. This was a time when
local governments found it advantageous to enter the market,
when one after another existing issues were converted at
lower rates.

The expansion in general activity that ran from 1894 to
the latter half of 1898 falls fully within the Great Depression.
Home investment rose; the yield on Consols fell; commodity
prices remained relatively steady; unemployment came down
to about 2 per cent. The rise in exports was spread fairly
evenly over the complex of British markets; and capital
exports were lower in 1898 than they had been in 1894.
These were years dominated by industrial investment, largely
within Great Britain. A bicycle boom was about the most
exciting new enterprise the City could offer the investor.
But the Spanish–American War came in 1898, and the Boer
War in the following year. Joseph Chamberlain was in the
Colonial Office; and the British economy was on the eve of
a new secular phase.

V

It is thus concluded that the central causal force in the
Great Depression was the relative cessation of foreign lending. In less precise terms the period might be entitled 'What
Happened when the Railways were Built'.[1] Of course, railway-building went on, but never in these decades on a scale
sufficient to dominate the British capital market and capital-
goods industries. Savings moved into other channels—
channels less profitable to the investor. The expectations
of 1871–3 had encouraged great expansion of plant. Cheap
money, new invention, and the need to reduce costs carried

[1] For the decisive importance of the end of railway-building in another
context, see R. Pares, 'Economic Factors in the History of the Empire', *Economic
History Review*, 1937, pp. 139–40.

on the process in the decade that followed. The expected marginal efficiency of capital declined.

The whole economic system conformed to the theoretical consequences of this process. There was no increase in the supply of labour, comparable to that of capital, and money wages fell but slightly. Reduced prices brought the benefits of increased productivity to the working man. Wealth was redistributed favourably to labour, despite the introduction of much labour-saving machinery.[1] The Stock Exchange was slack. It was forced to perform the process of revaluing downward the capital equipment of the community, as its quasi-rents declined. Business men were harassed with falling profit margins and increasingly severe competition. Everywhere they began to search for an escape—in the insured foreign markets of positive imperialism, in tariffs, monopolies, employers' associations. None of these trends advanced far in the Great Depression. But they were symptoms of the central ailment. The capitalist was to have a last fling at a rising interest rate in the capital export boom of the decade before the war.

The irritations of the declining yield on capital which accompany intensive investment were to reach a much greater intensity in the period 1919–39. In the Great Depression, however, there were still outlets for enterprise that yielded a rate high enough to entice the private lender. The Government was not then forced to assume the role of compensatory monopolist in the capital market; but the lines of future development were clearly forecast. The mid-century blandishments of the profit motive had begun to lose their force.

[1] See below, Chapter IV, pp. 103–7.

INVESTMENT AND REAL WAGES, 1873–86

I

IN Chapter III the economic characteristics of the Great Depression are explained as stemming from the changed direction of investment in Britain, at a time when the quantity of investment was sustained. Capital export, principally for the construction of railways, fell off severely, and was supplanted as the principal source of employment by various types of intensive domestic investment. Rates of interest, profit margins, and prices fell; money wages fell less than retail prices. This rise in real wages resulted from a process of capital refinement.

It was a situation where doses of capital were being applied to a relatively fixed quantity of labour.[1] The consequence was a rising marginal productivity for labour, a falling marginal productivity for capital. But real wages are not paid in kind. Nor are they directly or automatically associated with physical marginal productivity. The process can be considered automatic only under the assumptions of perfect competition, and even then requires the intermediary of markets: in this case markets where the prices of goods fall more rapidly than the prices of labour. This chapter will attempt to investigate how, in this period, money wages remained constant or fell slowly, while retail prices declined more rapidly.

The general conclusion that real wages were rising is supported by a *per capita* index of food consumption:[2]

(All figures 1900 = 100)

	Money wages	Retail prices	Real wages full work	Real wages allowing for unemploy.	Consumption index	Wages bill
1868	72·6	133·7	60·1	56·4	66·0	47·9
1873	86·6	137·1	69·9	70·9	77·0	68·3
1879	81·6	115·7	74·9	67·6	74·3	60·6
1883	83·2	114·6	76·0	76·0	78·9	66·2
1886	82·7	103·4	82·5	76·0	76·3	62·0
Average 1870–5	86·6	130·8	68·9	69·2	73·8	61·4
Average 1880–5	82·7	115·3	76·2	73·7	76·9	64·0

For notes 1 and 2 see opposite page.

It is clear that the extraordinary gains of 1868–73 were not only maintained in the decade that followed, but slowly increased. The annual average increase in real wages provides a rough measure of labour's relative progress during the three periods comprising the sixty-four years before the war. These figures, of course, do not take into account the benefits of shorter hours or improved social services:[1]

(1850 = 100)

	Annual average increase in real wages, full work	Annual average increase in real wages, allowing for unemployment
1850–73 . .	+1·17	+1·30
1874–1900 . .	+2·04	+1·85
1901–14 . .	− ·93	− ·71

Contemporary opinion, as reflected in the pamphlet literature, in trade reports, and in responses to the questions of royal commissioners, agreed that labour's position, aside from cyclical and frictional unemployment, was improving:[2]

'There is no feature in the situation which we have been called upon to examine so satisfactory as the immense improvement which has taken place in the condition of the working classes during the last twenty years . . . wages have not fallen to any great extent, the hours of labour are shorter, and most of the necessaries of life cheaper. . . . Those who may be said to represent the producer have mainly dwelt upon the restriction and even

---

[1] These figures were arrived at by the simple process of dividing the total net change in each period by the number of years contained in it. Compare these measurements with the calculations by annual average percentage rate of change, Chapter I, Table I.

[2] *Final Report, Committee on Depression* (1886), pp. xxi, xi, and xv. For an extended discussion of the relative level of unemployment in the Great Depression, see above, pp. 47–50. Layton and Crowther's conclusion (op. cit., p. 95) is: 'Looking at the whole period (1873–96) there seems to be no evidence that employment was less regular than in previous periods.'

Notes 1 and 2 of opposite page.

[1] The reader may wish to consult the Appendix, for a discussion of Mr. M. Kalecki's approach to the problem of income distribution in the period 1880–1913, a portion of which bears on the subject-matter of this chapter.

[2] W. Layton and G. Crowther, *An Introduction to the Study of Prices*, pp. 265–6, give G. H. Wood's wage calculations; A. C. Pigou, *Industrial Fluctuations*, pp. 387–8, Wood's index of *per capita* consumption; Pigou, loc. cit., pp. 383–4, A. Bowley's estimate of the wages bill, allowing for unemployment.

the absence of profit in their respective businesses. It is upon this class, and more especially from the employer of labour, that the complaints chiefly proceed. On the other hand those classes of the population who derive their incomes from foreign investments, or from property not directly connected with productive industries, appear to have little ground of complaint; on the contrary, they have profited by the remarkably low prices of commodities . . . a similar remark will apply to the labouring classes.'

Although the Great Depression years had their share of unemployment, the period would not have been thus named if labour's viewpoint alone were considered. It was a falling yield on capital which called forth royal commissions. The trades unions could pursue a relatively passive policy, strikes were rare. It was estimated that average hours of work had fallen three to four hours per week in the fifteen years before 1886.[1]

The social historian and reformer find much that was deplorable in working-class life of the seventies and eighties. Using less absolute measures of welfare, the economic historian, viewing the Great Depression in relation to the years which preceded and followed (1896–1914), sees considerable relative progress peacefully achieved. In many ways the economic environment favoured labour; certainly more so than the difficult pre-1914 decade.

We shall here first examine the market conditions for labour and retail commodities, attempting more specifically to trace the supply and demand conditions which produced slowly falling money wages, a rapidly falling cost of living, a favourable turn in the terms of trade. These phenomena will be linked where possible to the investment of 1873–86 and to the boom which preceded (1868–73). Some effort will then be made to explain the changed distribution of income in terms of current wage theory.

---

[1] *Final Report, Committee on Depression* (1886), p. x. Three typical examples from the *Third Report* (pp. 299 and 307) are the following: Hours per week fell from 59 to 54 in the Palmer's Shipbuilding and Iron Co., from 60 to 54 in the Jarrow shipyards, from 61 to 54 in the New Castle Chemical Works.

II

Major changes in the total volume of labour supply have no great causal significance in the Great Depression. The population had been increasing at an accelerated rate from 1855 on, and it is evident that by 1885 an increase in younger men on the labour market must have resulted. But this development had no striking consequences traceable in the reports or the statistics:[1]

	Population of Great Britain (in millions)	Increase in population (per cent.)
1845 . . .	27·8	—
1855 . . .	27·8	—
1865 . . .	29·9	7·6
1875 . . .	32·7	9·4
1885 . . .	36·3	11·0

It is difficult to generalize about changes in the manner in which the supply of labour may have responded to changes in wages and working conditions, i.e., in the shape or position of the labour supply curve. Two relevant facts, however, can be established. After the crisis of 1873, entrepreneurs successfully applied pressure in an effort to eliminate the inefficiency which prosperity wage rates had engendered. Especially in mining, but in other trades as well, there is no doubt that entrepreneurial watchfulness in the face of falling profits caused an increase in man per hour labour efficiency—this quite apart from economies achieved through the introduction of new equipment. The destruction of restrictive trades union regulations relating to apprenticeship, piece-work, and shop routine, is symbolic of the trend.[2] A counter-

---

[1] *Ibid.*, p. xxxii. W. Beveridge, *Unemployment*, 1930, pp. 458–9, estimates that the 'supply of labour' increased from 7·135 million in 1871 to 7·747 million in 1881.

[2] 'Review of 1874', *Economist*, pp. 1–2: 'The almost universal excitement of 1871–2 had thoroughly disorganised both labour and commerce. The working people became intoxicated and unmanageable under rapid advance of wages, and rapid diminution of the hours of work; and the excessive profits of the coal, iron, shipping, and some other trades introduced into ordinary business a degree of recklessness which can only end in mischief. The reduced demand for labour has not only brought down wages, but it has also put an end to many of the rules adopted, under pressure from the trades unions since 1871, directed to limitation of hours of work, abolition of piece work, restriction of the number

movement, however, was the almost universal tendency to shorter hours. The Nine Hours' Bill in the coal industry was typical of a movement which, in the course of fifteen years, cut three to four hours off the average working day. The extent to which this reduction in hours was balanced by an increase in efficiency (from the shorter day) and increases enforced by sharp-eyed foremen one can only guess. The verdict of the Royal Commission was that 'both the quantity and the quality of the work produced have largely increased. [Referring to longer hours and lower wages abroad.] The workman in this country is, when fully employed, in almost every respect in a better position than his competitors in foreign countries, and we think that no diminution in our productive capacity has resulted from this improvement in his position.'[1] Weighing trends in population and efficiency one can conclude that the general labour supply curve shifted slightly to the right.

At the same time, a falling price level and an end to conditions of full employment probably made the curve somewhat less sensitive to small reductions in wage rates. After the initial post-boom difficulties of adjustment, strikes were rare. Retail price movements were steadily revising upwards the value of a given money wage. An unseen hand (invisible, for example, among labour supply and demand curves in the coal and iron industries) was changing the real value of wage bargains. Labour as a whole could afford to accept gracefully such small wage reductions as competitive conditions occasionally allowed the entrepreneur. This was the Lib-Lab era.[2]

of apprentices, etc. In many trades these prohibitions, if persisted in, would have been fatal. The working classes are now learning by the sharpest and rudest experience that combinations among themselves are powerless to control the markets for the products of labour; and, therefore, powerless to maintain wages and rules which the market price of commodities will not afford. And the lesson has not come too soon.'

[1] *Third Report*, pp. xxi and x.

[2] The negative attitude of trades union leaders and the indifferent progress made in labour organization tend to support the contention of Mr. John T. Dunlop that movements in the cost of living play an important role in motivating trades union policy ('The Movement of Real and Money Wage Rates', *Economic Journal*, Sept. 1938). Arguing against Keynes's contention that trades union leaders keep their eyes almost exclusively on money wage rates, he

The nature of economic development in the Great Depression cheapened the cost of most commodities, caused chronic excess capacity, and increased the elasticity of their supply. The supply of labour showed no comparable tendency to increase: the demand for labour, as for other commodities, was maintained. And the price of labour does not follow the movement of the index for commodities in general. In the trade cycle, as abstracted for theoretical analysis, wages and prices tend to move roughly together (the former perhaps lagging). The processes of cyclical inflation and deflation are calculated to increase and to reduce the competitive value of all factors of production more or less together. The divergence between the course of general prices and money wages in the Great Depression is evidence against any interpretation of it as a chronic general deflation induced by monetary or other forces:

	(1900 = 100) Sauerbeck general prices	Money wages
1873 . .	148	86·6
1879 . .	110	81·6
1883 . .	96	83·2
1886 . .	84	82·7

Such wage reduction as could be effected came largely in the mining areas, where the famine conditions of the boom for a short time gave rise to exorbitant monopoly wage rates. A part of the miners was thereafter burdened with sliding-scale agreements, which associated wages with mineral prices. The consequent lowering of wages was the chief irritation in the labour market through these years. Out of resentment against the sliding scale was to arise the most important labour development of the eighties, the Miners' Federation.[1] In the one case where an institutional arrangement worked

adduced evidence showing the sensitivity of trades unions to declines in real wages caused by a rise in the cost of living. He concluded that it was inaccurate to hold that the lag of money wages behind retail prices in times of prosperity was sufficient to produce inverse movement between money and real wages.

[1] 'Review of 1886', *Economist*, p. 31; G. D. H. Cole, *A Short History of the British Working Class Movement*, 1925, vol. ii, pp. 152–3.

against the forces of the market a counter-institution appeared.

The position of entrepreneurs was such that they would certainly have forced wage reductions if it were feasible. With profit margins narrowing they searched for means of cutting money costs. There was none of the breezy atmosphere of 1871–2 when, despite complaints from industry and occasional strikes, wages were raised freely, and prices rose without a loss of new orders.[1] Nor was it the power of labour union organization which made wages sticky. The Royal Commission's dictum was that 'the unfavourable elements (among them narrowing profit margins) in the existing state of trade and industry cannot with any justice be attributed to the action of trades unions and similar organisations'.[2] Trades union membership languished through these years.[3]

Before the 1886 commission Lowthian Bell stated that 'the workmen were getting all the profit, the iron manufacturers none', but he added that he did not wish it to be inferred that he thought the workmen were too highly paid.[4] The competitive market for labour simply did not produce a falling wage. Even in 1884, when the cycle was well past its peak, an attempted agreement among cotton operators to lower wages by 5 per cent. was broken. The employers, one by one, 'found it prudent' to restore the former wage.[5] Output was expanding, the supply of men was limited. Capital was not

---

[1] *Economist*, 'Review of 1871', pp. 1–5; *Economist*, 1872, p. 771; 'Review of 1872', pp. 8, 10, 11, 15, 55.

[2] *Third Report*, p. xxi.

[3] Cole, op. cit., p. 202. Total Trades Union Congress membership moved as follows (in thousands):

$$
\begin{array}{l}
1868—114 \\
1873—735 \\
1879—522 \\
1883—561 \\
1886—638
\end{array}
$$

[4] *Third Report*, p. vii.

[5] 'Review of 1884', *Economist*, p. 29. Like the mine owners, cotton-mill owners had attempted to regulate wage scales 'by the returns yielded to the masters'. A strike resulted which the masters apparently had won. Some of them, however, began to bid labour away from competitors by offers of the former wage. As a result the old wage level was restored, 'the fruit of their hard earned victory' given up: 'Ever since peace has reigned in the domain of wages.'

sufficiently a substitute for labour. Although labour-saving machinery might be introduced, its results for industry as a whole were not on a scale large enough to reduce the demand for labour so sharply as to permit a reduction in money wages. In only two periods could that be done: immediately following the 1873 crisis, when temporary boom rates were lowered (wages fell from 87·2 in 1884 to 84·9 in 1876); in the collapse of 1878–9, when unemployment rose as high as 10·7 per cent. (wages fell from 84·4 in 1877 to 81·6 in 1879). Even the severe unemployment of the middle eighties (1886, 9·55 per cent.) produced only a fall from 83·2 in 1883 to 82·7 in 1886. The laws of marginal productivity and free competition operated, although the labour market was by no means completely competitive.

III

While money wage bargains kept up payments to labour, other developments in the system produced falling retail prices. In industry excess capacity, cheaper sources of raw materials, and new technical methods combined to create a régime of almost steadily falling prices. A conjuncture of parallel circumstances tended to lower the cost of the principal items among the working man's 'necessaries'.

The following are the price movements of chief grain products:[1]

| | (1900 = 100) | | | | | | | Household bread London per 4 lb. |
| | Wheat | | Barley | | Oats | | | |
	Brit.	Import.	Brit.	Import.	Brit.	Import.	Maize	
1873 .	218·0	191·3	162·2	143·9	144·5	154·7	155·2	8·0d.
1886 .	115·2	111·0	106·7	95·7	117·1	125·0	118·5	6·3d.

The expansion of Indian and American agricultural territory, the railway development throughout the American continent, and the cheapening of shipping rates were the

---

[1] W. Page, *Commerce and Industry*, 1919, vol. ii, pp. 216–23, for a variety of wholesale foodstuff prices. For figures given above, pp. 216–17 and 219.

principal agents in this decline.[1] Layton and Crowther quote the case of Minnesota wheat producers:[2]

the value of farm crops on the farm in inland states actually rose per unit in the twenty years preceding 1895, but owing to the fall in the cost of freight to the seaboard, the producers could place their produce on board ship at a lower price than before, while retaining a larger sum as their own share. This, of course, damaged the position of the seaboard farmers relatively to their inland competitors. But though the fall in prices on the seaboard was considerable, it was even more severe in Europe, owing to the steady but rapid fall in the cost of carrying grain across the Atlantic.

Here are the long-term cost-reducing effects of investment (in railroads and shipping) which, in the short period, caused sharply rising capital-goods prices.

The prices of tea and sugar followed a similar pattern as new production areas were opened:[3]

	(*1900 = 100*)	
	Tea	*Sugar*
1873 . .	131·9	264·0
1886 . .	97·6	130·3

The investment of British capital in Indian tea plantations accounts for the cheapening of that staple. Between 1879 and 1888 Indian exports of tea increased from 35 million lb. to 113 million lb. A contemporary observer commented that

herein we have another striking example of the inability of unskilled labour and labour following old processes, even at extremely low wages, to contend against intelligence and machinery; inasmuch as the English planter in India, by skilful cultivation and careful

[1] The opening of the Suez Canal (1869), of course, had lasting and important effect on all imports from China and India. The shipping booms of the early seventies and eighties, not only provided, or even over-provided, the trade with more economical vessels, but world competition was made increasingly severe and freight rates lowered by the practice of subsidies to the merchant marine indulged by continental countries. See *Third Report*, 10, 108–33 and 10, 571–5 (W. R. Price and J. Burke).

[2] Op. cit., p. 90, from *The Purchasing Power of Gold*, report by J. M. Powers, to the Bureau of Labour, Minnesota, 1897.   [3] Page, op. cit., p. 221.

manufacture with machinery, is now able to place in Europe a tea of good quality and greater strength at a price which the Chinaman, with his old methods, producing an inferior article, cannot afford.[1]

The subsidized development of beet sugar on the Continent caused the remarkable fall in its price. Britain's free market collected the premiums of a fierce international competition.[2] Tobacco, rice, butter (imported), spirits, among other basic consumers' commodities, showed the same falling tendency: retail prices as a whole were 137·1 in 1873, 103·4 in 1886.[3]

Faced with the competition of virgin soils, British grain agriculture met falling world prices at the expense of its rents and profits. The British cattle- and sheep-farmer confronted no such immediate rivalry; and British beef and mutton prices were maintained. Australian frozen meat did not begin to cut meat prices until well into the eighties:

	(*1900 = 100*)[4]		(*1865–9 = 100*)
	Beef	*British mutton*	*Economist index*[5] *butchers' meat*
1873 . .	126·7	111·8	120
1879 . .	113·8	109·7	105
1883 . .	125·9	120·8	121
1886 . .	100·0	100·0	90
1890 . .	100·0	104·2	—
1896 . .	91·4	90·3	—

Prices fell because capital development had reduced costs. The price reductions do not seem to be the consequence of a gold shortage. When investment did not reduce the cost of producing a commodity (i.e. labour), its price did not conform to the general movement.

[1] Layton and Crowther, op. cit., pp. 90–1.

[2] Ibid., pp. 88–9. Also *Third Report*, testimony of Messrs. Martineau, Duncan, Easton, and Neill, 13, 154–13, 327. These men represented the British sugar-producing interests, and dwell, therefore, on the hardships of foreign competition. The nature of the process at work, however, is clearly reflected in their bitter responses.

[3] Page, op. cit., pp. 216–17 and 219.

[4] Ibid., p. 220. Coffee, similarly, did not fall in price. A lack of new methods and series of bad harvests kept its price from showing a secular decline (Layton and Crowther, op. cit., p. 91).

[5] *Third Report*, Appendix, Table 26, p. 343.

IV

An element in the increase of real wages was the favourable trend of the terms of Britain's foreign trade. From 1873 to the turn of the century (roughly the Great Depression) they secularly declined. The Taussig–Silverman statistics give the movement of net and gross barter terms of trade as follows:[1]

	Import price index		Estimated physical quant. exports
	Export price index		Estimated physical quant. imports
	Taussig	Silverman	Taussig
1880 . .	124	109	129
1900 . .	100	88	100

Since British goods' exports in the pre-war period responded immediately to her capital exports,[2] this development is consistent with the tendency for home investment to increase relative to foreign investment. Mr. Colin Clark associates the improvement in the terms of trade with the increased productivity of British industry.[3] He notes a parallel trend in post-war years, a reverse tendency in the pre-war decade. In all cases productivity and the terms of trade move together. He does not, however, attempt to link the direction of investment with productivity, in as much as he holds that there is no causal connexion between the amount of capital invested

[1] F. Taussig, *International Trade*, Appendix I, pp. 412–13. A. G. Silverman, 'Index Numbers of British Export and Import Prices', *The Review of Economic Statistics*, 1930, p. 147. Also G. Haberler, *The Theory of International Trade*, pp. 161–6.

[2] Taussig, op. cit., chap. xxi, especially pp. 247 and 259–60. See also Silverman, loc. cit., 1931. 'Some International Trade Factors for Great Britain', pp. 123–4.

[3] *National Income and Outlay*, pp. 270–1. Clark states that the improvement in Britain's terms of trade from (*circum*) 1877 on was accompanied by 'a heavy downward trend in prices, increased unemployment, and a general atmosphere of trade depression'. He uses this case to support his doctrine of Economic Indigestion which holds that a large part of the gains from increased productivity or an improvement in the terms of trade is dissipated in unemployment. Although the existence of abnormal unemployment in the Great Depression is by no means established, the phenomenon to which he refers may be viewed causally as arising from the changed direction of investment, producing a shift in the terms of trade, falling prices, falling profit margins, 'a general atmosphere of trade depression'—and, perhaps, an increase in productivity as well.

and productivity.[1] In the three cases mentioned, however, the two dominated by rising productivity were notably slack in capital export, the pre-war decade dominated by it. Taussig has found a good inverse correlation between wages and the barter terms of trade in the forty-three years before the war.[2]

An improvement in the terms of trade would be expected to result from a sharp decrease in foreign lending. If one considers the adjustment as effected primarily through shifts in purchasing power, it follows that a decrease in capital export should produce, other things remaining equal, an increase in import quantities, relative to export quantities, and probably a relative fall in import prices. Over the period 1873–1900 this, in fact, occurred; and when capital export revived in 1904–5, a reverse movement was inaugurated. The process through which Britain's exports of railway iron, for instance, fell off as a result of reduced foreign lending is evident.[3] The manner in which consumers' purchasing power at home was maintained, and thus the quantity of imports, is also clear. The tendency for exports to lag in their increase behind imports—the improvement in the barter terms of trade—is consistent with the general view taken of the period.

The net barter terms of trade, however, escape such symmetrical explanation. It is virtually impossible to calculate the extent to which the secular shift in relative prices may be associated proximately with the direction of British investment. One can merely point to the existence of the expected correlation. It is quite possible that the following trend, important to British real wages, had no connexion with the changed direction of investment, except in so far as activity at home and high wages kept the price of British manufactured exports from further decline:[4]

Amount of manufactured exports given for a fixed quantity of food imports

1881	. .	132
decade ending 1890	. .	119
decade ending 1900	. .	107

[1] Ibid., p. 273.
[2] 'Great Britain's Terms of Foreign Trade,' *Economic Journal*, 1925, p. 10.
[3] See above, pp. 71–2.
[4] J. M. Keynes, *Economic Journal*, 1923, p. 478, in a rejoinder to Beveridge.

For the Great Depression as a whole the secular trend in the terms of trade is clearly established. For the years before 1886, however, the data are less decisive. The growth of an import trade balance and an improvement in the gross barter terms of trade appear between 1873 and 1886; but the relative fall in import prices does not develop until later in the period. In value terms, Hobson's approximations for the balance of payments are as follows:[1]

	(in £ millions)			
	Total of ships, shipping, insurance, banking, and government remittances	*Import excess*	*Balance of cap. and int. items*	*Capital export*
1873 . .	87·3	65·0	−22·3	72·3
1879 . .	74·6	109·8	35·2	12·1
1883 . .	83·4	122·3	38·9	16·9
1886 . .	69·1	80·3	11·2	61·8

An adjustment of the trade balance to foreign lending is evident.

The gross and net barter terms of trade are as follows:[2]

	Value net imports	*Value net exports*	*Import price index*	*Export price index*	*Quantity imports*	*Quantity exports*	*Gross barter terms*	*Net barter terms*
1868 .	247	189	152·8	114·6	161·7	156·2	96·6	133·3
1873 .	315	255	151·4	126·2	208·1	202·1	97·1	120·0
1879 .	306	192	124·5	88·6	245·8	216·7	88·2	140·5
1883 .	362	240	125·9	88·6	287·5	270·9	94·2	142·1
1886 .	294	213	96·3	77·2	305·3	275·9	90·4	124·7
	A	B	C	D	E	F	$\frac{F}{E}$	$\frac{C}{D}$

The gross barter terms of trade move generally in the expected direction. The net barter terms, however, are dominated by the extraordinary inflation of export prices in

Also Pigou, op. cit., p. 389 for annual figures, 1881–1914. See Silverman, *Review of Economic Statistics*, 1931, pp. 117–18 for a discussion of the Keynes–Beveridge controversy over the meaning of these figures.

[1] C. K. Hobson, *The Export of Capital*, 1920, pp. 197 and 223.

[2] The price estimates have been arrived at by linking the Giffen indices (*Third Report, Commission on Depression*, appendix B, p. 329) with the Silverman figures. Exports do not include bullion or re-exports.

1873 and their subsequent deflation. While export prices rose from 114·6 to 126·2 in 1868–73, import prices actually fell from 152·8 to 151·4. The period of adjustment before relative prices moved in favour of Britain is shown also in the following figures compiled by Beveridge:[1]

Food import price as percentage of manufactured export price

1868	. 107	1875	. 98	1881	. 123
1869	. 101	1876	. 105	1882	. 120
1870	. 98	1877	. 125	1883	. 119
1871	. 106	1878	. 116	1884	. 114
1872	. 92	1879	. 117	1885	. 111
1873	. 88	1880	. 115	1886	. 112
1874	. 94				

Not until the eighties did relative *prices* begin to exhibit the long-term trend, although the relative *quantities* of goods imported and exported responded immediately to the new investment conditions. It is significant that the increase in real wages did not await the favourable tendency in the net barter terms of trade. In the Great Depression money wages did not follow the movement of export or other prices. They remained steady enough to give labour a net advantage over the previous period from any retail price decreases that took place.

V

Two propositions have been thus far asserted: (*a*) that in the Great Depression the marginal return to capital fell, that to labour rose; (*b*) that the proportion of capital employed in production increased relative to the amount of labour. The distribution of shares in the national income remains still to be investigated. Any statements involving such quantitative judgement might well be prefaced with Mr. Bowley's conclusion on the available statistics:[2] 'I do not think that the statistics are sufficient for any fine measurements of income, earnings, of wages prior to 1880; there is indeed sufficient uncertainty after that date.'

Although the material is fragmentary, it clearly suggests that the national income changed in its distribution during the Great Depression. Examining the period 1880–1913

[1] 'Mr. Keynes' Evidence for Overproduction', *Economica*, Feb. 1924, p. 7.
[2] *Wages and Income in the U.K. since 1860*, p. 99.

Bowley found that the proportion of income going to property and labour was as follows: (per cent.)[1]

				Property	Labour
1880	.	.	.	37½	62½
1900	.	.	.	36 or 35	64 or 65
1913	.	.	.	37½	62½

He summarizes:[2]

The broad results of this investigation are to show that the national dividend increased more rapidly than the population in the generation before the war, so that average incomes were quite one-third greater in 1913 than in 1880; the increase was gained principally before 1900, since when it barely kept pace with the diminished value of money. The increase was shared with remarkable equality among the various economic classes. Property obtained a diminishing share of the home product, but an unchanged share of the whole income when income from abroad is included.

It would appear that changes in the relative proportions were largely determined by the extent to which Britain's income from abroad altered. Increased investment within the country produced lower yields on capital sufficient to give a larger share to labour, despite the total increase in capital; a relative increase in capital exports (as in 1904–13) countered the distributional trend at home.[3]

On the years 1873–86 the Commission on Depression concluded as follows:[4]

We have shown that while the general production of wealth in the country has continuously increased, its distribution has been undergoing great changes; that the result of these changes has been to give a larger share than formerly to the consumer and the labourer, and so to promote a more equal distribution. . . . While the share of the aggregate wealth produced in the country which now falls to labour is larger than it was twenty years ago, a corresponding diminution has taken place in the share which falls to capital: in other words that while wages have risen profits

[1] *Wages and Income in the U.K. since 1860*, p. 92.　　[2] Ibid., p. 26.
[3] The distribution of home-produced income gave property 34 per cent. in 1880, only 31 per cent. in 1913.
[4] *Third Report*, pp. xxiii, xxi, xv, and xvi. In the Report there may have been some tendency directly to associate changes in unit profit and unit real wages with changes in distribution, without considering carefully the more precarious problem of relative shares in the total dividend.

have fallen ... it would appear that the number of persons with incomes of less than £2,000 a year has increased at a more rapid rate than the population (which increased about 10 per cent.) while the number of persons with incomes above £2,000 has increased at a less rapid rate, and the number with incomes above £5,000 has actually diminished: and, further, that the lower the income the more rapid the rate of increase. ... The view, therefore, which we are disposed to adopt is that the aggregate wealth of the country is being distributed differently and that a large part of the prevailing complaints and the general sense of depression may be accounted for by changes which have taken place in recent years in the apportionment and distribution of profits.

Chief evidence for these statements, aside from the plaintive testimony of those deriving income from profit margins, was the following table:[1]

Schedule D—Trades and Professions

£ £	*1874–5 no.*	*1884–5 no.*	*Increase no.*	*Per cent. increase*
200–1,000 . . .	162,435	215,790	53,355	32·85
1,000–2,000 . . .	11,944	13,403	1,459	12·21
2,000–3,000 . . .	3,797	4,038	241	6·34
3,000–4,000 . . .	1,857	1,914	57	3·07
4,000–5,000 . . .	1,003	1,074	71	7·07
5,000–10,000 .	2,035	1,928	−107	−5·25
10,000 and up . .	1,283	1,220	−63	−4·91
TOTAL . . .	184,354	239,367	55,013	29·84

The same distributional trend holds for the period 1880–1900 as more recently calculated by Bowley.[2] His figures support the earlier generalization:

	The distribution of the national income			
	National income (in £ millions) (say)	*Percentages of total*		
		Over £160	*Intermediate*	*Wages*
1880	1,090	49	11	40
1881–5 . . .	1,160	48	12	40
1886–90 . . .	1,270	46	14	40
1891–5 . . .	1,400	44	14½	41½
1896–1900 . . .	1,620	45	14	41

[1] Ibid., p. xvi.   [2] Loc. cit., p. 92.

If the distribution between property and labour was $37\frac{1}{2}$ per cent. to $62\frac{1}{2}$ per cent., respectively, in 1880, one is permitted to include all of wages and intermediate income, and (in 1880) $11\frac{1}{2}$ per cent. (of total income) from 'Over £160'. The income-tax returns for Schedule D showed that among taxable incomes, a redistribution took place in favour of the lower brackets. It may be assumed then, that the net decrease in the proportion going to incomes 'Over £160' was due to the relative decline in incomes to 'property', not to that part of the category going to higher grades of 'labour'. Although these calculations are crude, there seems to be some justification for holding that the processes at work during the Great Depression tended to distribute wealth slightly in favour of labour.

The general theory relevant to this development is thus stated by Mr. Hicks:[1]

> If the amount used of factor B (labour) is kept constant, while that of A (capital) increases, the marginal product of A must fall (this is the ordinary law of diminishing returns). It follows directly from this that, if A is paid according to its marginal product, the total share in the product imputed to factor B must rise when the employment of A rises. Further, under constant returns to scale, an increase in factor A must raise the marginal product of factor B. . . . An increase in the supply of a factor will increase that factor's share in the social dividend if the elasticity of substitution between it and other resources employed is greater than unity.

These two dicta are made under the assumption of two factor production, perfect competition, constant return to scale, and without considering the consequences of 'keeping capital intact'. Although set in rigid limits it conforms roughly to the process apparent in the Great Depression.

In *The Theory of Wages* Hicks presents two illustrative cases.[2] In the first the relative amount of capital increases, but invention is stagnant. Total output increases, the relative share of labour rises, that of capital falls. In the second, the

---

[1] J. R. Hicks, 'A Revised Theory of Distribution', *Review of Economic Studies*, Oct. 1936, p. 3.

[2] pp. 127–30.

relative increase in the use of capital is accompanied by enough labour-saving invention to keep the elasticity of substitution above unity. Here total output increases and the total share of labour, i.e. real wages; but the relative share of labour falls, that of capital rises. Although new methods abounded, the facts of the period fit the first rather than the second case. Labour-saving invention in the period may be regarded in either of two ways: as induced invention, cushioning to an extent the fall in profits; or as 'the more extensive use of capitalistic methods' made feasible by a lower rate of interest. The distinction, one feels, is not sharp.

In any case, the net movement of $\frac{A/Pa}{B/Pb}$ (as reflected in the distribution of relative shares) seems to indicate an elasticity of substitution somewhat less than unity.[1]

The picture which emerges, then, is one of a society in which internal investment, devoted to the refinement and increase of the community's capital stock, rose relatively to total new investment, increasing labour's absolute and relative shares in the national income. It is a picture in many ways symmetrical to that of Britain in the period 1920–39. The expected marginal efficiency of capital, however, was sufficiently high for this process to be pursued through private investment channels, without the appearance of extraordinarily high or persistent unemployment. The Great Depression, in that way, contrasts sharply with contemporary industrial societies, within which it is doubtful if full employment will ever again be attained, over long periods, exclusively through investment motivated by expectations of private profit.

---

[1] Hicks, loc. cit., pp. 131–2: 'If we accept these figures [Bowley's, given above] then it is clear that the elasticity of substitution must at this time have been rather less than unity. Not necessarily very much less; quite a small difference would be sufficient to give the observed result.'

PART II

ECONOMIC FACTORS AND POLITICS

V

TRADE CYCLES, HARVESTS, AND POLITICS
1790–1850

You cannot get them to talk of politics so long as they are well employed.—
WILLIAM MATHEWS, 1833.

*I have observed during the whole time I have been in Lanarkshire that any
rise in the rate of discount at the Bank of England has been immediately, or
at least shortly, followed by an increase both of crime and of civil suits, and
if it continues long, of mortality and typhus fever. So much so, that, as I am
an official member of the prison board and of most of the Charities, I have
always made it a rule to say . . . 'Gentlemen, the Bank of England have
raised their discounts, you had better immediately take measures for enlarging
the prison accommodations and for extending the infirmaries and Poor houses.'
—*A. ALISON, *Sheriff of Lanarkshire, 1848.*

I

HISTORIANS of every shade of bias admit the importance
of the influence of economic situations on political and
social events. The weight attached to economic factors or,
more precisely, the mechanism of their action is, however,
by no means settled. The most familiar relation that has
hitherto been emphasized in the years 1790–1850 links the
mechanical inventions of the late eighteenth century to the
growth of the factory system and to the consequent rise of a
large urban proletariat and a powerful middle class. From
these relations, which are essentially sociological, efforts have
been made to explain the political forces that produced the
Reform Bill of 1832, the Chartist Movement, the repeal of
the Corn Laws. In the realm of cultural history, the rise to
dominance of a philosophy of individualism and a cult of
romanticism have been linked to the same forces, with ramifications in economic doctrine, religion, architecture, and
poetry. Such attempts at interconnexion represent a long-
run analysis of economic influences. For many purposes,

especially where economic influences operate at several removes, that sort of generalization is adequate.

Experience of the inter-war years, however, impressed observers with the tremendous impact of economic forces, acting over shorter periods. Changes in social structure, in political atmosphere and policy, and in intellectual attitudes can be more or less directly traced to the depression after 1929. While it is true that these trends (and the causes of depression as well) have a long history reaching back, at least, to 1873, their timing, their intensity, and their unique character are closely connected with recent short-run developments. Many historians have taken account of this type of influence, but rarely have they done so systematically.[1]

From 1790 to 1850 there were at least three major economic forces that contributed, at intervals, to British social and political unrest: cyclical unemployment, fluctuations in domestic harvests, and technological unemployment. The latter, by itself, was not likely to produce major disturbances; nor can it be sharply distinguished from cyclical unemployment. The underemployment of hand-loom weavers was, admittedly, an important element in the Luddite and Chartist movements; and the resentment of the hand-loom weavers against the introduction of machinery often gave a peculiar character to the activity of wider groups. The most serious unrest, however, was a product of cyclical depression and high food prices.

II

Good harvests with resulting low grain prices were calculated to call forth complaint from the landholders and from tenants burdened with fixed rent payments. The demand for grain was sufficiently inelastic to bring a decline in gross income when good harvests caused a sharp fall in price; and,

---

[1] Of the studies covering the first half of the nineteenth century G. D. H. Cole's *Short History of the British Working Class Movement, 1789–1927*, makes perhaps the most consistent use of a framework of business fluctuations and price movements. See, for example, vol. i, pp. 79, 88, 105, 177–88. But in describing strikes, and even phases of political development, many opportunities for relating the data to short-period fluctuations are missed.

until 1832 at least, the agrarian interest was disproportionately represented in Parliament. The simplest short-
period, economic-political relation is that between the wheat
price and the Corn Laws.

The Corn Laws were altered principally in the following
years: 1791, 1804, 1815, 1822, 1828, 1842. Repeal came, of
course, in 1846. A glance at the annual average wheat price
reveals the principal setting for these amendments.

The wheat price fell from 56s. per quarter in May 1790
to 42s. in October 1791. The movement continued to a low
point of 47·0s. in May 1792. The harvest of 1791 was 'one
of great abundance' and, under the prevailing corn law, the
fall in price was sufficient to cause the ports to be closed to
foreign grain:[1] 'but the low price was productive, as usual,
of complaint on the part of the landed interest, and was
the occasion of a fresh corn bill'. The inadequate harvests
of the following years, however, kept the wheat price at
or above 50s., and the Act of 1791 was not called into
operation.

The catastrophic fall in the wheat price, from 154s. per
quarter in March 1801 to 50s. in February 1804, produced
similar, though even more violent complaint. The Corn
Laws were again modified. The area under cultivation had,
of course, been greatly expanded between 1793 and 1804.
A succession of abundant harvests brought forth an unparal-
leled supply of wheat.[2] The import limit was raised to 63s.[3]
The cutting off of Baltic supplies resulting from the resumption of war, together with bad harvests, kept the wheat price
above the new minimum until 1815. Like the Act of 1791,
that of 1804 was never operative.

From August 1812, when the wheat price was 152s., to

[1] T. Tooke, *A History of Prices* (1838), vol. i, p. 81. This act provided for a
duty of 24s. 3d. if the price was under 50s.; 2s. 6d. at or above 50s. and under
54s.; 6d. at or above 54s., and a bounty of 5s. on exports at a price under 44s.
See also W. Smart, *Economic Annals of the Nineteenth Century* (1917), vol. i,
pp. 90–2; and D. Macpherson, *Annals of Commerce* (1805), vol. iv, pp. 219–20.

[2] T. Tooke, *A History of Prices* (1838), vol. i, pp. 237–9.

[3] Under the Corn Law of 1804 a duty of 24s. 3d. per quarter was imposed
when the wheat price was under 63s.; and 2s. 6d. per quarter, when at or above
that rate and under 66s.; and 6d. when above 66s. The lowest price reached
between 1804 and 1815 was 66s., in November 1807.

January 1816 a steady decline took place. The break-up of the continental system and finally, the return to peace, as well as good harvests, caused this fall.[1] Despite considerable opposition[2] it was judged that only an 80s. import limit could protect the capital newly invested in agriculture.

Until the close of 1818 the wheat price remained above 80s., aided largely by inadequate harvests on the Continent and considerable exports from Britain to France.[3] But good harvests then brought on a decline to 39s. at the close of 1822. The period of severe agricultural distress has coloured the whole view of British agriculture in the three decades after the Napoleonic wars.[4] In 1822, however, the Government was trapped between the farmers' petitions and the opposition to further protection from labour, commercial, and industrial interests. At Peterloo, three years before, 'No Corn Laws' had appeared on the banners. Unlike the position in 1815 the decline in agricultural prices (1818–22) was accompanied by a decline in import prices and non-agricultural domestic prices. The Corn Law of 1822 modified only slightly the terms of the Act of 1815.[5] 'The farmers had asked for bread and gotten a stone'; but there were others, too, asking for bread between 1818 and 1822.

From the second quarter of 1823 to the last quarter of 1828 the price of wheat hovered between 50s. and 70s. per quarter. Although the farmers were far from content, their relative position was, with respect to profits, probably no worse than that of the manufacturer or exporter; after the crisis of 1825, in fact, it was probably better. And those who sought a reduction in agricultural protection were victorious in the

---

[1] Tooke, op. cit., vol. i, pp. 322–5; vol. ii, pp. 2–4; also *Annual Register*, 1814, p. 219.

[2] T. Doubleday, *A Financial History of England* (1859), p. 227, notes that the protection of soldiers was required for members of the House of Commons, on the passage of the 1815 Corn Law, such was 'the fury of the people'.

[3] Tooke, op. cit., vol. ii, pp. 16–18.

[4] For a modification of the traditional view of unrelieved depression, see G. E. Fussell and M. Compton, 'Agricultural Adjustments after the Napoleonic Wars', *Economic History*, Feb. 1939.

[5] See Smart, vol. ii, pp. 117–18, for a detailed account of this Bill which, like those of 1791 and 1804, was never really operative. A feature of its terms was the application of a sliding scale of duties when the price rose above 70s.

Corn Law of 1828.[1] It is probable that the growing prestige of free-trade ideas and the parliamentary influence of industrial and mercantile groups played some part in moderating the 1815 bill.[2] There was, however, an immediate economic basis reflected crudely in the movement of relative prices in the twenties:[3]

	Domestic price index	Import price index	Wheat price (s. per quarter)
1823	97	99	52
1827	106	82	56

It is clear that, from 1823 to 1827, the wheat price did not share the net fall experienced in most other markets. After 1825, a peak year in general prosperity, this disparity was especially felt; and it was in the post-crisis atmosphere that antagonism to the Corn Law of 1815 developed.[4]

Until the last quarter of 1832 the wheat price remained well above 50s. and, although the farmers never ceased to complain, their position was not desperate. The three following years (1833–6), however, brought abundant harvests, low prices, and extensive parliamentary investigations. Although the pressure for further protection increased, no action was taken by a Parliament in which anti-agrarian interests had been materially strengthened by the Reform Bill of 1832.[5]

At the close of 1836 the wheat price again rose suddenly as the harvest of that year appeared inadequate.[6] Chronically

---

[1] Smart, op. cit., vol. ii, p. 439. The sliding scale introduced in 1828, after two years of controversy, ranged from a duty of 34s. 8d. when the home price was 52s., to 1s. when the home price was 73s. In fact this amounted to only a very slight modification on the preceding Bill, although the trend against agricultural protection had clearly set in.

[2] Their long-term significance was symbolized, perhaps, in the person of William Huskisson.

[3] Non-agricultural domestic commodities show, on the whole, a greater net decline than the domestic index, which includes wheat and a variety of other agricultural commodities heavily weighted.

[4] See Tooke, op. cit., vol. ii, p. 136, on food prices (1826–7), relatively high 'in the distressed state of the manufacturing population'.

[5] The Poor Law of 1834, however, may be considered, in part, as a concession to the hard-pressed landowners. It was in the agricultural districts that the burden of poor rates, under the old system, was most severely felt.

[6] Tooke, op. cit., vol. ii, pp. 157–8.

bad yields kept the price abnormally high until 1842. In this period the anti-Corn Law forces crystallized outside of Parliament, deriving additional strength from the generally depressed state of industry and the high level of unemployment, especially after 1839. This protracted pressure on real wages helped bring about the Whig tariff reforms of 1841: but 'Corn duties they left where they were, crying over their shoulders as they were being pushed out of office that a reasonable fixed duty . . . was the right thing'.[1] Peel was elected on the issue of the sliding scale, and in 1842 his modifications of the Corn Law of 1828 consisted in lowering the maximum duty and in making the sliding scale less steep.[2] He himself believed this arrangement to be a considerable reduction in protection, and it was put forward as such. There is no doubt that the high food prices and depression in the previous few years had, by 1842, helped to discredit the whole argument for agricultural protection and for tariffs generally.

The role of the Irish famine in the suspension and, ultimately, in the repeal of the Corn Laws is a familiar short-period sequence, as is also the tangled and dramatic political story of 1846. It is probable, in fact, that strictly economic considerations played a somewhat lesser part in the final repeal than in some of the earlier modifications. In 1845 and the first three quarters of 1846 the domestic wheat price ranged between 45s. and 59s. A few years before it had been over 70s. The Irish famine might have been dealt with by extraordinary measures short of actual repeal. The rise in the wheat price (to a peak of 93s. in June) in 1847, however, would almost certainly have ended agricultural protection then, if its end had not been accomplished earlier.

[1] J. H. Clapham, *An Economic History of Modern Britain* (1926), vol. i, p. 497. The Whigs went out of office in 1841, to be succeeded by Peel and the Tories, until 1846.

[2] W. Page, *Commerce and Industry*, vol. i, pp. 128–30. The new scale started with wheat at 50s. paying 20s. duty, diminished to 1s., when the price was 73s. (as in the scale of 1828). There were two 'rests' in the scale, wheat from 52s. to 54s. paying a duty of 18s. a quarter, and wheat between 66s. and 68s. paying a duty of 8s. This, it was hoped, would check the speculations of corn dealers, who had been tempted, by the steepness of the scale of 1828, to hold back corn in the hope of getting higher prices.

This account is not meant, of course, to deny the long-period factors making for a reduction in agricultural protection: the growth of population, the accelerated industrialization of Britain, the widening political power of the urban middle classes and their free-trade doctrines. But it is clear that the timing of the events leading up to repeal were closely connected with the British harvests and other short-run factors influencing the absolute and relative level of the prices of agricultural products.

III

1. *The Speenhamland System, 1795.* The years 1794 and 1795 saw some industrial recovery in Great Britain, from the depression of 1793. A more powerful force, however, affecting labour's position, was a rise in foodstuff prices, due primarily to bad harvests.[1] The wheat price was 43·2s. per quarter in January 1792, 108s. in August 1795. Cost-of-living indexes reveal this rise graphically.

	Gilboy-Boody (cost of living in London)	Silberling (wholesale prices of foodstuffs, &c.)
1793 · ·	148	106
1794 · ·	168	110
1795 · ·	179	130

Although money wages rose, there seems little doubt that they rose 'in a very inadequate proportion to the increased price of the necessaries of life'.[2] There was widespread evidence of physical distress,[3] and the wage-subsidy scheme for out-of-door relief was instituted, much in the tradition of the Elizabethan poor laws.

2. *The Combination Acts, 1799 and 1800.* From the last quarter of 1796 until about the middle of 1799 the price of wheat and the cost of living remained moderately low.

---

[1] Tooke, op. cit., vol. i, pp. 181–3 and 187.
[2] Ibid., pp. 185–6.
[3] Ibid., pp. 225–6. It is perhaps worth noting that the situation in 1795–6 had direct and immediate influence on the ideas of Thomas Malthus, Frederick Eden, and Thomas Paine, as well as many others.

Despite the brief but severe depression of 1797, these were, internally, years of relative peace. The wheat price (which, at the end of 1798 was down to 48s.) then rose to a peak of 154s. in March 1801. The cost-of-living indexes move as follows:

	Gilboy-Boody	Silberling
1798 .	165	121
1799 .	229	143
1800 .	252	170
1801 .	190	174

The government acted by offering bounties on grain imports, by sending agents to the Baltic ports, and by encouraging the process of inclosure. In 1799–1801, in general, the working classes were fairly well employed. Even the crisis in the Hamburg trade, in 1799, did not induce a prolonged deflation.[1] Under these circumstances the workers had considerable market leverage in contracting money-wage bargains.[2] In the attempt to maintain their real wage, at a time of rapidly rising costs of living, the men resorted to various types of combinations. Even agricultural workers banded together in certain areas, notably in Norfolk.

Although the combination movement was very much the outgrowth of a particular short-period situation, and although the typical expression of discontent was the local bread riot or strike, the unrest was, at times, successfully linked with republican ideas. The corresponding societies, particularly, attempted to shape and unify the general dissatisfaction around the current liberal platform. With the memory of the French Revolution fresh in mind the Government acted to repress the corresponding societies and the combinations.

---

[1] Willard Thorp's *Business Annals*, p. 152, seriously misrepresents the position of British industry from 1798 to 1801. Each of those years is headed 'depression', although output was almost certainly increasing and unemployment was low. This is not meant, of course, to deny the reality of the difficulties due to high living costs, from 1799 to 1801.

[2] For the role of a prosperity demand for labour in the unrest of these years see Macpherson, op. cit., vol. iv, pp. 475 and 500. Strikes for higher wages were, in this as in later periods, a familiar characteristic of the latter stages of business expansion.

The Acts of 1799 and 1800, reinforcing existing legislation,[1] made illegal all collective working-class activity except the guild functions of the friendly societies.

3. *The Repeal of the Combination Acts, 1824 and 1825.* From 1820 through the early months of 1825 a fairly continuous increase in output and employment occurred. In the latter stages of the boom prices rose, relieving manufacturers briefly from the chronic downward pressure that had existed since 1814. But the period 1820–4 saw a coincidence of increased output and a sagging price level. Foodstuff prices, too, were fairly low. It is not surprising, then, that in the four years after Peterloo British labour was relatively peaceful.

The fact of increasing prosperity, too, made it possible for the industrialists and the Government to afford a greater tolerance:[2] 'Exceptional measures of repression were allowed gradually to lapse; the activities of spies were relaxed; and the law was set less freely in motion against working-class attempts at combination'. It was in this atmosphere, early in 1824, that Place and Hume manœuvred the repeal of the Combination Acts.

The repeal immediately brought into the open the trade unions which had been operating under cover in the previous two decades; and it encouraged the formation of many others. A wave of strikes broke out and, in the following year, an aroused Parliament seriously limited the easy-going terms of the Act of 1824.

There can be little doubt that the strikes of 1824–5 can, in some measure, be attributed to the repeal of the Combination Acts. Two other factors, however, were then operating. In the first place, in the latter half of 1824, the boom was suddenly accelerated, pushing the major British industries close to full employment. Enormous exports to South America and to the United States, as well as widespread internal enterprise, created a typical, late prosperity situation. Strikes for higher wages would, normally be expected.

---

[1] For the position of the 'Combination Acts of 1799-1800', as part of a long tradition of limitation, see D. George, 'The Combination Acts Reconsidered', *Economic History*, 1926.

[2] Cole, op. cit., vol. i, p. 88.

This tendency was accentuated by a second factor, a sudden rise in living costs:[1]

	Tucker (London artisans)	Silberling
1823 . .	124	111
1824 . .	126	113
1825 . .	137	128

In 1825, with a confidence born of some five years of increasing employment, the unions instituted numerous strikes for higher wages—in the cotton, wool, coal, iron, building, and other trades.[2] At about the middle of 1825, however, the business cycle turned downward; and, although the strikes continued for some time, by the end of the year 'combination . . . was kocked on the head. Bradford weavers and combers went back to work at the old wages . . . so did the Renfrewshire colliers'.[3] In the bitter industrial conflicts that continued into 1826, labour was no longer on the offensive, but attempting to preserve wage rates in the face of a declining industrial demand.[4]

The repeal of the Combination Acts is properly regarded as an expression of the general trend toward *laissez-faire*, paralleled, in the twenties, by the Huskisson tariff reforms. Hume, in Parliament, presented the measure in such a light. Both Hume and Place regarded the unions as illiberal institutions brought into being by the repressive action of the Government; and they looked forward to their disappearance with the repeal of the Combination Acts.[5] Nevertheless, the tolerant action of Parliament in 1824 was directly connected with the previous years of prosperity; the violence of the

---

[1] For an account of the inadequate harvest which largely explains this rise, see Tooke, op. cit., vol. ii, pp. 132–5.

[2] For a detailed account, from contemporary sources of strikes in 1824–5, see Smart, op. cit., vol. ii, pp. 232–3, and 306–13.

[3] Ibid., pp. 312–13.

[4] See *Annual Register*, 1826, Chronicle, pp. 67, 109–12, 115, 149–51.

[5] J. L. and B. Hammond, *The Town Labourer*, pp. 134–6; Page, op. cit., vol. i, p. 77, quotes Place as follows: 'Combinations will soon cease to exist. Men have been kept together for long periods only by the oppression of the laws; these being repealed, combinations will lose the matter which cements them into masses and they will fall to pieces.'

strikes of 1824–5 was largely the outgrowth of the situation in the labour market on either side of the cyclical turning-point, accentuated by rising costs of living. It is possible, too, that the intemperance of the reaction of the Government in withdrawing, in 1825, a large part of the freedom granted in the previous year, may be linked to the change in the industrial outlook which occurred in that year. With commodity prices falling, and disillusion setting in with respect to the newly floated Latin-American mining issues, the doctrine of *laissez-faire*, as applied to labour organization, seemed somewhat more empty than in 1824.

4. *The Factory Act of 1847.* Factory acts in the first half of the nineteenth century were passed in 1802, 1819, 1833, 1842, and 1847. Each arose in a unique political setting; but each saw a similar combination of humanitarian and anti-industrial groups arrayed against the manufacturers. Within the ranks of the manufacturers there were, of course, notable exceptions: men like Peel and Whitbread and Owen, to whom the conditions of factory labour were ethically outrageous and/or who believed that shorter hours and better conditions meant great efficiency and profits. In parliamentary debate, humanitarian arguments led to rebuttal based on pleas for the freedom of the individual, or originating in attacks on state paternalism. To these the manufacturer would often add the claim that shorter hours meant a serious reduction or even the destruction of the existing margin of profit, and the loss of foreign markets.

There is, however, probably some significance in the fact that these acts were all passed at, or close to, a low point in cyclical fluctuations. The years 1819 and 1842 are such troughs in general business conditions, while 1833 and 1847 were also generally depressed years (the troughs were in 1832 and 1848).[1] To a limited extent the children and women working in the factories and mines were competing with the men available for the jobs. At a time of severe cyclical unemployment it would be natural, then, that the men should complain, and attempt to oust their competitors

---

[1] The Factory Act of 1802, which dealt only with the pauper children, was probably inspired almost exclusively by religious and humanitarian motives.

or to limit their working time. A major driving force behind the movement which led to the Act of 1833, for example, was, 'the hope of absorbing men who are "hanging on the trade idle" '.[1]

In the case of the Ten-hour Bill of 1847 the role of depression is even more clear. From 1845 onward unemployment was steadily increasing. In 1844 a Ten-hour Bill was defeated; in 1847 it was quietly passed:

The Times, in a leading article on the following day, said it was not to be imagined that there had been any considerable degree of conversion on the subject. The argument stood very much where it had done in 1844, and had, in fact, been almost exhausted in that memorable struggle. The absence of fierce opposition was attributed in a large measure to the fact that the chief argument of the opponents—namely, that the country could not spare the last two hours of industry—could not be brought forward in 1847 without inviting its own refutation, for so great was the depression of trade that the mill owners found it impossible to keep their mills working for so long as ten hours.[2]

From the side of the workers, too, a distinctly non-humanitarian factor can be detected in the ten-hour agitation. There seems to be little question that the labour unions viewed the measure as a means of restricting the labour supply and maintaining wage rates at a time of serious depression. At an early stage of the ten-hour agitation (December 1841) in a period of severe unemployment, Fielden was reported as having said:[3]

It is 'the duty of individuals to curtail the quantity of production when there is an over-abundant supply of the article they produce rather than increase it and reduce wages.' He considered that 'a reduction of hours of labour from twelve to ten would have this tendency,' and was therefore desirable, as they had already 'got mills and machinery to produce more than they could find a vent for at a remunerating price.'

[1] Quoted by Clapham, op. cit., vol. i, pp. 573–4, from First Report of the Factory Commissioners (1833), vol. xx, p. 849. See also Frederick Engels, *The Condition of the Working Class in England in 1844* (1892), pp. 134–48, on the competition between the men and their wives and children.

[2] See B. L. Hutchins and A. Harrison, *A History of Factory Legislation*, p. 70, with reference to *The Times*, 4 May 1847.

[3] Hutchins and Harrison, op. cit., pp. 63–4 n.

To some extent, then, the Ten-hour Bill was passed because unemployment existed and because it was believed by some to be a recovery measure. In markets other than that for labour the restriction of supply, in an effort to maintain prices, was a typical depression phenomenon in these years.

The long-run economic and social influences reflected in the debates are perhaps more familiar.[1]

In Parliament, the factory question, from this time down to 1847, was really a part of the wider struggle between the agricultural landlords and the manufacturers over the repeal of the Corn Laws. 'The Tories were taunted with the condition of the labourers in the fields, and they retorted by tales of the condition of the operatives in factories. The manufacturers rejoined by asking, if they were so anxious to benefit the workman, why did they not, by repealing the Corn Laws, cheapen his bread. The landlords and the mill owners each reproached the other with exercising the virtues of humanity at other people's expense.'

This is not to deny, of course, that sincere humanitarians worked within the Ten-hour Movement; nor does it underrate the importance of the strange political battle which led, finally, to the passage of the 1847 Bill. But it is clearly a case where the short-run position of the economic system—the degree of unemployment—played a part in determining the moment of its ultimate acceptance.

IV

Testifying before the Committee on Manufacturers (1832) William Mathews, Staffordshire iron manufacturer, was asked:

9991. Do you conceive that the depression of trade in late years has had any effect in producing . . . discontent?—Very great. 9992. Do you think the working classes of Staffordshire ever show political discontent so long as they are doing well in their particular trade?—Not at all; you cannot get them to talk of politics so long as they are well employed. 9993. Do you think any man could create discontent among them so long as they were doing well?—It is utterly impossible.

[1] Hutchins and Harrison, op. cit., pp. 61–2, quoting Morley's *Life of Cobden*, vol. ii, p. 300.

The converse of the dictum—'you cannot get them to talk of politics so long as they are well employed'—is not to be generalized without reservation; but within this period it serves to explain the political unrest of such years as 1811–12, 1816, 1819, 1826, 1830–2, 1837, 1839–42, and 1847–8. In each of these cases a fairly direct connexion can be traced between unemployment and mass dissatisfaction. In the case of the Reform Bill, for example, to which Mathews's questioners were referring, there can be little doubt that the intense depression of the latter months of 1831 and the early months of 1832 contributed significantly to the pressures that led to its passage.

The activities of the Chartists, covering more than a decade, offer an interesting, if somewhat crude confirmation of this thesis. General business conditions reached a peak in 1836; 1837 was a year of severe depression; some recovery followed through 1838, to a second peak early in 1839. From the latter months of 1839 to the end of 1842 Britain suffered almost unbroken depression, exacerbated in its effects on the working classes by bad harvests. A recovery set in during 1843 which culminated in a peak in 1845. Business activity then declined to a low point in 1848. The phases of the most important Chartist activity occurred within severe depression; its temporary, but almost complete disappearance in 1843–5 coincides with the prosperity of those years.[1]

The three focal points of Chartist activity came in 1839, 1842, and 1848. Beginning in 1837 the Movement gradually grew to the point where a petition boasting some million and a quarter signatures was presented to Parliament in 1839.[2] The failure of this petition, and the Government's prosecution of the leaders, caused a temporary stagnation; but in 1842 a petition containing almost three and a third million names was placed in the hands of the Government.[3] In that year, too, the Chartists helped lead a series of bitter strikes, marked by extensive sabotage.

The wheat price fell, with the advent of a promising

---

[1] This relationship has been traced in detail by Preston W. Slosson, *The Decline of the Chartist Movement*, pp. 115–37.

[2] Ibid., p. 60.

[3] Ibid., p. 61.

harvest, in the summer of 1842, and in the following year recovery was under way. For the Chartists 'a long period of discouragement and inactivity followed', until the return of depression in 1846.[1] Still another petition went to Parliament in that year, and throughout 1847 the strength of the movement increased. Early in 1848 there were large meetings in the principal cities, climaxed by the presentation of the signatures of what purported to be almost six million British men and women.[2] Threats of direct action, however, failed to materialize, and, in the following years, prosperity and inadequate leadership brought the movement to an end.

The demand for universal suffrage at this period in British history patently had roots deeper than cyclical unemployment. The chronically depressed position of the hand-loom weavers, many of whom were Chartists, was also more than a cyclical problem. Yet, apparently, depression was required before the political doctrines of the Chartist leaders could command wide or effective support.

These examples by no means exhaust the possibility of tracing important links between short-run economic fluctuations and political and social events in the years 1790–1850. There are innumerable other cases which might usefully be examined from this perspective, and those traced here deserve more detailed analysis. Even these brief summaries, however, reveal the manner in which cyclical fluctuations and cost-of-living movements served to detonate and to give expression to the familiar underlying trends. They should also emphasize the distinctive economic, social, and political atmosphere of each year, or even different parts of the same year. The use of long-run conceptions like 'the growth of the Free-trade Movement', or the 'development of working-class organizations', or 'the Industrial Revolution' tends to blur this type of distinction. A necessary, but by no means sufficient requirement for a thorough interrelation of economic and other factors is a knowledge of fluctuations in general business activity and in costs of living.

[1] *The Decline of the Chartist Movement*, pp. 78 and 94.
[2] On close examination it was later estimated that about two million bona-fide signatures were attached to this final petition.

A Note on the Statistics

The indexes of imported and domestic prices used here have recently been constructed in the course of a study of *The Growth and Fluctuations of the British Economy, 1790–1850*, under the direction of Dr. Arthur D. Gayer. The Gilboy-Boody index appears in 'The Cost of Living and Real Wages in Eighteenth-Century England', *Review of Economic Statistics*, August 1936. The Silberling index is from 'British Prices and Business Cycles, 1779–1850', *Review of Economic Statistics*, 1923. The Tucker index is from 'Real Wages of Artisans in London, 1729–1935', *Journal of the American Statistical Society*, March 1936.

The business-cycle index is an outgrowth of an extensive history of business fluctuations (also a part of Dr. Gayer's study). Each year is rated from o (deep depression) to 5 (major peak). The ratings represent judgements made on the basis of all available statistical evidence, as well as a large body of qualitative material. In addition, an index of business activity was constructed containing some half-dozen of the more significant series. To present that index as a cyclical indicator would have required the abstraction of secular trends from each of the series; the index misrepresented business fluctuations at several points, in the light of wider information. It was thus decided to use the semi-descriptive chart presented here. It is similar in many respects to those compiled from Thorp's *Annals* by Gottfried Haberler (*Prosperity and Depression*). The wheat price is an annual average, derived from weekly quotations (1790–1834) in the *London Gazette* and (after 1834) monthly quotations in the *Gentleman's Magazine*.

The so-called Social Tension Chart is of even more imaginative construction than the business-cycle index. The wheat price was first reduced to a o to 5 scale: o representing a year of abnormally high wheat price (and thus, like a o year in business activity, 'high social tension'), 5 representing a year of abnormally low wheat price. This abstraction of the wheat price was then added to the business-cycle pattern, and the total plotted inversely to a high wheat price and/or estimated severe unemployment thus tending to raise the level of the chart. This method makes the quite arbitrary judgement that cyclical unemployment and high food prices were equally responsible for unrest. Low wheat prices, of course, affected farmers unfavourably and probably, to a lesser extent, agricultural workers. At best, then, the Social Tension Chart summarizes influences operating on the industrial working classes.

It is perhaps unnecessary to emphasize the essentially approximate and descriptive nature of these calculations. They represent, however, a useful summary of a considerable body of evidence, and the results conform fairly well to qualitative political and social data. Intervals of 'high social tension' bred known symptoms of unrest,

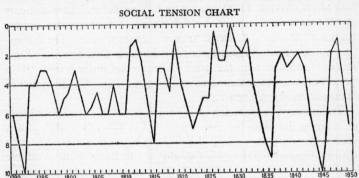

SOCIAL TENSION CHART

which, in many cases, expressed themselves in important legislation or in the activities of the Luddites, the Chartists, and other groups: intervals of 'low social tension' saw these movements fade from sight, although the low wheat prices that helped create them often brought the agricultural interests clamouring to Parliament.

'Social Tension' and its Components

	Trade Cycle Pattern	Wheat Price (actual annual average: s. per quarter)	Wheat Price (abstracted; inverse)	'Social Tension'[1]
1790 . . .	3	50·5	3	6
1791 . . .	4	45·0	4	8
1792 . . .	5	41·2	5	10
1793 . . .	0	47·7	4	4
1794 . . .	1	51·8	3	4
1795 . . .	2½	74·1	½	3
1796 . . .	3	77·1	0	3
1797 . . .	0	52·8	4	4
1798 . . .	1	50·2	5	6
1799 . . .	3	67·6	2	5
1800 . . .	4	113·7	½	4½
1801 . . .	3	119·0	0	3
1802 . . .	5	67·2	4	9
1803 . . .	1	56·6	5	6
1804 . . .	1½	59·8	4	5½
1805 . . .	2½	87·5	2	4½

[1] 'Low social tension' is indicated by high figures in this index; this series is designed to be plotted inversely.

	Trade Cycle Pattern	Wheat Price (actual annual average: s. per quarter)	Wheat Price (abstracted; inverse)	'Social Tension'[1]
1806 . . .	3	79·0	3	6
1807 . . .	2	73·3	4	6
1808 . . .	1 .	78·9	3	4
1809 . . .	4	95·4	2	6
1810 . . .	5	106·1	1	6
1811 . . .	0	94·6	1½	1½
1812 . . .	1	125·2	0	1
1813 . . .	1½	108·5	1	2½
1814 . . .	2½	73·9	3	5½
1815 . . .	3	64·2	5	8
1816 . . .	0	75·6	3	3
1817 . . .	3	94·8	0	3
1818 . . .	5	84·2	½	5½
1819 . . .	0	73·0	1	1
1820 . . .	1	65·6	3	4
1821 . . .	1½	54·3	4	5½
1822 . . .	2	43·2	5	7
1823 . . .	3	51·9	3	6
1824 . . .	4	62·1	1	5
1825 . . .	5	66·7	0	5
1826 . . .	0	56·9	½	½
1827 . . .	1½	55·9	1	2½
1828 . . .	2	60·4	½	2½
1829 . . .	0	66·0	0	0
1830 . . .	1½	64·4	0	1½
1831 . . .	2	66·3	0	2
1832 . . .	0	58·7	1	1
1833 . . .	1	53·0	3	4
1834 . . .	2	46·3	4	6
1835 . . .	3	39·4	5	8
1836 . . .	5	48·4	4	9
1837 . . .	0	55·6	3	3
1838 . . .	1	64·3	1	2
1839 . . .	3	70·6	0	3
1840 . . .	2	66·2	½	2½
1841 . . .	1	64·3	1	2
1842 . . .	0	57·2	3	3
1843 . . .	1	50·2	5	6
1844 . . .	3	51·1	5	8
1845 . . .	5	50·9	5	10
1846 . . .	4	54·6	3	7
1847 . . .	2	69·3	0	2
1848 . . .	0	50·5	1	1
1849 . . .	1	44·2	3	4
1850 . . .	2	41·8	5	7

See p. 124, n. 1.

VI

ECONOMIC FACTORS AND POLITICS: BRITAIN IN THE NINETEENTH CENTURY

I

VIRTUALLY all who work within the terrain of history or the social sciences must seek to relate economic forces to social and political events. Many have resolved the problem to their satisfaction within the context of particular investigations. There has been, however, relatively little generalized and formal treatment of the issue in recent years. All would now agree that economic factors, in some sense, are important for politics; virtually all would agree that, in some sense, economic factors are not sufficient to explain political events. From that point, however, the subject tends to disappear into the realm of *ad hoc* formulations and private faith. This chapter constitutes an effort to expose some of the complexities inherent in the relationships among the levels of activity which constitute the structure of society. It is an exploratory discussion, and presents no new self-contained system of analysis; it is, rather, an effort to make explicit some of the assumptions which appear to underlie a great deal of contemporary thought and writing, academic and otherwise.

A reviewer has recently criticized a study in which a rather rigid and whole-heartedly economic interpretation was applied to a complex set of political and social events. The reviewer concluded:[1]

Now, such an extreme position is neither science nor history. It is merely a new theology—not even good theology, because it is uninspired. It has faith in nothing but a verbal formula. It would rule Christ out of the Christian Church, Lincoln and the idea of national unity out of the Civil War, Roosevelt and the concept of human dignity out of the battle against the Nazis . . . even a great scholar knows only a very little and may not under-

[1] F. Tannenbaum, 'A Note on the Economic Interpretation of History', *Political Science Quarterly*, June 1946.

stand the little he know. Facts are easily acquired by industry and diligence. The meaning of the facts, all their meaning, is beyond the ken of any scholar—perhaps beyond the ken of mortal man.

It would be widely accepted that any satisfactory explanation of political events must leave a place for the role of ideas and for the individual; and the ultimate meaning of facts, indeed, belongs to philosophy, if not to religion, rather than with history or the social sciences.

The rejection of a rigid and monolithic economic interpretation of politics, however, is not in itself a satisfactory answer to the problem. The study of history moves towards general history, where a conscious effort is made to relate economic, social, and political phenomena; while social scientists seek increasingly to bring their various techniques to bear in a co-ordinate way on common bodies of data. Such communal effort within the social sciences demands, if it is to be fruitful, a minimum explicit agreement concerning the manner in which the various strands into which human society forms itself relate to one another.

A more refined view of society as a whole and of the interrelations among its parts is not merely an appropriate academic objective. Its achievement may prove prerequisite to successful resolution of major problems of policy at home and abroad which characterize the post-war period. A much expanded range of functions has now fallen into the hands of governments in both their domestic and foreign responsibilities. They are not likely to diminish substantially over the foreseeable future. Their exercise demands at bottom no less than the conscious manipulation of whole societies. Decisions of priority and of technique which have confronted governments in the tasks of domestic reconstruction have been made, explicitly or implicitly, on theories concerning the way society as a whole operates: the ends it will accept, and the stimuli required to produce the actions which will achieve them. Problems of policy in the occupation of Germany and Japan involve assumptions of equal breadth and inclusiveness, as do other aspects of contemporary foreign policy. The relationship between economic factors and politics is thus a matter of wide and not wholly academic concern.

II

A useful refinement can be achieved by distinguishing the economic forces which impinge on politics, directly or indirectly, with respect to the time-periods over which they persist. The number of categories one might derive by application of this criterion is obviously very considerable. As a first approximation, however, we shall distinguish and illustrate three types of economic impulse, operating over long,[1] medium, and short periods.

Long-period impulses are, for these purposes, those which proceed from the way people earn their living. Whether a man owns a large estate or is an agricultural labourer; whether he works in a cotton mill or a mine; whether he manages industry, engages in commerce, or goes each day to an office in a bank, obviously affects his outlook on society and on the political system; and it is one factor which enters into his judgement concerning particular policies and political events.

This long-run economic influence has much to do with the way people dress, the sort of houses they build, the standards of behaviour which govern their relations to one another, the literature and art and science which they generate. The nature of social life in, let us say, rural England, of the early nineteenth century cannot be deduced from the simple fact that it was an agricultural society proportioned in a certain way among large and small landowners and farm labourers. But its analysis would not be meaningful if it were not placed within such a framework. This is the sort of economic influence which is associated with the conventional analysis of the Industrial Revolution. The long process of industrialization shifted drastically the proportions of the population working at different occupations. The economic balance of society altered, and with that change came, gradually, shifts in the social life and the political structure of the

---

[1] It is evident that society is also shaped by forces operating over much longer periods than those distinguished as 'long' here: geography, climate, and the mysterious heritage of communal life persisting over centuries. These very long-run forces which form a large part of the subject-matter of anthropology, as well as history, are not considered here except briefly, p. 140 below.

country. In the study of the nineteenth century, volumes on literature as well as politics can begin, quite properly, by paying their respects to the Industrial Revolution.

The long-run economic impulse, among other factors, affects the judgement of individuals on particular political issues; but it may operate at several removes indirectly. And its influence may take various forms. When, for example, the Ten-hour Bill was under discussion in the 1840s, representatives of the landowning interests took various positions. Some, representing the strand of responsible public service embedded in the social tradition of their class, pressed for the Bill on paternal humanitarian grounds; others supported the Bill as a tactic of embarrassment to the manufacturers who were striving concurrently to repeal the Corn Laws; others joined the manufacturers in opposing the Bill as a general threat to men of property. In each case a part of the political position of the agriculturalists on this issue can be traced to the long-run impulse imparted by their general economic background; but the form of its expression, and even the net position taken, varied widely. There is no simple one-to-one relationship necessary between the long-run impulse and a given political judgement.

Perhaps the most important political influence of this type of economic impulse is in setting the political structure of a society: the nature of the electorate, and the distribution of power among the branches of government. The two great Reform Bills of 1832 and 1867 incorporate the effects of this long-run influence.[1] The link between the increase in relative economic importance of the industrial and commercial middle classes and the Reform Bill of 1832, the link between the rise of the industrial working classes and the Reform Bill of 1867 are, of course, familiar. The timing of the passage

---

[1] The passage of the Third Reform Bill of 1884, which enfranchised agricultural workers and some of the remaining industrial workers, notably miners, was not, of course, due to a growth in relative importance of the agricultural working classes. It was due, primarily, to the desire of certain groups of Liberals to strengthen the left wing of the party, as well as to a widening acceptance of the concept of universal suffrage. See G. M. Trevelyan, *British History in the Nineteenth Century*, pp. 389–91 and J. L. Garvin, *Life of Joseph Chamberlain*, vol. i, chap. xxi, pp. 459 ff.

of these acts, the role in their evolution of the concepts of modern democracy, and the complex political battles which preceded their acceptance cannot be deduced from a know-ledge of the changing composition of the British working force; one can deduce, however, a strong pressure to alter the balance of political power in definable directions.

James Madison, in the discussions which led to the adoption of the American Constitution, expressed clearly the predominant influence he assigned to economic factors in politics; and since the issue of a national Constitution was structural, long-run economic factors in these terms would be relevant.[1] Madison defined the function of government as the peaceful resolution of differences of opinion and interest within the community, or the regulation of factions, and he wrote:[2]

> . . . the most common and durable source of factions has been the various and unequal distribution of property. Those who hold and those who are without property have ever formed distinct interests in society. Those who are creditors, and those who are debtors, fall under a like discrimination. A landed interest, a manufacturing interest, a mercantile interest, a moneyed interest, with many lesser interests, grow up of necessity in civilized nations, and divide them into different classes, actuated by different sentiments and views. The regulation of these various and interfering interests forms the principal task of modern legislation. . . .

It is the long-run impulses from the economic system which change the balance of power among factions.

A second type of impulse imparted to the social and political systems by the economy can be described as operat-ing over the medium-run or over trend periods. The British economy in the period 1790–1914 operated in a manner such that trend movements of (say) longer than a decade existed which placed particular pressures on one part of the community or the other. In the period of the French wars, for example, agriculture prospered; but the

---

[1] The timing of the Constitutional Convention and the urgency which characterized its proceedings were, of course, related to the troubled course of economic and political events over the period 1783-7.

[2] *Federalist*, No. 10.

working classes suffered from chronically high food-prices. In general these years were pervaded by a contented spirit among agriculturalists and by a working class unrest out of which the conceptions and aspirations of the modern British working-class movement took their initial shape. The Speenhamland System and the Combination Acts reflect two of the diverse responses of politics to the pressures exerted by the working classes, generated in turn by very specific economic trends. From 1815 to the mid-century, on the whole, agricultural prices fell, and important segments of the farming community were discontented and defensive, with consequences which infected the whole sequence of political life. After 1873, for a quarter century, industrial prices tended to fall, and industrial profit margins as well. It is no accident that, in these years, the assumptions of mid-century *laissez-faire* were questioned not only by socialists, but also by the advocates of fair trade and by those who formed the international steel-rail cartel. In many ways the new imperialism of these years was a Great Depression phenomena; and it is a just, if fortuitous, irony that Joseph Chamberlain's battle for power was lost in 1906 because several basic trends of the Great Depression had, by that time, changed their direction: capital exports were very much on the rise, in part due to policies Chamberlain had previously sponsored in the Colonial Office; British exports were expanding; prices and profit margins were on the increase; tariff reform no longer appealed.[1]

The trend movements of the economic system generate new attitudes of mind among the classes and interests affected, and they lead often to the formulation of major legislative proposals which form, over considerable periods, the focus of political life, the concrete issues over which ministries fall and reputations are made and broken. The attrition against measures of protection from 1815 to the final repeal of the Corn Laws is a political sequence strongly

---

[1] See E. Halevy, *A History of the English People, 1905–1915*, p. 14. The election of 1906 was affected not only by the turn in the trends from their Great Depression pattern, but also by the cyclical expansion begun in 1904 which would be accounted a short-period phenomenon in the vocabulary used here.

affected by the trends within the economic system over the three decades preceding 1846. Another important example was the trend movement of real wages from 1900 to 1914. There were many deep and long-run influences which made likely the development, in these years, of a political party representing the British working classes, and the formulation in British society of a concrete programme designed to increase working-class security. But that development was given a special urgency and impetus because the economic system in its normal relatively free workings, yielded a more rapid rise in retail prices than in money wages. Much of the political pressure which was mobilized for the Liberal reforms in the pre-1914 decade derived its immediate strength from the desire of the working classes, conscious or otherwise, to redress by legislative action the balance of income distribution decreed by the economic system.[1]

A third type of impulse imparted to politics by the economy is the short-period impulse, associated with the fluctuations of the trade-cycle and of the harvests.[2] In the nineteenth century severe unemployment or a passage of high food-prices did not usually determine the nature of the major political issues nor the basic relative strength of the forces which arrayed themselves on either side; but they tended to detonate the underlying forces, by accentuating unrest, and to achieve some slight but occasionally significant shift in the balance among those forces. They thus affected the timing and character of political events. The introduction of the Speenhamland System in 1795 was, for example, connected with the two bad harvests which had immediately preceded; the appearance of the Luddites in 1811 and again in 1816 was directly connected with the severe unemployment of those two years. It is significant that the Peterloo massacre occurred in 1819, a year of severe depression; although the pressures which underlay it, as reflected in the banners which were carried, indicate the influence of long-run and

[1] Halevy, op. cit., pp. 270–3 for the combination of long-run and trend forces which affected the budget of 1907; and, more generally, for the basis of working-class discontent in falling real wages, p. 441.

[2] For a more extensive discussion of this type of impulse, covering the period 1790–1850, see Chapter V above.

medium-run forces as well.[1] Similarly, the Reform Bills of 1832 and 1867 both represented the adjustment of political pressures long in their generation; but they were passed at or close to cyclical low points preceded by intervals of working-class unemployment and unrest.

We have thus distinguished three types of impulse from the economic system acting on social and political life: a long-run force which constitutes the framework within which social life develops and which affects particularly the general balance of power within the community and the structure of its political life; a medium-run impulse, associated with economic trends, which often defines major political issues and generates movements designed to achieve certain concrete political results; and short-run impulses which in the nineteenth century affect the timing of political events and their colouring.

This rough and arbitrary formulation, based on the distinction of the time period over which an economic force operates on society as a whole, explains in part why the relation of economic factors to politics is complex. Embedded in any political event of importance one is likely to find not simply an economic factor, but a range of economic factors, with different and even conflicting impacts on the minds and public behaviour of men. The great gathering at St. Peter's Field, Manchester, in August 1819 was not simply a response to a period of cyclical unemployment; nor was it simply a response to several previous decades of painful social adjustment and restricted standards of living; nor was it simply the response of an increasingly large segment of the community to the lack of political representation. It was all of these things.

III

The multiplicity of economic impulses acting on political life is among the lesser complexities which surround the rela-

---

[1] The short-run influence was represented at Peterloo by the cry of cyclical depression, 'A fair-day's wages for a fair-day's work' which Carlyle made the occasion for extended reflection (*Past and Present*, bk. i, chap. iii, pp. 23–9). The trend impact of the war-time high food-prices can be detected in the call for 'No Corn Laws'; and the long-run aspirations of the working classes in 'Equal Representation or Death' (W. Page, *Commerce and Industry*, p. 47).

tion between economic factors and politics. More difficult is the mechanics of their operation. Here it is necessary to seek a rough outline of the structure of society which historians and social scientists can take as agreed.

It is a useful convention to regard society as made up of three levels, each with a life and continuity of its own, but related variously to the others. These three levels are normally designated as economic, social, and political. Each is itself capable of elaborate sub-division, and these sub-divisions, too, have their own life and continuity. Within the economy, for example, one can isolate for examination the evolution of its capital market institutions; or the development of iron and steel trades; or the course of wheat prices. Nevertheless the production and distribution of goods and services form a unified and interrelated operation; and the component parts of economic life may be studied in relation to a larger whole (e.g. the national income, or the level of real wages). Similar unity among discrete strands exists in the social and political levels of society although, lacking quantitative measures and refined analytic tools, it is less easy to define and to manipulate.

The economic level of society imparts, as is suggested above, a variety of impulses to social and political life; and these have been distinguished in three arbitrary categories according to the time-period over which they operate. But it also receives back from social and political life other impulses which affect its course. Such interactions are discussed briefly below. For the moment it is sufficient to note that the relations between the economic level of society and its other levels do not run merely in one direction.

The social level of society, as viewed here, is very broad indeed. It includes the way people live, the culture and religion which they generate and regard as acceptable, their scientific pursuits, and above all the general political concepts which serve to rationalize their relationship to the community.[1] In a passage which implies the use of an analytic

[1] A satisfactory definition of the term 'social' is difficult, although its accepted usage is tolerably clear. A. L. Rowse (*The Study of History*, p. 69) has defined social history, on a rough-and-ready basis, as how society consumes what it has

structure not very different from that developed here, Professor G. M. Trevelyan has written:[1]

... the social scene grows out of economic conditions, to much the same extent that political events in their turn grow out of social conditions. Without social history, economic history is barren and political history unintelligible. But social history does not merely provide the required link between economic and political history. It has also its own positive value and concern.

There are various senses in which this intermediate role for social life may be taken as meaningful. The limited aspect most relevant to present purposes, however, is the manner in which general ideas are formed which serve as the basis for a considerable array of political positions on particular issues.

It appears to be a general characteristic of education, in a broad sense, that the community equips the individual with a set of general ideas which he may modify, reject, or supplant, by which the multiplicity of situations he confronts is reduced to order, made explicable, or tolerable. These are the conceptions that relate man to his family, his fellow-men, to his church, and to the state. In terms of nations similar general ideas develop which set, let us say, a Britisher's conception of his relationship to the continent of Europe, or to the African colonies, or to the United States.

These powerful simplifications alter only slowly; but they alter in such a way that they appear adequately to conform to the society's range of interests, and to explain the phenomena which men confront daily in their lives. There is a hard long test of empiricism that societies, as opposed to individuals, apply to the large ideas they accept. Once accepted

produced. This is not wholly satisfactory; for the writer, the teacher, the dress designer, are all producing in an economic sense; and it would be an arbitrary distinction that would segregate the work of the scientist in an industrial laboratory from the scientist in a subsidized university laboratory. Social activities appear to arise from human needs or desires over and above the technical minima necessary for food, shelter, clothing, and reproduction. These needs are met by the production of goods and services; and the working force consists of men, not factors of production; therefore, 'social' qualities and objectives suffuse the process of production as well as consumption.

[1] *English Social History*, p. vii.

these ideas have an authority of their own and a great independent reality among the forces which move men to act.

The fact that such general ideas change slowly, and that men's attachment to them is often impervious for considerable periods to evidence of their unreality, irrelevance, or inapplicability, has led to a considerable literature of cynicism in which men's minds are regarded as an anarchic open market for large concepts, unrooted in solid judgement or empirical tests. Pareto's sociology and some of the subsequent literature of fascism enshrined this bias, as did some of the discussion of semantics in the United States during the 1930s.[1] While it is clearly necessary to take into account the very considerable time lags which attend the rise and fall of ideas, in relation to the situations which they are designed to explain, and to appreciate the independent power they exercise over the minds and behaviour of individuals, at bottom and in the long run, ideas appear to be rooted in

---

[1] J. M. Keynes closed *The General Theory of Employment, Interest, and Money* with a comment on the relative potency of vested interests and ideas in determining the course of history (pp. 383–4): '. . . the ideas of economists and political philosophers, both when they are right and when they are wrong, are more powerful than is generally understood. Indeed the world is ruled by little else. Practical men, who believe themselves to be quite exempt from any intellectual influences, are usually the slaves of some defunct economist. Madmen in authority, who hear voices in the air, are distilling their frenzy from some academic scribbler of a few years back. I am sure that the power of vested interests is vastly exaggerated compared with the gradual encroachment of ideas. Not, indeed, immediately, but after a certain interval; for in the field of economic and political philosophy there are not many who are influenced by new theories after they are twenty-five or thirty years of age, so that the ideas which civil servants and politicians and even agitators apply to current events are not likely to be the newest. But, soon or late, it is ideas, not vested interests, which are dangerous for good or evil.'

Keynes's observation is not at issue with the view developed here. It would be accepted that a given set of special interests confronting a given situation can find resolution in a variety of ways; that the course followed in fact may depend on the ideas current, especially in the short run; and that the long run, in history, is compounded of a series of short-run resolutions to particular issues and conflicts. The argument here would emphasize, however, that the ideas available, and their acceptability, depend on previous or current experience and interests, not excepting the 'General Theory'. For a comment on the independent power of institutions, apart from their 'original meaning or purpose', similar in its general implications to Keynes's observations on the limited rationality of political judgement, see L. B. Namier, *The Structure of Politics at the Accession of George III*, vol. i, p. 164.

real and substantial changes in the conditions under which
men live.

In the period 1790–1914 the eighteenth-century notion of
responsible aristocratic government gave way to concepts of
representative democracy; notions of *laissez-faire* and self-
help triumphed over older concepts of paternalism and then
quite promptly began to lose ground to a revived conception
of state responsibility for the general welfare. Similarly, the
mid-century hopes of permanent peace and of universal free
trade with the countries of the Empire dropping like ripe
fruit from the tree, hardened into a more exclusive conception of Empire and a defensive British nationalism *vis-à-vis*
Germany. Each of these massive changes was associated
with real events, economic in character in the first instance.
This does not imply that those who formulated the ideas
were personally motivated by economic forces; nor does it
imply that individuals accepted the new ideas by a Machia-
vellian process of rationalization. It does imply that the
complex of changes in society which in the end made the
new ideas acceptable to the majority of the British people
were, at their basis and in their origin, economic.

While these conceptions may have economic roots, they
often express the widest sensibility and aspiration of which
men are capable; and the shifts in conception which occur
affect men's attitudes towards issues wider than those of
politics. In reflecting genteel doubt concerning the sanctity
of mid-Victorian articles of faith, Gilbert and Sullivan were
no less a product of the Great Depression than Joseph
Chamberlain.

As suggested earlier there are many aspects of political life
which take their shape from the social level of society; but
for these limited purposes the most significant is the generation of wide conceptions in terms of which specific issues are
viewed, fought over, and settled. Social life furnishes to
politics its vocabulary.

Politics, the third level of society, emerges as the arena in
which the various interests and powers of the community
negotiate the terms of their common life. In the resolution
of any particular issue there is involved not only the network

of pressures and formulations arising from the economic and social levels, but also the technique of politics itself: the accepted methods of mobilizing and making effective these pressures according to the rules and procedures which constitute the political system. This is an absorbing human activity demanding special virtuosity. The life of the political system, like that of the economy and the social system, is in a sense autonomous. At any moment of time the terms within which it works are, it is true, given; and the balance of power within the community sets relatively narrow limits to the actions which are permissible to the politician. Nevertheless, within those limits, a complex process of formulation, persuasion, personal initiative, and compromise takes place which, in its detail, bears often relatively little direct relation to the large basic forces outside the level of politics.

In nineteenth-century Britain the types of issue which arose for political settlement can be grouped in three categories:

First, issues of the balance of power in society and of political structure. Of these the Reform Bills are the most obvious example. The great crisis in the early years of this century over the power of the House of Lords would, of course, also fall within this category. The various Acts, legislative and in common law, relating to the status of the trades unions are only a little less important, and might well be grouped with the basic constitutional issues.

Second, issues of the distribution of income in a broad welfare sense. This category would include the Corn Laws and their repeal; the Factory Acts; education bills; the social legislation of the pre-1914 decade; issues concerning the structure and incidence of taxation, most notably, perhaps, the question of the income tax. The effects of such legislation over a period of time may be to alter the balance of power in society, and thus to help induce structural changes at a later stage. But the issues actually arise and are settled fully within the existing political structure.

Third, issues concerning the security and relative power of the community as a whole. Foreign affairs fall within this category, and questions of war and peace; although one might include, for Britain in the nineteenth century, the problem of Ireland as well. This general category falls mainly outside the present discussion, although it is susceptible of analysis in similar terms.

As between issues of the balance of power and what are here called issues of income distribution a sharp line is, occasionally, difficult to draw. The final repeal of the Corn Laws involved pressures almost as various and profound as the passage of the Reform Bill of 1832; although there is a sense in which the Corn Laws were lost with the passage of the latter act. And a useful distinction can probably be made between them as distinct types of political issue. The Reform Bill of 1832 involved specific consequences which could not be fully foreseen, stretching far into the future. It was not an issue of measurable gains or losses, for the segments of the community concerned, like another penny on the income tax. It shifted political power at its bases and thus stirred very large hopes and fears. For the landowning gentry a whole way of life appeared to be at stake; and emotions were brought into play transcending economic factors in their limited sense. These are the issues in politics which involve the greatest dangers to the process of peaceful adjustment; and in countries outside Britain in modern times they have often yielded revolution or civil war.

In terms of the international community, and problems of diplomacy, many of the issues which have resulted in war have been of this nature. No significant, peculiarly economic stakes appear to be involved, but rather the relative power of states which, it is felt, will determine the decision in a whole range of particular future issues incapable of exact prediction. The role of economic factors in a matter of Corn Laws, taxation, or tariff adjustments between nations is evident and fairly direct. The overtones of high moral or political principle which are occasionally invoked on such occasions are a relatively thin and conventional veneer. In the case of the Reform Bill of 1832, or the German invasion of Belgium in 1914, however, the basic balance of power appears in question for classes within a community and as between different communities. And with the balance of power there enters legitimately the whole way of life to which men are attached and the large ideas to which they owe allegiance.

Much of the dissatisfaction with analyses which place an exclusive emphasis on economic factors in politics arises from the obviously complex nature of the forces and motives which enter into these basic struggles for power, either within states or between them. Men do not usually fight and die for finite economic gains. They are, more generally, moved by a loyalty to ideas. These ideas, in turn, may be largely generated from economic life, and from a social life substantially shaped by the economy. But in war men are often moved by a simple sense of community quite independent of a particular economy or society, except that it is theirs; and in combat soldiers are often dominated by a loyalty that extends not much beyond those who are at their side. In times of peace this primitive loyalty to the community, though muted, can constitute an independent element in politics, acting as a powerful solvent in moments of acute domestic conflict, as the Duke of Wellington showed in 1832 and 1846.[1]

IV

The argument has thus far roughly defined the nature of the impulses generated by the economic system; it has sketched briefly the social and political structure on which they have their impact; and it has indicated some possible routes by which they may find their way, directly and indirectly, to the arena of politics. As suggested earlier, however, the economic system receives as well as imparts impulses; and these interactions are an additional element of complexity.

One of the more important interactions lies in the field of education. One can trace in nineteenth-century Britain a dynamic reinforcing process: the rise of an industrial and

[1] On the eve of the American Civil War the symbols of community were widely invoked, notably in the closing passage of Lincoln's first Inaugural Address; but they failed to produce a resolution.

commercial middle class; its insistence on improved facilities for education; and the consequent strengthening of that class in both its economic activities and in politics. In the latter half of the century a similar process affected the economic and political strength of the working classes. Religion, too, and science, and other aspects of social life tended, over the century, to reinforce the economy whose structure and direction of change gave them their special bias. In its broadest sense it is the social level of society which produces or fails to produce men of the type required for the efficient working of the economy.

The influence of politics on the economic system is, of course, very considerable. It sets, in the first place, the framework of law within which goods and services are produced. Among other major issues of the century, British politics was called upon to decide whether the basic framework of the economy was to be one of protection, or of free trade; and whether bargaining in the labour market was, in part, to be collective, or as between individual working-men and firms.

More than that, the structure of government taxes and disbursements, decreed by politics, constituted an authentic part of the economic process; and the government's intervention was meaningful even when it took the negative form of a Gladstonian obsession with economy. In many of the most important activities of government it is accurate and convenient to regard politics as a way of taking economic decisions alternative to private markets. This is patent in the case of war; notably, in this era, the French wars, when the society, having become engaged in large military enterprise, transferred to the government a significant range of economic decisions (e.g. the scale and terms of foreign loans and subsidies). These decisions, in turn, shaped indirectly many other aspects of economic life. Although the direct role of government in the economy is less marked during times of peace in the nineteenth century, the nature of political intervention, as a minor but real instrument for the taking of economic decisions, is much the same.

Society emerges, then, from this schematic analysis, as a

dynamic structure of three levels, each with a quasi-auto-
nomous life of its own, each receiving and imparting impulses
from and to the other levels. In the formal sense with which
economists are familiar the analysis of society is a dynamic
problem: the impulses which are generated within society
require time in which to work themselves out.

. Movements within the economic system, long-run in
character, set the framework within which social life and its
concepts evolve, pursuing, on the whole, a sluggish life of
their own. The long-run impulses have their main impact
on politics, having worked through the social structure, where
they have been generalized, associated with non-economic
aspirations, and crystallized into ideas and particular, often
structural, political objectives. Similarly, the medium-run
or trend impulses imparted from the economic system
become associated with wider concepts and objectives before
they make their full appearance in politics, often in the form
of particular non-structural acts of legislation. The short-
run economic forces tend to strengthen or weaken the relative
forces making for or resisting political change; and they thus
affect the timing and character of political events. The
political level of society receives from the other levels this
complex of impulses and by rules and conventions and ideas
which are themselves partially the product of long-run
economic and social influences, sorts them out, and seeks to
resolve conflicts among them in a manner such as to avoid
resort to settlement by trial of brute strength. In performing
these functions the political level of society sets the basic
terms of both social and economic relationships in society;
and, in receiving and disbursing income, it actively engages
in current economic activity of significance.

V

It is evident that the unity of the structure of society, and
its shape, derive from the character of man: his desires and
motives and aspirations. Any complete theory of society
would have to begin, formally, with psychological hypotheses.
No attempt to supply them will be made in this limited and

exploratory discussion. But two observations concerning the position of the individual, in the structure outlined above, appear germane.

It will be noted that, of its nature, this structure is determinist in a loose-jointed way at the most. The economic system imparts certain impulses to the social system; and it constitutes a framework within which social life must develop; but it does not determine the particular manifestations of social life. Romantic poetry may have been connected, by various remote and proximate links, to the coming of the Industrial Revolution; but it was not written by Arkwright or Ironmaster Wilkinson. Similarly, the nature of political problems, and within limits, the nature of their possible resolution is given, at any moment of time, by forces external to political life. The particular solution arrived at, however, may vary substantially; and its particular form may have important consequences for the future. The area for freedom of action afforded to the individual in politics is certainly not infinite; but it is real. Referring to an incident that involved F. E. Smith, Mr. Churchill once wrote:[1] 'This probably turned the scale in favour of Mr. Bonar Law's leadership, and may traceably have altered the course of history. However, it is always being altered by something or other.'

Within economic life, as well, technical conditions and the economic environment are given, but progress is achieved by the efforts of men stretched to the limit of their energy, imagination, and competence, as the history of any great firm will attest. There is, in short, a considerable place for the individual within each level of this structure. On occasion it may be proper to regard the course of history as inevitable, *ex post*; but not *ex ante*.

Secondly, there is the question of motives. Is man in society basically economic man? Here only a very limited observation will be hazarded. It appears necessary to distinguish the behaviour and motives of individuals from those of economic, social, and political groups. In devoting his efforts to the repeal of the Corn Laws John Bright was no doubt helping to effect a shift in relative economic advantage

---

[1] W. S. Churchill, *Great Contemporaries*, p. 151.

among the economic and social classes of Britain. One can scarcely imagine an issue more purely economic in its character or intent; and without its economic substance there would have been no such well-financed agitation. Yet Bright, the Quaker, threw himself into the great crusade out of the broadest of motives, as a whole man; and as his later positions on the Crimean War, the American Civil War, and the Second Reform Bill indicate, he regarded the repeal of the Corn Laws as part of a larger political conception for Britain and the world. There is little doubt that many of his followers shared the Free Trade vision, with its full penumbra of hopes for peace, democracy, and universal prosperity.

More generally, the personal economic motives of a political figure appear often to have little relevance to his position on particular issues. The profession of the politician or statesman, as one who helps press forward or resolve peacefully the pressures thrust from below into the arena of politics, is, in one sense, intrinsically disinterested. The politicians who directly benefit economically from participating in politics are, for Britain in the nineteenth century, rare. And in other countries and in other times, the fact of the connexion rarely appears to be the decisive element in shaping major political events. Men may seek in politics the opportunity to exercise powers of leadership or of oratory; they may enter politics from a sense of service or out of family or social tradition, like Namier's 'Inevitable Parliament Men' of the eighteenth century. The interplay of personal motives and impersonal political forces is, surely, a relevant and interesting aspect of the study of society. It appears necessary, however, to avoid treating them as identical.

At every stage, then, the individual appears to work out his destiny within limits which, while narrow from the perspective of the whole evolution of society, provide, more or less adequately, for the expression of his full energies and aspirations. History seems to be tolerant of the individual if he avoids the larger illusions of grandeur.

PART III

ECONOMIC THEORIES

VII

EXPLANATIONS OF THE GREAT DEPRESSION

As a result of developments in economic theory during the 1930s no sharp distinction now exists between the theory of money and the theory of value and production. This article proposes to trace the destruction of a discrete monetary theory by examining the explanations that have been offered for the secular fall in the British price level from 1873 to 1896. It is an appropriate case because it attracted substantial interest and analysis, both contemporaneously and in retrospect. Many of the great figures in the history of doctrine, from Marshall on, have spoken their piece about it. An examination of the application of their theories to a single body of data is calculated to reflect the paths by which monetary analysis has come to its present position.

I

The types of theory illustrated will be divided into the following categories:

1. Those which argued directly from gold to the price level.
2. Those which took into account changes in $M'V'$, dealing explicitly with the monetary and banking system.
3. Those which looked explicitly to the interest rate as the lever by which price movements were achieved.
4. Those which explained movements in the general price level in terms of a supply-demand analysis of individual prices.
5. Finally, three cases will be examined in which attempts have been made to combine the various strands into a consistent general explanation: those of Marshall, Wicksell, and Keynes in the *Treatise*.

It is obvious that no reputable theorist has been content to interpret price movements simply in terms of gold production, or even of the amount of gold held by the banking system. All were led, to a greater or lesser degree, to examine the mechanism by which gold affected individual price movements. Most writers might be placed in several of the categories. But the confusions, the sort of data selected as relevant or left unused, the movements in variables assumed implicitly to have taken place, all point the consequences of the lack of co-ordination between monetary theory and value theory.

1. Fisher writes:[1]

Between 1873 and 1896 prices fell. This fall was presumably due to the slackening in the production of gold; to the adoption of the gold standard by nations previously on a silver basis, and the consequent withdrawal of gold by these new users from the old, to the arrest of the expansion of silver money consequent on the closure of the mints to silver; to the slackening in the growth of banking; and to the ever-present growth of trade. . . . It is not that the left-hand side of the equation did not increase, but that it did not increase so fast as trade. . . . It will be seen that the history of prices has in substance been the history of a race between the increase in the media of exchange (M and M') and the increase in trade (T), while (we assume) the velocities of circulation were changing in a much less degree.

In both the *Purchasing Power of Money* and the *Theory of Interest* Fisher explored the relation between the interest rate and price movements; yet, in a so-called 'statistical verification', he finds a correlation between gold stocks and price-level movements a sufficient test.[2] There is no investigation of capital market conditions calculated to reveal whether, in fact, the money rate was lagging behind the 'real' rate of interest.

---

[1] *The Purchasing Power of Money*, pp. 243 and 246–7. See also Mr. R. G. Hawtrey, *The Art of Central Banking*, pp. 199–200. After a statement of the gold situation, implying the usual consequences on prices, he shifts to a discussion of central bank policy and its ramifications—presumably the active agent in the price decline, pp. 200–7. More recently (*A Century of the Bank Rate*) Hawtrey has attempted to show that monetary crises, caused by gold shortages, and consequent unemployment, were required in this period to keep Britain in international exchange equilibrium (see especially pp. 100–2).

[2] Ibid., pp. 242–5.

Cassel's explanation follows precisely the same pattern. He finds a nice correlation between gold stocks and the price level, discovers the mystic 3 per cent. rate of gold production which, in conjunction with a 'normally' increasing T, will keep prices steady, and rests his case.[1] He immediately refers to the manner in which the automatic manipulation of the bank rate on gold-reserve criteria brings about the necessary price changes; but that proposition is not tested historically.[2]

2. Cassel makes an attempt to bring M' into the explanation, by assuming explicitly that the volume of bank money varied with the stock of gold in reserve.[3] But it is a half-hearted effort; and it has been painstakingly demolished by J. T. Phinney, who says:[4]

The conclusion of this analysis of bank statistics is that such data as are available show that little or no correlation existed between the rate of growth of the gold supply and the rate of growth of either bank reserves or bank notes and deposits. Between variations in gold production and variations in the rate of growth of the most important part of the circulating medium there seems to have been almost no correlation that is assumed by all studies of the problem of price trend that deal in terms of gold and price alone. This absence of correlation is especially striking in the period from about 1875 to 1913, when so many of the statistics examined show a relatively constant rate of growth of bank reserves and bank currency, quite unaffected by variations in gold production or by trends in prices.

Layton and Crowther, using the same sort of theoretical framework, were aware that banking statistics did not reveal the expected stagnant (and thus deflationary) tendency. They trace briefly the development of banking institutions and practices to find that in a considerable measure 'Great Britain had substituted credit instruments for gold'.[5] Banking developments were working in the opposite direction to the alleged gold shortage. With the type of analysis they employ, however, the fact that the price level did fall forces them, by

[1] *The Theory of Social Economy*, pp. 467–94.
[2] Ibid., pp. 494–502.   [3] Ibid., pp. 481–9.
[4] 'Gold Production and the Price Level: the Cassel Three Per cent. Estimate', *Quarterly Journal of Economics*, 1933, p. 677.
[5] *An Introduction to the Study of Prices*, pp. 85–6.

definition, to conclude that the expansion in banking was 'quite overshadowed by the absorption of gold'.[1]

3. The explanations of Fisher and Cassel appeared in general theoretical texts. The author could select without a historian's full responsibility such data as he chose, to illustrate elegantly a long-run generalization. Readers and reviewers, too, were not essentially critical of the historical implications of the illustrations. But this secular fall in prices was, in its day, a burning short-run issue, with political implications. Economists who put forward their views in the Press or before the royal commissions found themselves in heated debate, and sharply questioned. In the course of the controversy over the causal process by which prices were lowered, short- and long-run monetary analyses were brought closer together than they were again to be for many years.

One of the best of these controversies involved Sir Robert Giffen, Marshall, and the *Economist*. Giffen had maintained that the fall in prices was due to a stationary amount of money, at a time when the amount of commodities coming on to the market was steadily increasing.[2] This relationship was illustrated by a diagram showing money (1873–96) as a horizontal line, commodities sloping steadily upward, prices downward.[3] In subsequent debate it was argued that if a gold shortage was being felt it would have operated through the money market; but long- and short-term capital rates were, on the average, patently lower than they had been in the decades before 1873. Giffen realized, too, that the long-run consequences which he ascribed to a gold shortage must be the cumulative result of a series of short-period deflations induced from the centre of the banking system:[4]

The way scarcity or abundance of gold would tell upon the money market would be by producing monetary stringencies and

---

[1] *An Introduction to the Study of Prices*, p. 86.

[2] 'Recent Changes in Prices and Incomes Compared', *Essays in Finance*, vol. i. A. Sauerbeck, before the Royal Commission on Precious Metals, argued on precisely the same lines: '1067. You said, I think, that the increase of the supply of gold has not been as great as the increase in the supply of commodities, and therefore prices have fallen?' 'Just so.'

[3] Ibid., p. 214.

[4] 'Trade Depression and Low Prices', *Contemporary Review*, 1885.

periods of temporary difficulty and discredit, by which, perhaps, the tendency to depression would be aggravated. The average rates over the whole period, when these stringencies were occurring, might be lower than at times when they were fewer, but the mere fact of successive stringencies would help to produce the effect described on prices.[1] Now the course of the money market since 1871 has been full of such stringencies.

The final sentence, backed by a few vague references, constituted Giffen's only proof. And the *Economist*, with a barrage of carefully prepared statistics (comparing 1860–71 and 1872–83), showed not only that money rates on the average had been easier,[2] but that the number of rate changes and the average range of rates was about the same in both periods, despite the fact that 1872 and 1873, years of rising prices and high and frequently changing Bank rates, were included in the latter decade. These statistics, in addition to a re-examination of its own weekly money market reports, led the *Economist* to conclude:[3]

The whole of the evidence, therefore, adduced in support of the theory that we have been suffering from a great gold scarcity, which has exercised a severely depressing influence upon prices, seems to us to break down upon examination.

Giffen began by contemplating an increase in commodities set against a stagnant amount of money. So long as he was able to remain on the level of quantity theory terminology there were no problems of detailed explanation: gold production had tapered off, there had been an increased demand for gold, as the gold standard was widely adopted, prices had fallen. What more could one ask? But the dissatisfaction of opponents who had their eyes fastened on individual prices —the dissatisfaction Cantillon felt with Locke, Tooke with Ricardo—forced him into short run. Simplicity and sureness were gone. The case fell to the ground.

[1] See also G. D. H. Cole, *British Trade and Industry*, pp. 91 and 96–7, for a similar explanation of the role of gold, and monetary influences.
[2] *Economist*, 1885, pp. 687–8.

	Average Bank Rate.
1860–71	4·12%
1872–83	3·46%

[3] Ibid., p. 688.

Marshall, commenting on the *Economist*'s article in reply to Giffen, emphasized that a low rate of interest was not in itself sufficient evidence against the existence of a gold shortage. He believed that the interest rate had not fallen so far as it might have—that a 'gold shortage was felt a little in the Bank parlour'.[1] But neither his analysis nor his conclusions differed in any important respect from those of the *Economist*, which held that gold, from 1873 to 1885, was 'an influence of a very minor kind' on prices.[2]

Like Giffen, Layton and Crowther, after reciting the usual monetary statistics, felt called upon to deal somehow with the problem of the interest rate:[3]

It has frequently been argued that the low rate of interest which prevailed, together with the fact that the combined bullion reserves of the leading countries of the world increased during these years, are signs that there was no lack of gold. Falling prices are, indeed, commonly associated with a low rate of interest, which is not necessarily incompatible with a relative shortage of the precious metal. The test of sufficiency or otherwise of the gold supply is the relative levels of the bank rate of discount and the general rate of capital (as indicated by the yield on an approved security) over long periods. Both may be low, but if the former is consistently above the latter, it indicates a shortage of gold.

A comparison of the Bank and Consol rates reveals the 'former above the latter' except at occasional cyclical periods of easy money. The years after 1896, when the gold shortage was presumably no longer operative, show, if anything, a greater gap between market and Consol rates than those before. But it is not the inadequacy of the verification that is to be noted here, so much as the authors' faith in the sufficiency of the quantity theory framework. Pages are devoted to the gold question, a perfunctory paragraph to the interest rate.

4. Although, in quantity theory terms, it was admitted by most writers that T was the 'dynamic' force in the price decline—that the volume of trade was increasing against a stagnant amount of effective money—discussion centred on the left-hand side of the quantity equation. The *Economist*

---

[1] *Official Papers*, p. 128.   [2] 1885, p. 688.
[3] Op. cit., pp. 86–7.

noted that Giffen only 'tersely summarized' what he himself had believed the active agent in the price fall:[1] 'a great multiplication of commodities and diminution of the cost of production due to the progress of invention, improved facilities of communication, lower freights, international telegraphy, and the like circumstances'.

Giffen in this list not only mentions the increase in T, but he includes, as well, forces which tended to lower costs. Here is a kind of double counting which lies at the heart of the duality. In the theory of production, falling costs shift supply curves down and to the right. If the demand curves facing individual firms remain unchanged, increased output and lower prices result simultaneously from the change in cost conditions. Marshall had pointed out this redundancy. In a written reply to preliminary questions submitted by the Royal Commission on the Depression of Trade and Industry (1886) he wrote (after quoting Tooke on the fall in prices from 1814 to 1837):[2]

I think that there is an objection to Tooke's mode of wording which applies also to many recent writings on the subject. He has not made it clear that the diminution of the cost of production of commodities must not be counted as an additional cause of the fall in prices, when its effects in increasing the supply of commodities relatively to gold has already been allowed for separately. This is a point of some difficulty, and its interest is theoretical rather than practical.

This theoretical confusion in reverse appears in the method by N. G. Pierson in examining the same problem.[3] He separates influences from the side of 'commodities' from those of 'money'. Taking the price of silver as an example, he finds no residual fall in its price to be explained after supply and demand conditions have been investigated, concluding that there was, therefore, so far as silver was concerned, no bullion shortage operative. David Wells battled the bi-metallists

---

[1] *Economist*, 1885, p. 688. More than anything else it was the inability to deal analytically with T in quantity theory terms which led to a concentration on the factors of the 'left-hand side', an identification of the quantity theory with a causal explanation almost completely in terms of money.

[2] *Official Papers*, p. 5.

[3] *Principles of Economics*, vol. i, pp. 384–99.

in the same way.[1] Neither realized that what the quantity theorists were saying was that the price fall was caused by a chronic deflation—a shifting down of individual demand curves—which was a result, in turn, of an artificially high interest rate. It is no wonder that the Royal Commission on the Depression, confused by the monetary theorists, took refuge in *ad hoc* explanations of individual price movements, turning the whole question of the precious metals over to another commission.[2]

II

The theory of general equilibrium towards which these writers were moving was obviously in an embryonic stage in Marshall's time. And it was to remain so until much later. Keynes has remarked that, 'It was an odd state of affairs that one of the most fundamental parts of the Monetary Theory should, for about a quarter of a century, have been available to students nowhere except embedded in the form of question-and-answer before a Government Commission interested in a transitory practical problem.'[3]

Marshall himself, confronted by a Commission dissatisfied with the long-run vocabulary of the quantity theory, anxious to suggest short-run remedies for the fall in prices, was facing some issues in monetary theory almost for the first time. He was asked:[4] 'We are supposing that there is a scarcity of gold and prices have fallen by reason of scarcity of gold?' to which he replied, 'I want to try and trace that if I can and see how it comes to affect prices, which puzzles me down to this moment'. His analysis contains most of the elements that have found their way into current general theory, but it is an uncoordinated and scattered statement at best. These were, for Marshall and his contemporaries, new issues; and the classical framework of theory was slow to adjust itself.

Marshall began bravely: 'I look with some scepticism on any attempt to divide the recent fall of prices into that part which is due to changes in the supply of commodities and that which is due to the available gold supply.'[5] He insisted that

---

[1] *Recent Economic Changes*, New York, 1890.
[2] Third Report, pp. 3–5.
[3] *Memorials of Alfred Marshall*, p. 30.
[4] *Official Papers*, p. 126.
[5] Ibid., p. 5.

he would use the term appreciation of gold to mean simply a fall in general prices. He desired to imply no causal monetary effect, he was eager to avoid the duality of which he was sharply conscious.

But the term 'general prices' proved quite as difficult to manage as 'appreciation of gold'. He came at one point close to the kind of causal statement he deplored, with the dangerously popular dictum:[1] 'The gold prices of all commodities fall together in consequence of the scarcity of gold.' He was asked: 'How many commodity prices must fall before there is an appreciation of gold?' 'That is what I wanted to guard myself about in my first answers. I quite admit that it would be possible for there to be a general fall of prices without anything that you could call a rise in the real value of gold. But on further consideration I see I need not pursue the point further. I can alter my wording so as to avoid the necessity for recalling the distinction I then made between the different uses of the term "appreciation of gold" and say there is a fall in gold prices. That is all I want. I do not want the scarcity of gold.'

From this point Marshall was pushed by the Commissioners (concerned with possible bi-metallist legislation) into the question which most interested them: In what way and to what extent did bullion influences operate to affect prices? As noted above, Marshall felt that to some extent the Bank rate had been kept artificially high, and that this had depressed the demand for goods through its effects on the willingness of merchants to hold stocks of goods. Several other types of influence on general activity stemming from the Bank rate were hinted, but the theory of its operation was left inconclusive.

Marshall evaluated the gold shortage as a minor influence on prices; yet he was incapable of discussing in other than the terms of partial equilibrium what he regarded as the major force, the reduction in the real costs of production. He refers

---

[1] Ibid., p. 79. Further evidence that Marshall did not free himself from the duality of approach is the following: '9978. So that in the long run, although trade influences appear to affect prices, really the reduced or increased supply of gold tends to bring about a lower or higher average level of prices?—Yes.'

to 'an improvement in the methods of production of many commodities, leading to a fall in their real cost', admits it as a 'true cause', but concludes that 'when we regard the average level of prices as dependent, other things being equal, upon the ratio of the volume of the standard metals to that of commodities, we count in the action of this cause through its influence in increasing the amount of commodities. There is some danger that its direct influence in reducing cost may be counted in as an additional cause of low prices; and this would, I submit, be to count the same thing twice.'[1] No more was heard from Marshall about the reduction of costs.

At the same time, in his discussion of the movement of the long-term interest rate, Marshall showed that he had grasped the essential character of the depression:[2] 'A depression of prices, a depression of interest, and a depression of profits. I cannot see any reason for believing that there is any considerable depression in any other respect.' Now the interest rate and profits were clearly linked in theory by Marshall:[3]

My position is that the mean rate of discount is governed by the mean rate of interest for long loans, that again is determined by the extent and the richness of the field for investment of capital on the one hand, and on the other by the amount of capital seeking investment.

Marshall attributed the falling real rate of interest to 'a difficulty of finding good openings for speculative investment', to an increase in the amount of savings available for investment, and, partially, to the fact that the price level was falling, and the expectation of further fall injured the confidence of investors. But the strands were never pulled together. A causal line in this dynamic process was never clearly traced by him, the elements remained unweighted, discrete.

Wicksell's is a less elaborate but more consistent explanation:[4]

Since 1871 . . . railway building, though it was continued on an enormous scale, took place mainly in countries outside Europe,

---

[1] *Official Papers*, p. 23.   [2] Ibid., p. 99.
[3] Ibid., p. 81.   [4] *Interest and Prices*, pp. 174–7.

or in more remote regions. In short, there was a considerable lack of really profitable opening for the additional capital which arose out of the savings of almost all classes of the community. The increase in real capital served rather to raise real wages. . . . The natural rate of interest consequently fell, but whether it fell to a *corresponding degree* must be regarded as doubtful.

This statement does centre attention on the changed direction of investment. It is developed, moreover, in a set of unified terms. It fails, however, to indicate that the type of investment 'increasing real capital, serving to raise real wages', would, in itself, lower prices whether a lag in the money rate of interest caused a chronic deflation of demand or not. Unless Wicksell contemplated two separate pressures downward on prices—one from the side of supply ('increasing real capital, lowering costs and prices, raising real wages'), the other from the side of demand ('a lagging money rate of interest')—there is a real conflict here.

In terms of theory Wicksell's view differs essentially from current analyses in its assumption of an equilibrium position where an appropriate rate of interest, by definition, achieves a steady price level and full employment. Aside from the assumptions this proposition makes about the demand for loanable funds, it holds only for the short period. The neutral rate of interest is that which would maintain constant *per capita* income. In the long run that rate is expected to fall, and prices with it. Assuming for the moment that the demand for capital was such as to produce full employment at some rate of interest, then only chronic unemployment, not merely a falling price level, would be evidence of the lag Wicksell assumes. Under short-period assumptions, of course, a falling price level might be sufficient evidence. The grip that the short-period analysis has held on theorists is indicated by the fact that none conscientiously investigated such employment statistics as were available; all ignored the royal commissioners' conclusions, and Marshall's, on the point.

Wrestling still with these issues, Keynes, in the *Treatise*, remained attached to several conceptions which defeated his attempt to make monetary and value theory homogeneous:

a concern with the general price level; a belief that general dis-equilibrium could be defined usefully (i.e. causally) in terms of an inappropriate interest rate. In addition, unlike Wicksell, he was hampered still by a residue of old-fashioned quantity theory, unco-ordinated with the body of his theoretical structure.

His judgement on the Great Depression was that 'a failure of the market rate of interest to fall as fast as the natural rate, has been more important than a shortage of gold supplies'.[1] He does not indicate that if a gold shortage was operative, it would have been effective through an artificially high market rate. Now, it is possible to distinguish two types of lag: that induced by a gold shortage, and consequent chronic pressure on the central bank's reserves; that due to institutional 'stickiness', symmetrical with the conventional lag assumed to exist between money and real wage rates. Without other evidence one might assume that Keynes was merely isolating out the two kinds of lag.

But earlier in the *Treatise* he dealt with the same period. He stated that the decline of prices from 1873 to 1886 was due to a failure of new mining to keep up with the demand arising from the adoption of the gold standard by a number of countries.[2] No justification, historical or theoretical, is given for the acceptance of 'the story on which we were brought up'.[3] He proceeds at that point, however, to discuss the depression of 1890-6 as a case of commodity deflation proceeding under a regime of easy money and abundant gold. The third of the Great Depression slumps is distinguished from the earlier ones presumably because the influx of new gold had already begun, making nonsense of any explanation simply in terms of the precious metals. The other cyclical depressions within the period, however, might have been equally well interpreted in the vocabulary of the *Treatise*. In them one can also trace clearly 'the effects of a prolonged withdrawal of entrepreneurs from undertaking the production of new fixed capital on a scale commensurate with current savings'.[4] The data offer no justification for such arbitrary division of cause.

[1] Vol. ii, p. 206. [2] Ibid., p. 164. [3] Idem. [4] Ibid., p. 206.

The duality appears even more sharply in Keynes's discussion of the Gibson paradox. He attributes the correlation of interest rates and general prices to a market rate of interest lagging frictionally behind the natural rate. But an allowance is made in prices for 'monetary influences as distinct from the influences of Profit Inflations and Deflations'.[1] The price index is corrected 10 per cent. from 1875 to 1884 for the downward pressure exerted presumably by monetary influences, i.e. a bullion shortage.[2] Even Giffen had admitted that the bullion shortage, if it operated at all, operated through something very close to a profit deflation. On this point, one can see clearly why Keynes described the composition of the *General Theory* as 'a struggle of escape from habitual modes of thought and expression . . . which ramify, for those brought up as most of us have been, into every corner of our minds'.[3]

III

Keynes of the *Treatise* emerged, then, like most monetary theorists before him, with an explanation of the price fall in terms of an inadequate demand for commodities, caused by a lagging money rate of interest. Many commentators on the period, however, were impressed from the beginning by the profound changes in cost and supply conditions. They knew that individual prices had fallen simply because freight rates were lower, new sources of supply had been opened, new machinery was in use. This sort of change, in a sense, defined the Great Depression to common-sense observers. They were baffled and angered by monetary theorists who, at best, could talk only in terms of a lagging interest rate, implying a chronic deflation of demand.[4]

The monetary theorists were severely hampered in their efforts to persuade. They were obsessed with the criterion of a constant price level, a monetary and interest rate policy

[1] Vol. ii, p. 206.   [2] Ibid., p. 199.
[3] *General Theory*, p. viii; and, also, pp. 292–4.
[4] See, for example, the testimony before the Commission on the Precious Metals, of N. L. Raphael, bullion broker. Questions 6908–7061. He could see no justification for all the talk about gold and monetary influences when costs had obviously fallen, new supplies were coming on the market, and cheap money lay idle in London.

'neutral' in its effect on prices. Any fall in prices automatically was 'caused' by an interest rate 'not low enough' or a failure of the effective amount of money to 'increase fast enough'. This was due to the fact that they were employing a short-run and essentially static analysis. In the analytic short run the quantity of fixed equipment does not change. Fluctuations in income, employment, and prices can be virtually identified. It was the application of a theoretical framework, developed under short-period assumptions, to deal with an abstracted 'trade cycle', that led them astray when it was applied to a period when long-period forces were at work. They could not indicate that the acts of investment in Period I, which caused a shifting up of demand curves and rising prices, in Period II would be shifting down cost curves, causing falling prices. In the secular analysis of the gold-prices theorists, changes in T could be used to deal with increased productivity, lower costs. The short-period analysis left such factors untreated. Wicksell's long-period analysis, as applied to the Great Depression, alone seemed to offer the economist a way of getting at changes in cost conditions without forsaking a monetary vocabulary.

When the *Treatise* was written Keynes was much concerned with Britain's inability to achieve full employment after the return to the gold standard in 1925. His comments on Bank of England policy in that period make it clear that he saw in the Great Depression an analogy to chronic post-war unemployment as he then interpreted it.[1] That analogy was justified in that complaints of excess capacity, a searching for new markets, characterized both periods; abnormal unemployment, however, was not present during the Great Depression. In both cases Keynes concluded that the interest rate was 'too high'. A disillusion with the efficacy of interest-rate manipulation and an analysis which relieves causal emphasis from it came together.[2] It would be interesting to know whether Keynes of the *General Theory* would have placed greater emphasis on the demand for capital in the post-

---

[1] *Treatise*, vol. ii, pp. 207–8.

[2] For the central causal importance of the interest rate in the *Treatise* formulation, see vol. i, pp. 156–9: 'The Causal Direction of Change'.

war years—a low and inelastic expected marginal efficiency —than he did at the time.

It is obvious that this analysis has implied a 'correct' approach to the treatment of price movements as well as historical judgement about 'the real causes' of the price decline from 1873 to 1896.[1] To set forth the theoretical approach fully lies outside the scope of this chapter. Certain of its tenets, however, may be stated:

1. No distinction in vocabulary is made between the analysis of the long and short run. A long-run movement in prices, in time, is regarded as an accumulation of short-run movements; analytically, 'long-period' factors are introduced into the analysis of price movements over short periods of time.

2. No distinction is made between the treatment of individual prices and the price level. Index numbers of prices are regarded as a summary of individual prices, not as 'the value of money'.

3. The analysis attempts to be dynamic in the sense that the movements of the chief variables are traced through periods of time and causal forces are evaluated in that movement. An important example of this is the tracing of the long-run consequences (i.e. consequences for cost and supply curves) of investment, which, in the short run, affect demand curves.

4. A maximum amount of the analysis, formulated in terms of income flows, is brought to bear on the factors affecting the position of the individual firm.

Perhaps the most useful lesson in this rehearsal of explanations is not for economists, but for historians. Men observing honestly the same set of data emerged with quite different explanations. Each explanation depended directly on theoretical presuppositions. But more than that, the data selected as relevant depended on those presuppositions. The royal commission reports contain pages of statistics on price movements, practically no statistics of investment. Fisher and Cassel were content with prices and gold stocks. Keynes of the *Treatise* was content with prices and interest rates. None

[1] See Chapters III and IV, above.

of the theorists (with the possible exception of Wicksell in his reference to rising real wages) could talk about interest rates and costs at the same time, or, at least, not in the same chapter.

In many historical terrains convention has marked out useful frameworks of organization, containing implicit assumptions of relevance and cause, which leave the writer free to exercise his talents for the collection of fact. The economic historian, if he is to go beyond the great institutional studies of the line which runs from Thorold Rogers to Clapham, must concern himself consciously with the problem of adapting such a framework from the corpus of current economic theory.

VIII
BAGEHOT AND THE TRADE CYCLE

I

To the economic historian the unique position of the *Economist* in the lore of nineteenth-century Britain consists not only in the special information it contains, information often inaccessible elsewhere, but also in the fact that it surveys systematically, week by week, the changing aspects of a whole economy. Its interest, it is true, was heavily weighted towards the problems of the capital markets and foreign trade; but the flow of reports from agriculture, and from the coal, iron, engineering, and textile industries, was regular and progressively more detailed, and in them can be traced the changing forces which governed the position in the various labour markets. All the relevant variables can be followed, in greater or lesser detail.

It would have been inconsistent with the coherence the *Economist* brought to political and social affairs for these reports to have been left to languish discretely side by side. It was inevitable that the editors should draw from them some generalized view of the course of the economy as a whole, and some sense of the typical relations governing the interplay of events in the various markets. Any journal committed to the regular reporting of the events which concerned the *Economist* would become, perforce, a chronicle of the trade cycle. The *Economist*, however, was more than a chronicle. Out of its accumulated experience it developed a lively sense of the causation of events. Unlike the typical Lombard Street operator or Midland industrialist it was not freshly surprised and affronted by each succeeding cyclical crisis and depression. If the *Economist* was to make sense of the changing scene week by week, if the journal was not to be an inchoate compendium of odd facts and statistics, an analytic framework was required. The *Economist* was forced, in a sense, to tell its readers where they stood at any moment in relation to the trade cycle.[1]

[1] This, in effect, the *Economist* regularly did, in the opening issue of each year,

It would be surprising, therefore, if the nineteenth-century *Economist* did not generate for its own needs some kind of trade-cycle theory. It would be equally surprising, however, if that theory were to be, as a theory, either highly explicit or highly abstract. The good reporter—even if he is a philosopher—must conceal the fact; and it would be a great philosopher indeed who could place the events of a complex economy into their ultimate analytic perspective as they developed, in their full detail.

The trade-cycle theory that emerged in the *Economist* was thus pitched on an intermediate level of abstraction, close to the language in which economic affairs were conducted, close to the data that were readily at hand. The *Economist* permitted itself no empty boxes. It employed only those analytic terms that carried an operating meaning to its readers. The most abstract and complete rendition of an *Economist* trade-cycle theory—chapter vi of *Lombard Street*—is entitled, 'Why Lombard Street is Often Very Dull and Sometimes Extremely Excited'.

II

Bagehot's view of the trade cycle is worth examination for several reasons. It is, for one thing, better articulated than those of either James Wilson or of his successors, before 1914; and we have the benefit of a chapter in *Lombard Street* addressed explicitly to the subject. Further, it was under his guidance that the modern *Economist* largely took shape. Echoes of his views can be heard through the four decades between his death and 1914. Finally, the period of his régime, 1860–77, coincides with the culmination of mid-Victorian prosperity; and if we would contrast sharply the problems of two centuries it is better to look there than to the last quarter of the century, with its evident foreshadowing of the major economic issues of later days.

Bagehot, after two years of apprenticeship, became editor of the *Economist* in September 1860, succeeding his father-in-

and later (from 1864) in the annual *Commercial History and Review*. In its role as analyst, and thus prophet, the *Economist* maintained, however, a becoming humility: 'We do not like to be Prophets in the money market; it is an indication of immaturity to be sure of the future' (1862, p. 533).

law, James Wilson, who had died while serving as Financial Member of the India Council. He remained editor until his death in March 1877. His régime thus embraces fully one major trade cycle (1862–8) and most of a second (1868–79). He drew, further, on his own considerable business experience, as well as upon the then meagre literature of economic history. His views on the trade cycle developed, however, mainly from observation of the economic system whose movements he professionally knew and reported.

These views incorporate his special gifts of generalization. One never loses touch with the institutions Bagehot is describing, nor the human motives and actions which suffuse them. Few latter-day cycle theorists, even those who have explicitly dealt with the so-called 'psychological factors', have permitted themselves such a bland and relevant observation as: 'All people are most credulous when they are most happy.'[1] The easy interplay of persons, institutions, and theory in Bagehot's exposition makes the abstraction from it of a formal structure difficult, as well as something of a violation. Chapter vi of *Lombard Street* still makes fresh reading, as do the *Economist* files themselves.

Bagehot begins by noting the failure of mid-century political economists to deal adequately with the trade cycle.[2] He points simply to the central cause of that failure, a diagnosis most modern economists would endorse: 'Our current political economy does not sufficiently take account of time as an element in trade operations.' Goods, in an advanced economy, are produced for consumption at some future time by persons other than the producer. From this observation Bagehot adduces two basic elements in his theory: the interdependence of markets ('the partnership of industries') and the central role of expectations about the future,[3] operating through the institutions of credit.

[1] *Lombard Street* (ed. Withers, 1931), p. 151.
[2] The existence of broadly regular cyclical fluctuations was not universally accepted at this time. See, for example, the letters of 'A Political Economist', *Economist*, 1864, pp. 1577–8 and 1428–9. This correspondent directly challenges the conception of any systematic general movement in the economic system and regards crises as uniquely determined catastrophes.
[3] This tribute to the entrepreneur, quoted in the *Economist*'s memorial leader

Using the first of these tools he launches a lively account of the workings of the cumulative upswing and downswing of the cycle. He takes, by way of example, the effect of lean or abundant harvests—a likely detonating force—with their repercussions on the volume of spending for commodities other than foodstuffs; and he shows that they alone could set in motion a minor business cycle which might, however, require several years to work itself out, in each direction.

The second tool—expectations, and thus credit—is then introduced: 'Credit—the disposition of one man to trust another—is singularly varying'. It is the preponderant role of credit that Bagehot finds peculiar to Britain of the seventies when compared with the other Great Powers. When the general view of the future is optimistic, credit is good, commodities change hands more quickly, and the volume of production increases. Here the banking system plays a major part, bridging the gap between present and future.

The effect of good credit Bagehot regards as a cause of 'real prosperity'. False prosperity comes when capital flows to uses which fail to produce their expected yield. Here Bagehot calls on rich historical illustration, including Macaulay on the South Sea Bubble, to indicate the credulousness of happy people. The element of mania, which he finds present even in more modest booms, like that which ended in 1866, he places as a factor setting the stage for the crisis and slump.

But the mania is not *deus ex machina*. He shows it growing naturally, in a modern society, from real factors. The mild and general prosperity, caused by (say) a good harvest, increased consumer spending on non-foodstuffs, and an improvement of credit, brings forward idle savings eager for a good return. The forms of fixed investment which are

to Bagehot, reflects the large part allotted to expectations in his system (1877, p. 348): 'Men of business have a solid judgment, a wonderful guessing power of what is going to happen, each in his own trade; but they have never practised themselves in reasoning out their judgments and in supporting their guesses by arguments; probably, if they did so, some of the finer and correcter parts of their anticipations would vanish. They are like the sensible lady to whom Coleridge said, "Madam, I accept your conclusion but you must let me find the logic for it".'

thus encouraged—especially in the latter stages of expansion —take time to mature. In the short period, however, they make demands on the money market for working capital and upon the basic industries, which are already strained; Bagehot points especially to the relative inelasticity of the coal and iron supply. The consequent rise in prices and interest rates creates a situation different from that in which many medium- and long-run projects were undertaken, and one less favourable. The pressure exerted by 'the sanguine and ardent' against limited financial and physical resources creates a prosperity 'precarious as far as it is real, and transitory in so far as it is fictitious'.

This is the setting for crisis, the chief characteristic of which is a general loss of confidence and a desire to reduce commitments. The decline can be set in motion by a bad harvest, or a local crisis anywhere within the economy. The changed view of the future spreads out from the first impact, and the volume of activity, in industry and in the capital markets, declines.

The limitation of depression, and then recovery, flow smoothly in Bagehot's system from the description of crisis. Money cheapens as industrial and commercial demands fall off and commodity prices decline; credit improves as the 'remembrance of disaster becomes fainter and fainter'; 'quiet people continue to save part of their income in bad times as well as in good',[1] and the irritation of John Bull with 2 per cent. stirs the adventurous; finally a good harvest comes.

---

[1] *Lombard Street*, p. 143. Bagehot notes that, as between bad and good times, 'people of slightly varying and fixed incomes have better means of saving in bad times because prices are lower'. At another point, however, Bagehot comments on the tendency for savings to diminish during depression; although there is no doubt that the net result of movements on the supply and demand sides of the capital markets made for lower interest rates (*Economist*, 1869, p. 1). '. . . in a year of depressed trade the monied savings of the country are not nearly so great as usual . . . most people do not deny themselves their customary indulgences till they have ceased to save; they arrest their provision for the future before they change their customary life. The small savings decline before the tea and sugar duties decline at all.' As indicated below, it is a characteristic especially of Bagehot's writing in the *Economist* that he distinguishes consistently the forces determining, at any moment, the volume of intended savings from those determining the volume of investment. And he is quite aware of the significance of their partial independence.

The terms of this dynamic system are familiar and modern with two exceptions: the considerable role of the harvests and the absence of the Hamlet of current theories—the marginal productivity of capital.

With respect to the harvests, it appears to have been true of the whole period from 1790 to Bagehot's day that a good harvest was a necessary if not sufficient condition for the beginning of general and sustained recovery.[1] Bagehot depicts its operation through the volume of consumers' money incomes—assumed to vary less than foodstuff prices —available for the purchase of goods other than foodstuffs. It is possible that harvests in fact had their chief impact on the economy as a whole through the volume of food imports required, the pressure or easing of pressure in the money market, and thus on the rate of interest.[2] In any case, repeal of the Corn Laws or no, the harvests were still in Bagehot's day an important factor in the trade cycle, even if their part was permissive and contributory, rather than central.

The absence of any extended discussion of the productivity of new investment is, of course, itself significant; and it may be taken by some virtually to define the difference between the nineteenth-century cyclical problem and that of the inter-war years. The concept appears briefly in one passage as part of a capital market trilogy:[3] 'In most great periods of expanding industry, the three great causes—much loanable capital, good credit, and the increased profits derived from better-used labour and better-used capital—have acted simultaneously.' On the whole, however, Bagehot assumes, as he was indeed entitled to assume in the early seventies, that the opportunities for profitable private investment were ample, and that the worst that had to be dealt with was the relatively mild irregularity of the rate at which they were

---

[1] See above, pp. 50–52.

[2] This is explicitly suggested in the *Economist* leaders. See, for example, the discussion of the consequences of the poor harvest of 1860 (1861, pp. 1–3); also (1863, p. 1205)—'in spite of our excellent harvest, which is generally the most potent of monetary agents, it [i.e. the rate of interest] has not fallen'.

[3] *Lombard Street*, p. 143. As noted below, the scant attention given to investment opportunities characterizes the generalized discussion of the trade cycle in *Lombard Street* more than the *Economist* itself.

exploited in an economy where investment decisions were taken by individuals, acting under self-defeating common impulses.

III

The treatment in *Lombard Street* cannot, of course, be taken to represent fully either Bagehot's or the *Economist*'s view of the trade cycle. It is a useful starting-place, and it suggests the considerations the *Economist* of the sixties and seventies regarded as most relevant. Chapter vi was written, however, for a special purpose: to explain and to reinforce Bagehot's plea for the maintenance by the Bank of England of a larger gold reserve.[1] His trade-cycle discussion centres disproportionately on the significance of credit and on the part played by Bank and other capital market policy in determining the extent of its fluctuation.

Although they reflect the same crusade, the *Economist*'s leading articles, taken over the course of a full trade cycle, present a better balanced view. Bagehot became editor of the *Economist* late in 1860, close to the trough of the slump which followed upon the crisis of 1857. The bad harvest of 1860, and then the opening of the American Civil War, set back the gathering revival; and considerable editorial attention was given to an analysis of the relative stagnation.

In the period 1860–3, before recovery was clearly under way, a recurrent theme in the *Economist*, and one not fully developed in *Lombard Street*, was the relation between saving and investment.[2]

The annual savings of the country, which some statistical writers are bold enough to specify, amount to many millions. By the most received computation—that of Mr. Porter—they amounted to £5,000,000 a month. It is only by a continually augmenting trade that this sum can be employed. Commerce

---

[1] *Lombard Street* has so long and honourably held its place as the classic description of the institutions of the City that it may not have been fully realized that its campaign for a larger gold reserve at the Bank had its roots in a particular analysis of the business cycle; and that the measure was regarded, by Bagehot at least, as a means of limiting the severity of crisis and depression. See below, pp. 174–5.

[2] The first of these quotations is from the *Economist*, 1862, p. 254; the second, 1860, p. 1; the third, 1862, p. 879.

must constantly extend itself in various directions, or a certain portion of the new capital will, of necessity, be unused.

The desirable and natural course is that year by year the inventive business talent of the country should open new fields sufficient to employ its new capital. In every year the new investments that are suggested ought to absorb the new capital that is saved.

But in 1862, with the market still depressed:

. . . we consider it exceedingly desirable that a considerable part of our spare English capital should just now be embarked in loans to foreign governments. We do not want the money; money in the open market is 2 per cent., and has been less; and foreign governments do want it.

Bagehot, patently, was using the conception of an equilibrium balance between savings and investment that would maintain an even prosperity. He did not define that equilibrium in terms of the full income flow as it is now conventionally defined; but he saw the cycle as arising from the fact that the decisions to save and to invest were taken by different sets of individuals, acting under motives that were not identical.

The major difference between Bagehot's analysis and that of modern economists is, however, his relative lack of concern about unemployment. The focus of his analysis is 'the value of capital':[1]

As we have often explained, an augmenting trade is necessary to a high, perhaps even to a fair, value of money. The savings of the country are constantly swelling the loanable capital to be disposed of, and, unless an increasing trade gives a new opening to our new resources, there will be a momentary superfluity, and a momentary depression in the money market in the value of capital for brief periods.

That Bagehot brings his analysis to bear upon unemployed money and low interest rates, rather than upon unemployed

---

[1] 1863, p. 533. It will be noted that implicit in this statement is the assumption that, without new investment opportunities, on an expanding scale, the value of capital would fall over long as well as short periods. There is enough here, and in similar references, to make one feel that it is only by fifty years in one direction and seventy in the other that Bagehot managed to avoid the accents of the Rev. Mr. Malthus, Lord Keynes, and Professor Hansen.

labour, is to be taken in part, of course, to reflect the concern of his subscribers. But there is little doubt that unemployment in the depression of the early sixties was relatively mild. The *Economist* was not simply the hard-bitten advocate of the mid-Victorian capitalist: with respect to the Nine Hours Movement it admitted the right of labour to wage an organized fight for a larger share in profits;[1] it emphasized the reality and measured the extent of the distress of the workers in the cotton districts during the famine caused by the American Civil War in its early days;[2] during the boomtime agitation of the trade unions, in 1865, it urged the case for organized labour as a means of equalizing otherwise disparate bargaining positions in the labour market;[3] it favoured the development of the co-operatives.[4] On the whole it seems fair to take the *Economist*'s lack of attention to general cyclical unemployment as properly indicating its lesser amplitude in the depression it was reporting.

The year 1863 was, clearly, a period of expanding prosperity, with its repercussions now felt strongly in the heavy engineering trades and the coal and iron industries.[5] The *Economist* recognized the widening effects of new enterprise, and correctly placed this phase of the cycle as part of the sequence, growing out of the good harvest and cheap money of 1861-2; but it was not complacent. The mood of optimism was bringing forward a spate of finance companies and banks. By February 1864, when the editors issued the first of the annual *Commercial Histories*, the *Economist*'s view of these

[1] 1860, p. 586. The *Economist* did not, however, believe that the reduction in the working day by one hour would result in a sufficient increase in efficiency fully to compensate the employer; but it was quite capable of regarding that outcome with equanimity.

[2] 1862, p. 479.

[3] 1865, pp. 1456-7. True to its political liberalism, however, the *Economist* also emphasized that the manner in which trade-union decisions were taken was not wholly democratic. It did not advance this as a general argument against the unions.

[4] 1862, p. 480.

[5] See especially 1863, p. 1246, 'Fluctuations in the Scotch Iron Trade'. This article traces, in some detail, the impact of business cycles on the iron industry, from the early forties on. It recognizes, in 1863, the relation between the contemporary prosperity of the iron districts and previous developments in agriculture and the markets for short- and long-term capital.

enterprises was already faintly jaundiced: 'Under any circumstances prudent observers will not fail to prepare for
contingencies the exact date of which is alone uncertain.'[1]
This theme had been elaborated in even greater detail in the
opening leader of 1864:[2]

Credit is the life of trade, but every sudden growth of new
credit is always tainted with an admixture of evil. The late
extensive credit has fortunately fallen upon a period of very
prosperous trade—of trade stimulated by cheap food, and, therefore, we may hope that the alloy of evil may not be large. Still,
some alloy general considerations warn us to expect, and what
alloy there is, a long period of dear money, especially of oscillating
dear money, will be sure to display and detect. On the whole,
therefore, we anticipate that the year 1864 will be a serious though
not an alarming year. Our trade will probably be very large and
very profitable, but against this we shall have to set the possible
consequences of a long period of dear money—the gradual
detection of undue credit—and the gradual failure of any trade
which such credit may have fostered or created.

The *Economist* could not be accused of leading its readers up
the garden path.

The first of the anticipated failures came in September
1864, when the Leeds Banking Company went down. That
shock, however, and concurrent difficulties caused by the
bullion policy of the Bank of France, were successfully
weathered. And 1865, with its revival of exports to the
United States, was another good year. Beneath the growing
tension of the capital markets, a general expansion in domestic
and foreign enterprise, including a major shipbuilding boom,
made for increased industrial output, higher wages, and a
typical prosperity outbreak of trade-union expansion, with
strikes for higher wages widely successful.

From late 1864, with their eyes firmly fixed on the middle
future, the editors began to concern themselves with the
developing financial crisis. In September 1864 the question
of Bank policy with respect to the gold reserve was reopened:[3]
'The good of Peel's Act is that it alarms the Bank Directors;
the harm, that it alarms other people also; the advantage,

---

[1] *Review of 1863*, p. 2.　　　[2] 1864, p. 2.　　　[3] 1864, p. 1195.

that it may prevent a panic; the curse, that if it does not prevent, it enhances it.' And in 1865 the case was vigorously put for a Bank rate policy that would discriminate between an internal and an external drain on the bullion reserve, a concept that lay behind Bagehot's recommendations for Bank action during crisis.[1] At the same time it noted 'the preliminary oscillation—the warning symptom—which suggested to every one under large liabilities the expediency of making preparation while there was yet time, and before the real crisis had set in'.[2] In the opening leader of the next year, the *Economist* expressed obliquely the hope that its message had been well read in the proper quarters: 'The management of the Bank of England has improved; they know that confidence is based on cash—that credit requires gold.'[3]

In May, however, 'like a spark falling on tinder', Overend, Gurney & Co. failed, giving rise to a panic 'more suitable to their historical than to their recent reputation'.[4] The Bank Act was suspended and the worst of the crisis was soon passed; but in London, the commercial centres of the provinces, and the industrial areas depression had set in. The *Economist* regarded the crisis of 1866 as having been generated in the credit system, rather than within industry or in the foreign balance:[5]

... credit is an unsubstantial phenomenon; it is like a woman's reputation; the moment it is suspected it is gone. ... The crisis of 1866 was in its essential character not a capital panic arising from an exhaustion of our actual resources, or a bullion panic arising from the excessive diminution of our national cash balance, but a malady of credit inherent in such credit.

In a limited sense this was obviously true: the failure of Overend, Gurney & Co. was decisive. But the condition of virtually full employment that had persisted over the previous year, the rapid rise of industrial prices in the months before the crisis, and the tension in the labour markets indicate a

---

[1] 1865, pp. 1266–7. [2] 1865, p. 1026.
[3] 1866, p. 2. [4] 1866, pp. 581 and 553, respectively.
[5] 1866, pp. 613 and 818. There can be little doubt that the crisis of 1866, as interpreted by Bagehot, strongly affected the formulation of his trade-cycle theory in *Lombard Street*, just as it reinforced his advocacy of a larger Bank reserve.

general background of instability in all the principal areas of the economy.

The *Economist*'s leaders of 1867–8, in the period of depression, follow much the same lines as those of 1860–3. The fall in interest rates came quickly, and in the depressed state of enterprise money hung heavily in the market:[1] '. . . for our present purpose, the cardinal fact is that our credit, which was last year so good as to raise the rate of interest by the ease with which it conducted money to those who could use it, is now so bad that it clogs up money in the hands of those who do not dream of themselves employing it.' There was, as well, considerable soul-searching of the kind that followed most nineteenth-century panics. For three long columns the *Economist* examined the 'Alleged Degeneration of England in Commercial Morality';[2] and it offered this observation to the already sorely tried country vicars, retired military gentlemen, and other amateur investors:[3] 'The fact is, that there is a real pleasure to the mind in slight pecuniary danger. It has the character of gambling and the delight of gambling; and to that temptation experience shows very quiet, grave-looking people are often susceptible.'

By modern standards, however, the depression was not severe. It was confined to business of an enterprise character: 'the optional business of the country so to speak'.[4] There was a 'regular continuance of profitable industry'; and this contributed a steady flow of savings to the institutions of the money market. The answer that was to be found to the pressure of 2 per cent., in the course of the subsequent five years, was clearly foreshadowed:[5]

An old saving country like this ought to lend to new countries where there are no sufficient savings to employ. A new colony, with virgin soil, untouched mines, and a whole wealth of nature waiting to be used, ought to borrow if it can; an old country which has no fresh soil, and no untried opportunities, ought to lend if it can. We ought to send capital abroad, if we can do so safely. We shall thus get a good interest for our money, for virgin communities can pay better than others; we shall thus get better

[1] 1867, pp. 1–2.   [2] 1868, pp. 1–3.   [3] 1867, p. 1408.
[4] 1867, p. 1.   [5] 1867, p. 141.

imports, for the capital we lend will raise produce for civilized countries, and very much for ourselves; and we shall augment our exports, for we can not have these new imports without paying for them.

In its opening leader of 1869 the *Economist* was able to note a tentative revival of confidence:[1] 'A really sound investment is now sure of fair attention; it will not be unreasonably pooh-poohed'; while the *Review of 1870* indicated 'constant and full employment for the working classes' in the textile industries.[2] With the ending of the Franco-Prussian War, however, the expansion took on a new and more intense character. Britain's export trade increased to record levels, responding to the booms in central Europe and the United States; while the export market was further supported by loans floated in London on behalf of numerous foreign enterprises and governments. An enormous trackage of railways was laid throughout the world, and capital facilities, in Britain and elsewhere, were overtaxed despite their extraordinary growth in the course of the expansion. Prices and wages rose astronomically in the coal, iron, and engineering trades—'the instrumental articles'—and, briefly, miners drank champagne.

IV

All this was explicable in the analytic terms the *Economist* had earlier developed, as was the crisis of 1873. The expansion of 1868–73 had been simply the greatest of the mid-century booms. In the years that followed, however, profits appeared to lose their resilience. As early as 1877, the year of Bagehot's death, the main problems of the Great Depression were apparent and had been defined:[3] a strong downward trend in prices and profits, increased foreign competition in the export markets, the intensive character of new investment opportunities.

In terms of public policy the *Economist* was to resume the battle of the early forties against the Protectionists. Having helped create the mid-century system, the *Economist* was not

---

[1] 1869, p. 3.   [2] *Review of 1870*, p. 32; also p. 29.
[3] See especially *Review of 1877*, pp. 1–2.

likely to abandon it in the face of a frightened minority. Its recommendations continued to run in terms of unsubsidized efficiency and enterprise; and while the thirty years that followed 1873 lacked, for British entrepreneurs, the exhilaration of the two preceding decades, the opportunities proved sufficient to support a high average level of employment and a rising standard of welfare.

The *Economist* continued, however, Bagehot's vigorous campaign for a more responsible Bank of England policy. In general, it saw the trade cycle as an unfortunate but not insupportable process, deeply rooted in the basic procedures of the economy. The cycle's chief manifestation, from the *Economist*'s perspective, was the irregularity of profit margins, and that irregularity it was willing to accept as a toll for continued capitalism. It clearly recognized, however, that the Bank's part in the economy was not atomistic; and it believed that the interest rate and lending policy of Threadneedle Street could affect the duration of cyclical expansion and the intensity of the crisis and contraction. In a different context the *Economist* of the sixties and seventies was still preaching, and with little greater success, the lessons of social responsibility defined in the Bullion Report of 1810.

Bagehot wanted the Bank to keep during prosperity a larger gold reserve, and to respond sensitively, in its interest rate policy, to drains upon it, especially to drains abroad. In its lending policy the Bank was to preserve its high qualitative standards, avoiding the 'unsound' business of the market and thus serving somewhat to temper the general extravagance of expectations. When crisis came, however, the Bank was to assume a more positive role. Its reserve was the final rock on which credit might be preserved. Within the country lending on good security was to proceed on an openhanded basis. In this way a crisis might consist, ideally, in the weeding out of only those investments which were unsound. The subsequent depression would be shorter and less intense. Bagehot concluded his chapter on the trade cycle in *Lombard Street* by bringing the argument to this focus:[1]

Now too that we comprehend the inevitable vicissitudes of

[1] *Lombard Street*, p. 152.

Lombard Street, we can also thoroughly comprehend the cardinal importance of always retaining a great banking reserve. Whether the times of adversity are well met or ill met depends far more on this than on any other single circumstance. If the reserve be large, its magnitude sustains credit; and if it be small, its diminution stimulates the gravest apprehensions. And the better we comprehend the importance of the banking reserve, the higher we shall estimate the responsibility of those who keep it.

By a modification of Bank reserve and lending policy, then, Bagehot hoped to see the trade cycle converted into something approximating Prof. D. H. Robertson's 'slooms and bumps'. That represented the limit of centralized trade-cycle policy the *Economist* of the sixties and seventies would support. It is significant, however, that the condition which justified this advocacy was that Bank policy, consciously or otherwise, affected the interests of the community as a whole. As the decades passed, the application of that criterion was capable of justifying, without violation of the *Economist*'s liberalism, an expanding scope for centrally planned economic action.

V

For those burdened with problems of post-war economic readjustment, a glance at Bagehot's day may appear almost wholly irrelevant, evoking, at best, a certain envy and nostalgia. There are obvious senses in which the mechanisms of Britain's mid-century economy are, and have long been, inapplicable to our own day. We have abandoned almost beyond recall a flexible interest-rate policy, sensitive to short-run movements of bullion in and out of the central bank reserve. Foreign trade and foreign investment will be affected substantially, both with respect to volume and direction, by centrally taken decisions of national policy; even if the relation between 'sanguine and ardent' promoters and 'quiet grave-looking gamblers' persists on the level of chancelleries or within the various institutions of the United Nations. Domestic investment, and, more broadly, the allocation of all resources, will be more largely a matter of communal decision than it has been for several centuries, at times of peace in the western world. The peoples will undoubtedly insist that a variety of services, formerly, in large part, a function of individual incomes, be systematically provided, at minimum levels, for all. In short, a generation facing issues which call for consciously conceived policy of great intricacy, which must blueprint vast administrations and readjust radically the techniques and terrain of political decision, may be tempted to look up only briefly from the drawing-boards at Britain of the sixties.

Although we would now apply different and perhaps stricter standards of social security and welfare, its economy had one virtue which justifies a certain amount of current attention: it worked. It gave a rising standard of life to a rapidly increasing population; it provided a tolerable level of employment; its mode of operation was not necessarily inconsistent with democratic development at home and with international peace.

The conditions of its success are familiar, and clear in Bagehot's writing, both in *Lombard Street* and the *Economist*. The growth of populations, the opening of new areas, and the application of new inventions and industrial methods, offered wide opportunities for investment; and these were exploited, with intermittent vigour, by persons and institutions, acting under the motives of private profit. A machinery was provided for setting the order in which potential new projects were undertaken; and the resultant sequence of development was adequately rational. Crude but effective means operated to expose errors in foresight and judgement and to cut the losses of individuals and the community. The system as a whole was sensitive to changes in taste, and to changes in knowledge. The accepted procedures of foreign trade and the exchanges prevented any nation from pursuing an international economic policy outside a fairly well-ordered framework. These remain the relevant criteria.

Founded on the rock of expanding investment opportunities, the required institutions grew with a minimum of central guidance or control. That fact, however, should not blind us to the combination of intelligence and spirit that infused their operation. The mid-Victorians believed in their system and its future. They felt that the rules of the game, if followed, would yield benefits to themselves and to their neighbours; and in the sixties the game was sufficiently successful, and the rules sufficiently well kept, to give their vision vitality. It is only in later times that their slogans, when confronted with the facts, ring hollow.

Roughly from the crisis of 1873, a new set of influences altered the assumptions and changed the pattern. America and Germany emerged as major industrial powers, and the era of Britain's almost monopolistic railway building came gradually to a close. The physical frontier of America was reached by 1890. Increased powers of production and enlarged institutions for the mobilization of savings made for lower profit yields when they confronted the existing range of investment opportunities. The flexibility of commodity prices and money wages was compromised. Working, for the most part, in opposite directions, two great political forces began to affect the operation of the economy: the rise of the working classes as a political force, and the sharpening of national rivalries among a group of first-class powers.[1]

The operation of these forces, in the seventy years after 1873, shattered the institutions upon which the British economy of the sixties was based. Movement was made towards a new pattern. But even at times of greatest relative success—1896–1912, 1920–9—the compromise system failed to recapture fully the old confidence. The mid-century slogans, developed out of the battles of 1832 and 1846, with even deeper revolutionary roots in the preceding centuries, were employed defensively. The newer ideas, often formulated in remote terms, were only dimly reflected in measures of economic control and planning, and in action towards social security and welfare. Those who viewed

---

[1] As early as the *Review of 1879* the *Economist* noted the increasing diversion of resources to armaments (p. 2): 'In fourteen years the military expenditure of Europe has risen at the rate of 3 mill. a year, or from 117 to 160 mlns., and, as far as can be judged, will go on increasing with the same or greater velocity till arrested by some combination of three events, viz. (1) a decisive victory by one or more of the Armed States over the other, (2) the exhaustion of the means and patience of the unfortunate populations who bear the burden, or (3) (most unlikely of all) such a return of common sense as will produce a pacific policy.'

events from the older viewpoint were perennially fearful, the reformers fuzzy and frustrated.

Post-war developments will not, of course, end the days of compromise. The war has, however, both lessened many inhibitions to centralized action and it has stimulated productive energies. While the goals of peace are not as simple or as easy to define as those of war, there is a wide, if rough, area of agreement in Britain with respect to objectives; and the technique of planning in a politically democratic society is being generated cautiously day by day. It is possible, that in the decade after the war Britain may come near to resolving, in its ideas and institutions, conflicts which have sapped the vitality of the western world for some seventy years.

If this success is to be achieved it must, clearly, be grounded in a spirit of individual and collective enterprise as impatient of some newly defined '2 per cent.' as were the mid-Victorians. Bagehot's expression of that spirit speaks strongly over the intervening years:[1]

The area for employing our capital being thus enlarged, the physical opportunities for it being augmented by science, the mental opportunities being increased by the growth of civilized organization and the improvement of individual intelligence, we must not expect to go back to the old times when capital was not employed, or was scarcely employed.

[1] 1865, p. 62.

PART IV
NARRATIVE

IX

THE DEPRESSION OF THE SEVENTIES:
1874–9

I. GENERAL

THE famous depression in Great Britain of the 1870s, traditionally regarded as a period of unrelieved economic decline and difficulty, in fact falls into two quite distinct parts. The first, embracing the years 1874–7, is marked by maintained or slowly rising levels of production, with activity at home compensating losses, direct and secondary, due to the cessation of railway building and other new development in America and elsewhere. Britain's position in the preceding boom had been that of supplying capital goods and capital to developing areas. When such orders fell drastically and the inducement to invest abroad slackened, funds were diverted into home and public building, the opening of new mines, a variety of technical improvements involving the manufacture and use of steel, and the installation of new machinery of all kinds. This immediate shift in the character of investment helped sustain average annual employment above 95 per cent. until 1878. From the last quarter of 1877 to the middle of 1879 output in almost every branch of trade declined and unemployment rose to severely high levels. This secondary phase is paralleled closely by waning activity in the building trade, where a peak was reached late in 1876.

In the money market a variety of factors tended to keep the market from the ease of depression and a revival of confidence. Foremost among these were the gold purchases from Paris and Berlin; in the former case to acquire a reserve for the resumption of gold payments, in the latter to shift from a silver to a gold coinage system. The maintenance of high purchasing power in Britain, with bad harvests at home, and relatively falling exports created, until 1877, a growing net balance of imports. A greater fall in the price of Britain's capital-goods exports than in her consumption-goods imports accentuated this tendency. An unfavourable American exchange especially proved an embarrassment. Internally the banking system came under suspicion in 1878 with the crash of the Glasgow Bank. Lastly, war in Eastern Europe, with England playing an irresolute neutral hand, contributed to an unstable market atmosphere. A conjunction of these pressures produced in 1878 a rise of almost a full per cent. in the average Bank rate.

The floatation of foreign issues had dominated the long-term capital market in London to 1873, but crises on the Continent and in the United States, a knowledge of the exotic financial techniques of various of Britain's debtors, and an accumulation of defaults brought about an almost complete cessation of foreign lending. 1876–8 were years of net capital import. Home investment as reflected in new issues and the formation of companies fell off, but not on a scale comparable with foreign floatations. Much of the investment, moreover—in houses, machines, iron ships—which maintained output and employment did not appear in the capital market. The boom in house-building, in fact, was stimulated in part by the uncertainty of the market and the disrepute into which foreign investment had fallen.

Despite the maintenance of moderately high output until 1878, business, for the employers, was unsatisfactory. Especially was this so in the heavy industries. Almost every influence playing on the market made for lower prices and smaller profit margins. In 1871–3 the coal industry had undertaken tremendous expansion. The increased possibilities of supply, coupled with a relaxation of the 'famine' demand of 1871–3, brought the price down continuously. And although coal output did not decrease until late in the depression, men could not be kept employed at full time. Cut-throat, profit-reducing competition was conducted for the limited orders available. In iron the manufacture of railway materials came to a virtual standstill after 1873. The building of iron ships and of new machinery bolstered many sections of the industry, but unemployment among iron-founders rose steadily, accelerating in the latter stages, until it reached 23·9 per cent. in the first quarter of 1879. In this setting the steel revolution was conducted. By 1879 steel rails had eliminated iron, and the first steel ships were under construction. Only in the last year of the period did output from the Bessemer furnaces decrease. The textile industry had not enjoyed in 1871–3 the same kind of boom as the capital-goods trades. For a time, despite bad harvests in the East and the painful depreciation of silver, Chinese and Indian orders increased; the demand at home remained strong until 1878–9. But prices fell and operators described trade as 'dull and profitless'. Profit margins, like the yield on Consols and other fixed-interest securities, fell steadily in almost every branch of trade.

Falling prices, and competition made more acute by the development of capital industries in Germany, the United States, and elsewhere, forced on entrepreneurs the necessity of lowering costs wherever possible. Increased attention to workers' efficiency, the weeding out of less competent men, the use of labour-saving machinery, and, above all, wage cuts carried on this process. Efforts to lower wages resulted in a series of bitter and often long-drawn-out strikes. Union funds had been built up rapidly in prosperity, employment in many sections remained good until 1878, and the men were willing to fight.

The real wages of labour, measured by *per capita* consumption or calculated from money wage and retail price indices followed the movement of production rather than of prices and profits. In various districts short time limited the men's earnings, as did almost universal wage cuts. Until the latter stages of depression the general position of labour was well maintained, aided, despite bad harvests, by reduced retail prices. But with the building boom over, and internal investment low in 1878–9, unemployment mounted to the highest point in the half-century before the First World War.

II. THE MONEY MARKET[1]

	Bank rate per cent.	Bank's reserve ratio	Bank reserve	Net foreign gold movements (in millions)	Business cycle index
1873	4¾	95·3	55·8	+ 1·53	+1·32
1874	3¾	100	51·2	+ 5·73	+0·94
1875	3¼	100	54·0	− 0·32	+0·51
1876	2⅝	120·9	74·4	+10·21	−0·42
1877	2⅝	100	58·1	− 3·54	−0·76
1878	3¾	86	50·7	− 2·70	−1·50
1879	2⅜	114	85·1	+ 0·55	−2·35

1. Rates in the money market were easier in 1874 than in the previous year of crisis. The supply of commercial bills for discount abated, but the bullion policy of France, like that of Germany in 1873, put such pressure on the reserve that the Bank was compelled for some time to maintain rates above those which normally prevailed in an easing market. Open market borrowing was necessary to preserve Bank of England control.[2]

In 1874 the Bank of France acquired (net) £16·27 million in gold bullion.[3] Of this amount fully £7·47 million came from London. The French Bank was building up its reserves in preparation for a return to specie payments, which had been suspended since the Franco-Prussian War. Bullion was attracted to Paris by a careful manipulation of the Bank rate there. The average rate of the Bank of France was ¾ per cent. above that of the Bank of England for the year. Directors of monetary policy in Paris were careful not to create panic conditions in the course of accumulating gold. Their shrewd judgement in timing the liquidation of their holdings in Lombard Street earned the grateful praise of London's bankers.[4] In June the demand from Paris slackened, after

[1] For statistical sources used in this and the following sections see below, 'The Principal Statistical Indexes', pp. 222–5.

[2] *Economist*, 1874, pp. 1393, 1477.

[3] *Economist, Commercial History and Review of 1874*, p. 4.

[4] *Economist*, 1874, pp. 337–8; also *Review of 1874*, p. 3: 'The Directors of that establishment (the Bank of France) have manifested the highest skill and judgment in the way in which they have quietly and effectively accomplished their object of increasing the cash reserve.'

dominating the early part of the year, and the Bank rate remained at 2½ per cent. until the first week in August, when further French withdrawals pushed the rate to 4 per cent.[1] After a short period of ease the autumnal drain set in during October, when the reserve in the Banking Department fell below £10 million, the accepted symbol of safety.[2]

The autumn situation was complicated by a rise in the rate of the Bank of Prussia which was experiencing difficulty in holding stocks of gold previously acquired for coinage. Constant rumours of actual or impending German withdrawals ran through the City.[3] Financial operations in Berlin threatened an uncertain market. Bankers knew that if gold coins were to be substituted for silver in Germany more gold would be required, London was the market where the pressure would be felt,[4] and, for the moment, the supply of bullion in Berlin was ebbing away despite high rates. By 12 December German withdrawals of gold materialized in London,[5] but the reserve was rising in the Bank. The seasonal drain was over, although a six per cent. rate remained until the year-end.

When the Bank rate rose defensively in the last quarter of the year, open market borrowing on Consols and Indian bonds was required to raise the rates in the outer market.[6] With bills relatively scarce and idle funds available, the Bank directors feared that the enforcing of protective stringency might be difficult. In fact operations on a relatively small scale sufficed to keep rates up.

2. In 1875 easier conditions settled in the money market.

[1] Ibid., pp. 957-8.

[2]

	Bank rate per cent.	Banking department reserve		Bank rate per cent.	Banking department reserve
30 Sept.	3	10·81	11 Nov.	4	9·04
7 Oct.	3	10·04	18 Nov.	5	8·82
14 Oct.	4	9·41	25 Nov.	5	9·29
21 Oct.	4	9·42	30 Nov.	6	8·64
28 Oct.	4	9·60	30 Dec.	6	10·35
4 Nov.	4	8·83			

See also *Banker's Magazine*, 1874, pp. 798-9.
[3] *Economist*, 1874, pp. 1249, 1398-9; and *Banker's Magazine*, 1874, pp. 934-5.
[4] *Economist*, 1874, p. 1449.   [5] Ibid., p. 1477.
[6] Ibid., pp. 1393 and 1477.

The Bank of France built up its reserve another £12 million and the Prussian Bank drew gold for minting; but the strain on London's reserves was not comparable to that in 1874.[1]

Against the continuous and forceful opposition of Bagehot, in the editorial columns of the *Economist*, the Bank reduced its rate early in the year.[2] From 17 February to 7 July it remained at 3½ per cent. from where it sank to 2 per cent. through most of August and September. The autumnal drain was mild in October, but aggravated by stringency in Berlin. The energetic withdrawal there of small notes and the change of the standard coinage from silver to gold created a demand for gold reflected in some exports from London and rumours of exports to come.[3] On 20 October the Bank rate moved to 4 per cent., still under the fear of German coinage needs. A small rise in the reserve encouraged a 3 per cent. rate on 17 November, but by the end of the year French and German demands for bullion set the rate back to 4 per cent.

The Bank's protective policy again operated against a market where 'two great difficulties impeded the usual action of the Bank—the excess of deposits as compared with good bills, and the independence of the rates for deposit given by the bill-brokers and banks of the Bank of England's discount rate'.[4]

3. For 8½ months of 1876 the Bank rate was 2 per cent. The autumnal drain, although reducing the reserve somewhat, called forth no change in the official rate.[5] In Paris, Berlin, and Amsterdam the same ease prevailed.[6]

The year opened with the rate at 5 per cent., still under the threat of further French and German withdrawals. The end of this type of bullion drain was, however, in sight. In

---

[1] *Review of 1875*, pp. 4–5.
[2] *Economist*, 1875, pp. 29, 57, 204. The Bank lowered its rate too rapidly and suddenly found in February that Paris had drawn off several millions. The Bank rate went promptly to 3½ per cent., and the reserve was again safe; but the *Economist* (p. 205) did not fail to point the moral. By the middle of the year, however, the editors were convinced that the reserve was adequate and 2 per cent. proper (pp. 957–8).

[3] Ibid., pp. 1216–17.   [4] Ibid., p. 1360.

[5] *Review of 1876*, p. 40. Notes in Banking Department (in £ millions): 20 September, 21·43, 20 December, 15·62.   [6] Ibid., p. 7.

January the *Economist* could predict 'a general preponderance
of cheap money during the present year'.[1] The supply of
funds continued to flow into the market, but the floatation
of home issues and the value of foreign trade had become
less, while foreign lending was virtually at an end.[2] Initiative
in the capital market was paralysed.

When the immediate threat of German withdrawals
ceased, in the spring of the year, a net influx of gold built up
the coin and bullion reserve from £21·98 million on 19 January to £26·26 million on 26 April: 'gold continues to come
hither, and to stop when it has come, no other European
money markets offering better inducements for its employment'.[3] In October the fear that Great Britain might inter-
fere in the Russo-Turkish War interrupted the market's
stagnant ease. This tightening was accentuated by the withdrawal of gold from London's cheap market on a small scale
to Germany, on a large scale to the United States.[4] Exports
to the United States had fallen 37½ per cent. in value in two
years, upsetting the balance of payments, and gold moved
to New York.[5] Coin and bullion holdings at the Bank
decreased as follows (in £ millions):[6]

20 Sept.	.	. 35·0
18 Oct.	.	. 33·4
22 Nov.	.	. 30·5
27 Dec.	.	. 28·4

But the Banking Department reserve was fully £5 million
over the conventional £10 million limit, and no action was
taken to check the withdrawal of funds.

4. In 1876, with the Bank rate at 2 per cent., there were

---

[1] *Economist*, 1876, p. 35.   [2] Ibid., p. 34.
[3] Ibid., pp. 515–16.   [4] Ibid., pp. 1291 and 1393.
[5] Ibid., p. 1393.
[6] Ibid., p. 1515. An unusually large part of the reserve of notes and coins
was made up of bankers' balances in 1876. For most of the summer and autumn
the proportion of bankers' balances to reserve hovered between 75 per cent.
and 85 per cent., with a tendency to fall off as the year ended. The increased
balances were 'the result of an unusual accumulation in the hands of bankers,
who, being unable to employ this surplus in any beneficial manner, allowed it
to lie dormant in the hands of the Bank' (*Economist*, 1877, p. 661). The tendency
for the proportion of bankers' balances to grow had been under way at least
since 1871, but the accumulation of idle funds in a depressed market stimulated
the development of the practice (*Banker's Magazine*, 1876, pp. 1001–3).

signs that the demand and supply of money were moving towards the kind of adjustment which might precede an upturn in new long-term floatations and a general commercial revival. In fact the last quarter of 1876 showed a modest general improvement.[1] At this crucial juncture, however, confidence was shaken by war in Eastern Europe, political disturbances in France, a slump in American railway shares, and a famine in Southern India. In addition, gold withdrawals began seriously in the autumn of 1877. The Bank, as in 1874, was forced to create an artificial demand for funds in the market by borrowing on Consols.[2]

Until 2 May the Bank permitted its reserve to fall. At that time coin and bullion holdings were £25·1 million, the Banking Department reserve just under £11 million.[3] The rate was raised to 3 per cent., meeting a stiffening tendency in both Berlin and Paris.[4] A period of relative ease followed in which the Bank rate faded to 2 per cent., lasting from 11 July to 29 August. A seasonal internal drain then brought the rate back to 3 per cent. On 3 October, the reserve having lost £2·17 millions in a week, it moved to 4 per cent.[5] A week later, with the reserve well under £10 million, the Bank discount rate rose to 5 per cent. where it remained until the end of November. An improved reserve position appeared then, permitting 4 per cent. through December.

The anomalous position of the Bank, fighting to make its rate effective in a period when the market had funds it was willing to lend more cheaply, produced at times market rates fully 2 per cent. below the official discount rate.[6] The tendency of the Bank to force up rates artificially at a time when bills were few and funds plentiful created great antagonism in the City against the central institution. Private bankers agitated against the publication of an official rate, and the

---

[1] *Economist*, 1877, p. 2. Also *Banker's Magazine*, 1876, pp. 981–3.

[2] *Review of 1877*, from the *Railway News*, pp. 39–40. An excellent account of the condition of the market in 1877 is given, and the manner in which Bank policy reacted, or failed to react, on a slack market is described. See also *Economist*, 1877, pp. 1273–4.

[3] *Review of 1877*, p. 30, for Banking Department reserve: *Economist*, 1877, p. 512, for coin and bullion.

[4] Ibid., p. 1177. Also *Banker's Magazine*, pp. 963–5.

[5] *Economist*, 1877, p. 1177.   [6] Ibid., p. 1312.

Economist closed an editorial: 'It is undeniable that the Bank rate is no longer the exact index of the value of money which it used to be. It is not that anyone desires to dethrone the Bank, far from it; but if the Bank rate ceases to be a sure guide, is there not a close approach to an abdication of the position.'[1]

5. A threatened reserve and high rates, projected on a market in which commercial activity was on a depressed scale, again characterized 1878—the year of bank failures, and the sixth successive year of rising average unemployment.

Early in 1878 the stagnation of the capital market asserted itself, and for the fourth time in four years the Bank rate was at 2 per cent. A sharp rise in deposits,[2] and some slight decrease in reserve made that rate untenable, and on 27 March the Bank rate moved to 3 per cent.[3] At the end of May, despite a dollar exchange that tended to draw gold to New York and large unstable floating balances held by Paris, the Bank lowered its rate to 2½ per cent.[4] Through the summer the Bank rate moved upwards in four stages. On 14 August, with the reserve at £8·9 million, it stood at 5 per cent.[5] Holdings in Paris on London were being liquidated, suspicion was spreading about the position of various private banks; and again, despite 'no increase in inquiry for discount in the market', high rates prevailed—and this in a period of seasonal ease.

On Wednesday, 2 October 1878, the City of Glasgow Bank closed its doors. Some £7 million in notes and bullion were withdrawn from Threadneedle Street, the reserve was £8·5 million (16 October), and the Bank rate was 6 per cent. Fearing a run on their deposits, bankers all over the country were keeping their assets on hand: 'A feeling that the times

---

[1] Ibid., p. 1274 and pp. 1329–30. Also letter by 'Bullionist', *Banker's Magazine*, 1874, pp. 821–3. A review of monetary developments in 1874 (*Banker's Magazine*, 1875, p. 95) describes a growing sentiment among bankers against the system of centralized reserves. The existing relationship to the Bank, it was believed, left the market victim to artificially high rates which made competition for a diminishing business in bills more difficult. A detailed proposal for a special bankers' reserve to be formed co-operatively in London, outside the Bank, is printed in *Banker's Magazine*, 1876, pp. 129–34.

[2] *Economist*, 1878, p. 369.   [3] *Banker's Magazine*, 1878, pp. 439–40.
[4] *Economist*, 1878, p. 369.   [5] Ibid., p. 977.

were anxious, that it was desirable to be prepared at all points, has been at the bottom of all this.'[1] Since frightened private bankers refused to lend even to sound customers, the Bank was called upon for advances, which were granted on a large scale.[2] As none of the reserve had been drawn out of the country, a 6 per cent. rate seemed adequate at the time. Moreover, high rates in London drew funds from the gold hoard at Paris, where a 3 per cent. Bank rate prevailed. A rumour persisted in the City that the Bank had borrowed £3 million in gold from the Bank of France in addition. By 20 November the reserve was back to £12·3 million and the Bank rate was lowered to 5 per cent.[3]

A second large bank failure occurred in the first week of December when the Caledonian Bank closed. Its portfolio contained £400 of City of Glasgow Bank stock. The unlimited liability condition under which it was held brought 'this sound, steady, and successful business' to its knees.[4] The West of England and South Wales District Bank followed in the next week. 'Heavy and reckless advances to concerns of a dubious nature' earned for it little sympathy in disaster.[5] By the end of the year caution had become paralysis in the market, the mercantile demand for money was 'languid'.[6]

In June the Court of Directors of the Bank officially abolished the principle of the minimum rate.[7] For the greater part of the year it was understood in the market that the Bank, using a qualitative discretion, had made advances at rates below the official minimum. Several banks complained that their deposits were being used to underbid them in the open market. Although strong resentment continued, bankers realized that nothing could be done to prevent the Bank from following the general practice of the market if it so desired. In fact the Bank's action was not motivated by a

[1] *Economist*, 1878, pp. 1221–2 and *Review of 1878*, p. 37. The note circulation of the Bank increased fully £6·4 million in 1878.

[2] *Review of 1878*, p. 37.

[3] *Economist*, 1878, p. 1369.   [4] Ibid., pp. 1429–30.

[5] Ibid., p. 1457. For an account of other firms affected at this time see *Review of 1878*, pp. 36–7.   [6] *Economist*, 1878, p. 1486.

[7] *Banker's Magazine*, 1878, p. 608. For the full significance of the change, as an admission by the Bank of 'its inability to discipline the market', see W. T. C. King, *History of the London Discount Market*, pp. 291–6.

desire to compete in the open market. For some time the publishing of a minimum rate, more or less rigidly adhered to, had served to alienate the Bank from the market. The published rate was so far out of touch with other prices for short-term money that the Bank's business was negligible, control only possible for short periods, after prolonged open-market operations. As noted above, the Bank was forced to relax, even before the official step, its system of a rigid minimum. The non-adherence to a published minimum merely confirmed a system which gave the Directors wider scope for more subtle rate and loan manipulation in the protection of the central reserve: 'The Bank retained at least the opportunity for re-establishing its supremacy'.[1]

6. An immense rise in the reserve, a fall in money rates, and a recovery of confidence characterized 1879. An increase in new capital issues and an autumn influx of American railway orders marked the third quarter as a turning-point for commerce and industry as well.[2]

A fall in 'other securities' and the note circulation, a rise in the reserve, permitted the Bank rate to fall to 3 per cent. by the end of January. The funds held by banks in the crisis of 1878 trickled back; advances made at that time in the interest of liquidity were being repaid.[3] The rate of interest, predicted the *Economist*, would soon be at its 'natural' level.[4] In March the reserve touched £20 million and on 9 April the Bank rate was 2 per cent. But even at that rate the Bank could not compete in a market where first-class paper was placed as low as $1\frac{1}{4}$ per cent.[5]

---

[1] King, op. cit., p. 296.   [2] *Review of 1879*, pp. 1–2.

[3] *Economist*, 1879, p. 57.

[4] Idem. 'All indications are in favour of a belief that the immediate period of tension is past. We may look forward to greater ease. The mere mercantile demand would certainly not justify a rate of 4 per cent., but the influences of our money-market are so intricate and frequently so little connected with mercantile demand, that we may very likely see money kept for a time above the price it would naturally stand at.'

[5] Ibid., pp. 425–6. A money-market correspondent writes: 'The prospects of the money-market are now quiet in the extreme, an inevitable result of the crisis of last autumn; and until the present cheapness of money has stimulated trade, led to the introduction of new foreign loans, or a considerable accession of speculative activity on the Stock Exchange, the present low quotations are likely to continue'.

The exchanges at last were in Britain's favour and 2 per cent. was maintained until 5 November. Higher rates in Paris (3 per cent.) and Berlin (4½ per cent.) caused the withdrawal of funds. The reserve fell £6 million in the two weeks preceding 5 November,[1] but a 3 per cent. rate instituted then kept the reserve hovering safely about £15 million until the end of the year. As the revival gathered momentum, however, there was some tendency for rates in the outer market to rise. The Bank's 'other securities' show an increase in the residual discounting that fell to its lot.[2] A reflection of the direction of recovery was the tightening of the money market in New York; the American railway boom, with the consequent imports from Great Britain, was to be the primary stimulus of British recovery in 1880.[3]

7. The notable characteristic of this downward cycle in the money market is the length of time required and the difficulties surmounted before cheap and easy rates steadily prevailed. In the preceding chronicle a non-commercial demand for gold, bank failures, and political uncertainty appeared to impede the normal adjustment of rates to an abundant supply of short-term funds and a slackened demand. In addition the American exchanges, turned unfavourable to Britain, seemed occasionally to draw funds from London.

This latter movement reflects the frictions generated within the balance of payments during the rapid shift of Great Britain from a large-scale exporter to a small-scale importer of capital (1876–8). Hobson's balance of payments estimates are as follows (in £ millions):[4]

	Total invisible items	Estimated income from capital abroad	Import excess	Capital export
1873	87·3	50·0	65·0	72·3
1874	80·9	52·0	79·9	53·0
1875	75·0	49·5	98·0	26·5
1876	76·0	46·5	125·9	− 3·3
1877	76·6	47·5	139·5	−15·4
1878	80·7	47·0	129·0	− 1·3
1879	74·6	47·3	109·8	12·1

[1] *Economist*, 1879, p. 1286.   [2] Ibid., p. 1490.   [3] Idem.
[4] C. K. Hobson, *The Export of Capital*, p. 197.

The two 'asset' items—invisible payments and income from abroad—moved in a fairly orderly way, with the former well maintained, the latter influenced by interest repudiations. Britain's liabilities to other countries, however, fluctuated extraordinarily with an increase in net imports racing up to balance the virtual cessation of new foreign investment. This was accomplished by a decline in the value of exports, with imports rising slowly to 1877, then fading slightly. Although Britain did succeed in halting the flow of funds abroad, the money market found itself in the position of having more payments to be made abroad than could easily be 'matched' in the market. This situation—with foreign lending at an end—need not have created an artificial tightness. But a relative abundance of bills on London made the continental task of acquiring gold easier and helped prevent the Bank rate from settling to the low level which money conditions outside the Bank would have permitted.

III: LONG-TERM INVESTMENT

	Yield on Consols	Index of enterprise	New issues in United Kingdom	Capital export	Industrial securities' prices	Fixed interest securities' prices	Business Cycle index
1873	3·24%	111·0	24·7	231·7	84·3	81·5	+1·32
1874	3·24	107·3	24·1	169·9	81·8	81·5	+0·94
1875	3·20	101·8	15·7	84·9	77·1	83·0	+0·51
1876	3·16	83·5	16·1	−10·6	72·1	84·6	−0·42
1877	3·14	79·8	21·1	−49·4	68·3	85·3	−0·76
1878	3·15	68·8	18·3	− 4·16	62·9	84·2	−1·50
1879	3·08	78·9	15·7	38·78	58·0	85·5	−2·35

1. In 1874 new capital issues, formally floated in London, were far below those of the two preceding years. The general reaction of 1873 developed only slowly into full depression, but confidence was immediately shaken as prices of goods and securities fell.[1] The following are the statistics of issues during the year[2] (in £ millions):

[1] For the state of confidence in 1874, see *Review of 1874*, pp. 1–2.
[2] Ibid., p. 2. A table of the amount and distribution of new issues is given, collected by Messrs. Spackman & Sons.

	Capital offered by new companies	New issues by existing companies	Foreign loans
1872	44·2	31·9	227·8
1873	44·4	36·0	128·8
1874	20·5	25·0	29·1

On the capital offered for new companies, deposits payable on application and allotments amounted to £5·5 million in 1874; of the £25 million in new issues of old companies £20 million were called up; of the foreign loans, which had dominated the market in 1872, and fallen heavily in the course of 1873, only £15·2 million were paid up. Sixty-one manufacturing and trading companies and eight railways absorbed half the funds for investment in new companies, while railway securities constituted most of the issues of existing companies. The foreign loans went to Belgium, Canada, Hungary, the Ottoman Empire, and the Santa Fé Railway. A 43½ price for the 5 per cent. Ottoman loan indicates the distrust under which such issues were presented.[1]

The Stock Exchange lists reflect sharply reduced profit expectations:[2]

	Heavy industry	Textiles	Lighting and Power	Transport and Com.	Total
Jan. 1874 .	145·0	145·7	59·4	128·8	127·2
Dec. 1874 .	134·2	141·7	67·1	120·2	120·2

The moderate fall in textile securities' prices is evidence of that industry's less abrupt cyclical movement, apparent in price and production statistics as well.[3] Lighting and Power shares, unaffected directly by changes in foreign trade, and in a wave of great secular development, continued to

[1] See also *Economist*, 1874, pp. 193, 654, 444, and 719 for sceptical comments on the Turkish deficit, financial methods, and outstanding debt. 'Turkey', it is concluded on the eve of the new loan, 'has been on the brink of bankruptcy for two or three years past' (p. 719).

[2] Smith and Horne, op. cit., p. 9. 'Heavy Industry' includes Iron, Coal, and Engineering shares. The monthly figures given in the text are an index in which July 1890 = 100; the annual figures have been recalculated in the table at the head of this section with 1900 = 100.

[3] See below, Section IV.

rise until the final stages of depression. Securities' prices in this branch moved as follows:[1]

Jan.	1874	. . .	59·4
„	1875	. . .	69·0
„	1876	. . .	75·5
„	1877	. . .	82·3
„	1878	. . .	78·1
„	1879	. . .	66·2

In the price of fixed interest securities the rate of interest revealed a tendency to fall. The index moved as follows:[2]

Jan.	1874	. . .	84·2
Apr.	„	. . .	84·6
July	„	. . .	84·6
Oct.	„	. . .	85·0
Jan.	1875	. . .	84·9

The yearly average, however, like that for the yield on Consols, is at the same level as 1873.

2. With certain of the more speculative markets virtually eliminated, investment statistics in 1875 show a further deterioration in expected profits, reflected, it is to be noted, on both the supply and demand sides of the capital market:

The money asked for by new ventures has been only scantily supplied, small though its amount has been. If the country had been moving at only half the ordinary pace, it is clear from these figures that there must be an enormous amount of money wanting employment, for the sums asked for by all kinds of borrowers last year reached little more than a tenth of that sought in 1872, and are not half the amount borrowed in 1874 . . . but it has been difficult during this period to float anything but the very best schemes.[3]

The following are statistics of issues during the year (in £ millions):

	Capital offered by new companies	New issues by existing companies	Foreign loans
1874	20·5	25·0	29·1
1875	7·4	14·0	14·0

[1] Building trade shows a parallel belated depression, idem.
[2] Smith and Horne, op. cit., p. 7.
[3] *Review of 1875*, p. 30. The *Report of the Select Committee on Foreign Loans* (reprinted *Banker's Magazine*, 1875, pp. 796–835 and 878–907) helped deter the

Only £2·5 million in deposits were laid against new issues, and £11·0 million called up on issues of old companies. Foreign loans were to the more or less financially respectable governments of Brazil, Russia, and Sweden; on these £13·1 million were paid up. A feature of the new floatations was the appearance of three building firms, which offered £0·76 million of which £0·31 million was taken—the third largest category.

The Stock Exchange continued weak except for the period March to May when prices remained moderately steady.[1] But there was nothing hearty about the recovery and prices proceeded to sink to the last quarter:[2]

Index of Total Security Prices

Jan.	1875	.	.	.	119·8
Apr.	„	.	.	.	119·6
July	„	.	.	.	114·2
Oct.	„	.	.	.	112·2
Jan.	1876	.	.	.	112·4

The miscellaneous item, containing for these years the shares of food, drink, and building companies, among others, shows no such drastic decrease:

Jan.	1875	.	.	.	114·1
Jan.	1876	.	.	.	111·1

A decisive fall in the rate of interest appears in both the yield on Consols and the prices of fixed interest securities generally.[3]

3. New issues in 1876 were again at a lower level than in the previous year (in £ millions):[4]

	Capital offered by new companies	New issues by existing companies	Foreign loans
1875	7·4	14·0	14·0
1876	8·5	6·5	3·6

floatation of foreign issues. The methods of contractors in floatation and the 'misstatement and suppression to be found in the prospectuses' were particularly condemned. See also *Banker's Magazine*, 1876, pp. 272–4.

[1] *Economist*, 1875, pp. 526–7, 555, 585.

[2] Smith and Horne, op. cit., p. 9. At the end of May rumours in the City of difficulties in the iron trade, the failure of the Deutsche-Brazilianische Bank, and the collapse of American railway shares started the market down again (*Economist*, 1875, pp. 645–6).

[3] See above, table at head of this section.   [4] *Review of 1876*, p. 32.

£2·9 million in deposits were set against new issues, £5·5 million were called up on issues of existing companies, and £3·5 million were paid up on foreign loans. These latter went to China (8 per cent. issued at 100), Norway, Sweden, and the U.S. Existing building companies drew from the market the relatively large sum of £1·1 million. Other substantial borrowers were again the railways and 'manufacturing and trading companies'. In 1876 holders of Eastern and South American government securities reaped their 'harvest of insolvency'.[1] Turkish, Peruvian, and Egyptian stocks, for example, depreciated 36 per cent. in the six months preceding April 1876 (in £ millions):[2]

	Amount outstanding	Value Oct. 1875	Value end Mar. 1876	Depreciation	
				Amount	Per cent.
Turkish . .	176·4	55·5	30·6	24·9	44·8
Egyptian . .	56·7	38·1	30·6	7·5	19·6
Peruvian . .	25·5	10·9	5·7	5·2	47·6
TOTAL .	258·6	104·5	66·9	37·6	36·0

The era of foreign government loans had come to a belated end. The *Economist* lamented:

It is melancholy to think that transactions which have done the lenders so much harm should have done the borrowers so little good. But we fear that in Turkey and Peru there is almost nothing, and in Egypt nothing sufficient to show as an equivalent for the expenditure of these enormous sums. The truth is that Lombard Street has been to these semi-civilized countries what the London money-lender is to young men at Oxford; it has given them a premature command of money which they have not the judgment or experience or stability of character enough to spend well, which, accordingly they spend ill, and which does them almost unmixed harm.[3]

---

[1] L. H. Jenks, *The Migration of British Capital to 1876*, p. 291.

[2] *Economist*, 1876, pp. 393–4.

[3] Ibid., p. 393. The Select Committee on Foreign Loans wrote: 'It is true that the credulity and cupidity of certain classes of the community have blinded them to the danger of embarking in speculations such as your Committee have described. They appear to have measured the value of the promises held out to them not by any rule of experience but their own sanguine expectations and

This disillusion explains almost completely Hobson's estimates, showing a net import of capital for 1876.[1]

Under the stimulus of a 2 per cent. Bank rate and generally undisturbed conditions, the stock market rallied hesitantly in the latter half of the year:[2]

Jan. 1876 .	. 112·4		Oct. 1876 .	. 107·1
July ,, .	. 106·6		Nov. ,, .	. 108·8
Aug. ,, .	. 107·2		Dec. ,, .	. 108·0
Sept. ,, .	. 106·6			

With 'much money ready to be placed', there seemed a real possibility of steady recovery;[3] but continued uncertainty and a tight money market ended the hope of immediate revival early in 1877.

The rising price of fixed interest securities and a falling yield on Consols continued. Their prices were sustained 'by a pressure which arises from the extraordinary abundance of money'.[4] With old outlets for funds tightly closed and new types of enterprise scarce, an assured yield commanded a rising price. But for the fear that Britain might become involved in an Eastern war the price of Consols would have risen even farther.[5]

4. The Macgregor index of enterprise (joint-stock company formation) shows initiative falling away in 1877;[6]

thus have fallen a prey to those who, by trading on their credulity, have obtained their money and then betrayed their interest.'

The extent to which foreign loans were ultimately defaulted is given by this summary table calculated from the *Review of 1878*, p. 4 (in £ millions):

Total issue	Partial default	Total default	Wholly fulfilled
505·2	66·2	157·2	281·8

This does not include losses from depreciation in market value.

[1] Op. cit., p. 223.

[2] The armistice in November between Russia and Turkey helped strengthen the tone of the market (*Economist*, 1876, pp. 1292–3); but the fear of further conflict harassed the market until April 1877, when doubts were settled by the outbreak of war. Speculators were operating largely on rumours: a settlement in Bulgaria, the Czar's abdication, Turkey joining or refusing to join a Conference of European powers, &c.

[3] Ibid., p. 292.

[4] Ibid., p. 743.   [5] Idem.

[6] See above, table at head of section.

bankruptcies remained at the high level of the preceding years in the cycle:[1]

1873 .	. 273
1874 .	. 328
1875 .	. 408
1876 .	. 356
1877 .	. 356

New issues were again on a small scale. Hobson's figure for capital issues slightly increases in both 1876 and 1877;[2] Beveridge's estimate of capital per head of new joint-stock companies registered a fall in 1876, a rise in 1877;[3] the following contemporary estimate, an increase in 1876, a marked fall in 1877 (in £ millions):[4]

1875 .	. 13·32
1876 .	. 13·65
1877 .	. 11·89

From these figures of relative movement, it may be concluded that 1877 was somewhere in the trough of the cycle in long-term capital issue.

In every branch of the market industrial securities gave way. The total index moved as follows:

Jan. 1877 .	.	.	107·4
Apr. „	.	.	103·6
July „	.	.	101·4
Oct. „	.	.	99·5
Jan. 1878 .	.	.	97·9

Market reports reveal operators again following avidly the movements of European diplomacy.[5] They found little comfort. In December stock market reports are still discussing Russian victories in the Balkans and the doings of Marshal Macmahon.[6]

Political uncertainty accounts also for the failure of Consols to rise. With Europe hovering on the brink of

[1] Macgregor, op. cit., p. 198. This figure includes compulsory bankruptcies, those caused by owners unable to meet liabilities, and two-thirds of other voluntary liquidations.   [2] Op. cit., p. 233.

[3] *Unemployment*, p. 456, col. 12 (1930 edition).

[4] The complete Spackman table, used for other years in this section, is not available for 1877. The figure here used comes from *Herpath's Journal*, reprinted in the *Review of 1877*, p. 40.

[5] For a fairly complete statement of the factors affecting the stock market at the time see *Economist*, 1877, pp. 787-8.   [6] Ibid., p. 1432.

general warfare, unemployment rising, business profit margins decreasing, it was difficult to find buyers for the safest securities. Even fixed-interest securities could not maintain the level of the latter months of 1876:

	1876	*1877*
Jan. . . .	86·9	88·8
July . . .	88·2	88·4
Dec. . . .	88·5	87·9

5. The exact movement of new issues in 1878 is obscure. There appears to have been some revival in foreign issues, none for use within Britain. The Macgregor joint-stock index falls, as does Hobson's estimate of new issues. Beveridge's figure remains as in 1877. These three statistics reflect movements in internal investment. Hobson's capital exports show a smaller net import than in the preceding two years, his figure for new foreign issues rises. The *Herpath* figure for total issues, quoted in the *Economist*, rises from £11·8 to £33·7 million.[1] But no important revival in capital investment was apparent in the City. Reports indicate that until the autumn bank failures, the previous depression conditions prevailed—falling security prices, a rising tendency in Consols and other fixed-interest securities. But the latter group weakened and a near panic occurred in industrial shares in the last half of the year:[2]

	Fixed-interest securities	*Industrial shares*	*Price Consols*
Jan. 1878 .	87·5	97·9	95⅝
Feb. ,, .	87·9	97·4	95⅝
Mar. ,, .	87·9	95·7	95¼
April ,, .	87·9	95·2	94⅞
May ,, .	88·5	94·3	96¾
June ,, .	88·3	96·3	95⅞
July ,, .	87·8	96·5	95¾
Aug. ,, .	87·4	96·5	94⅞
Sept. ,, .	86·9	94·7	94⅞
Oct. ,, .	86·3	91·3	94¼
Nov. ,, .	87·4	89·7	95¾
Dec. ,, .	86·4	86·9	94⅜

[1] *Review of 1879*, p. 55. This figure bears, of course, an unknown relation to the amount of capital actually subscribed.

[2] The average monthly price of Consols comes from the Statistical Abstract.

The irregular movement of securities in the early part of the year was another product of political alarms.[1] Rumours of impending peace alternated with those of the Russian capture of Constantinople. The market, eager for speculative activity, remained in a state of flux. After peace had been assured some tightening of money rates tended to hamper trade.[2] Nevertheless, an upward movement continued until August,[3] encouraged by the successful conclusion of the Berlin Congress.[4] In these midsummer months there was even some pre-revival shifting from Consols and fixed-interest securities to equities.[5]

The high money rates of the late summer and a few small failures in the City broke the spell of revival. 'Speculation was at a standstill, members of the House away in the country.'[6] Further failures in the City and finally the Scottish Bank catastrophe kept activity down until the end of the year. Bankers liquidated their holdings, even Consols in some cases. Finally in early December the closing of the West of England Bank ended a sporadic upward movement earlier in the month.[7] Once again the large cash balances which had been piling up since 1874 were prevented from finding employment either in speculation or in the floatation of new issues.[8]

6. In the latter months of 1879 the capital market revived. Hobson's total figure for investment declined from the level of 1878, as did the average price of industrial securities.

---

[1] *Economist*, 1878, pp. 70, 155, 213, 215.

[2] Ibid., pp. 370 and 770. All sorts of political mishaps continued to trouble the sensitive market. One report (ibid., p. 676) begins, 'Had it not been for the second attempt upon the life of the German Emperor it is probable that a further improvement in market prices . . .' The confidence of the summer helped produce a large number of new issues in June and July (p. 1121). Also *Banker's Magazine*, 1878, pp. 608–9 and 740.

[3] *Economist*, 1878, p. 706 and *Banker's Magazine*, 1878, p. 740. In a report for August: 'A feature of the month is the appearance on the scene of a crop of applications for foreign and colonial loans; with the successful settlement of the Berlin treaty it is to be expected that an abundance of every description of these demands will turn up, and it may be hoped that a gradual increase in trade bills will also follow as a result of a legitimate expansion of commercial transactions which have been kept in abeyance whilst the late political anxieties hung over the prospect.'

[4] *Economist*, 1878, pp. 860–1.   [5] Idem.   [6] Ibid., p. 1121.
[7] *Review of 1878*, p. 37.   [8] *Economist*, 1878, pp. 1440 and 1497.

The monthly figures for the latter, however, fall until July and recover rapidly afterwards. The Macgregor and Beveridge annual average indexes rise, as does Hobson's estimate of capital exports.

In its review of 1879 the *Economist* concluded:[1]

The amount of new capital created in 1879 was larger than in any year since 1874.[2] In the face of the general indisposition to invest money in new enterprises there has still been considerable activity in the promotion of new companies at home, while foreign and colonial governments—the latter in a marked manner —have offered inducements more or less tempting for the investors of surplus capital. Among the borrowers New Zealand still maintains its leading position. There have been loans of municipalities or corporations and one of £5 million by the government of the colony. Victoria has raised £2·9 million, N. S. Wales £3·1 million, Queensland £1·07 million, Western Australia £0·19 million. The Dominion of Canada has raised £4·5 million, and the Cape Government £2·6 million. There have been some foreign loans not wholly subscribed in this country such as the Hungarian issue of £15 million; the balance of the Egyptian State Domain Loan, and the large issue of 4 per cent. by the U.S. government. The calls made by railway companies make up a total somewhat less than 1878.[3]

The indexes of various groups of industrial shares moved as follows:

	Heavy industry	Textiles	Food	Building	Transport	Total
Jan. 1879 .	71·6	102·0	83·2	64·7	113·6	86·5
Apr. ,, .	70·3	96·4	101·4	61·6	115·4	86·2
July ,, .	59·8	94·0	103·5	56·5	115·5	82·1
Oct. ,, .	80·6	90·5	103·0	53·8	123·1	89·4
Jan. 1880 .	111·7	114·6	123·5	77·7	129·9	107·1

The revival in food shares came first, transport shares rose steadily. The building-share revival lagged a half year

[1] pp. 33–4.

[2] The estimate on which this statement is based is not available. Hobson's figures show new floatations higher in 1879 than in any year since 1875.

[3] By the end of 1879, the London *Times* was already expressing concern over the development of another railway mania. France, Italy, Switzerland, Russia, the Balkans, the near East, and India, as well as the U.S., planned the expansion of their railway systems for the coming year (reprinted, *Economist*, 1879, pp. 51–2).

behind the general upswing, textile shares one quarter. Cheap money brought some general increase in activity during April,[1] but trouble in Egypt and a minor crisis on the Austrian and German bourses prevented a revival from developing in the following months.[2] The summer was quiet. September reports still complained of the slackness of the Stock Exchange.[3]

By October a firm revival was under way: 'Business transacted has been extensive in most departments and speculators for the rise have found the public willing to swallow bait which a short time back would have been held before them in vain.'[4] The most active rise of the year occurred in November and continued more slowly towards the year-end with much profit taking.[5]

With the bank-rate easy and confidence returning the prices of Consols and fixed-interest securities rose. The average price of the former, $92\frac{1}{2}$ in 1873, was $97\frac{1}{2}$. A reaction against unlimited liability in banking and other fields following on the bank failures late in 1878, was bringing a new group of borrowers into the capital market;[6] and the floatation of such issues, and others as well, was aided by the prevailing low rates of interest.

IV. COMMERCE AND INDUSTRY

	Business cycle index	Capital goods' production	Consumers' goods production	Unemployment per cent.	Exports value	Imports value	General prices
1873	+1·32	55·3	68·8	1·2	77·8	71·0	148
1874	+0·94	56·2	74·5	1·6	74·0	70·7	136
1875	+0·51	56·5	72·3	2·2	79·5	71·5	128
1876	−0·42	58·7	71·8	3·4	72·4	71·7	127
1877	−0·76	61·4	73·0	4·4	71·2	75·4	125
1878	−1·50	57·6	69·2	6·3	69·3	70·5	116
1879	−2·35	56·5	64·7	10·7	70·2	69·4	110

[1] Ibid., p. 481.

[2] Ibid., pp. 656, 685, 713: 'The fact that money is so exceedingly abundant and readily obtainable has stimulated purchases in various directions. Not that buying has been at all active, but the wish to buy has certainly predominated' (p. 772, 5 July). [3] Ibid., p. 1086. [4] Ibid., p. 1203.
[5] Ibid., p. 1459. [6] *Review of 1879*, p. 33.

1. 1874 was the first full year of the Great Depression. Falling prices, complaints of high costs and narrowing profit margins dominate trade reports, especially in those industries where the pressure to expand had been most severe. Production levels fell off slightly in iron; but continued to rise in coal and textiles.[1] Ship-building was active, but felt a lack of new orders.[2] The home building trade and engineers maintained activity at prosperity levels.[3] Problems of wage adjustment received attention in almost every industry, but particularly in coal and iron.[4]

The rail branch of the iron trade found orders from the U.S. heavily decreased. In railroad iron alone the value of British exports to U.S. fell off from £2·4 million to £1·3 million.[5] The falling price of new iron rails, moreover, reduced profits:

... it is not merely a matter of impossibility under these circumstances (falling prices, high labour costs) for railmakers to make a profit, but the chances are that working under such conditions would entail a loss. Many of them, therefore, prefer to keep their works idle till wages and prices of materials shall have regained their normal position.[6]

The textile trade, which had not experienced (1868–73) a boom on the same scale as the capital industries, enjoyed a year, 'although not very brilliant, slightly better than 1873'.[7] But relative over-production is reflected in the report of Messrs. Ellison & Co.: 'Throughout 1874 the actual supply of the raw material has constantly exceeded the demand. The result has been an almost continuous readiness of holders to sell, in the face of a nearly chronic indifference on the part of consumers to buy.'[8] Falling prices cast a shadow on the industry, the value of cotton exports declined in the face of increased sales.[9]

[1] W. Page, *Commerce and Industry*, vol. ii, pp. 150 and 154.
[2] *Review of 1874*, pp. 17 and 21.
[3] Ibid., pp. 27 and 17, respectively.
[4] Ibid., pp. 1, 16, 17, 19–20, 26. Labour difficulties centred in the coal and iron industries. The rail trade in the north reported 'thousands of unemployed workmen'.
[5] *Economist*, Trade Supplement, January 1875, p. 7.
[6] *Review of 1874*, p. 18.   [7] Ibid., p. 22.   [8] Idem.   [9] Ibid., p. 24.

Home trades—unconnected directly with export fluctuations—enjoyed a year of maintained prosperity. Reports show building 'brisk', with unemployment among carpenters and joiners lower, in fact, than in the previous year, at 0·8 per cent.[1] The Huddersfield woollen-mills, catering particularly to home trade, found activity 'fully sustained'.[2]

A report of the chemical trade illustrates the confusion of industrial trends in 1874: 'There have been great complaints of dulness and of losses, those who bought either on speculation or in anticipation of their wants have suffered greatly.... Notwithstanding these facts the trade, taken as a whole, has undoubtedly further developed.'[3]

2. 1875 was a depressing year for business. Although production levels did not fall far and in some cases actually rose, many companies failed, prices and profit margins fell.[4] The building trade alone reported unmixed prosperity with a low record for unemployment of 0·6 per cent.[5]

The *Economist* lists five specific causes for the preceding boom and contemporary depression: the entrance from 1871 of Germany, Austria, Hungary, and Italy upon a 'newer, freer and more enterprising national career' and the demand in English markets which followed, especially in coal and iron; the American railway building boom (1868–73); a similar period of transportation expansion in Russia; a shipping boom stimulated by the opening of the Suez Canal and the general activity in foreign trade; a rapid rise in prices and wages which caused 'more expenditure and less work to take the place of frugality and diligence, the acquirement of riches seemed to have become so easy that the old virtues of diligence, skill and patience could be laid aside

---

[1] A. C. Pigou, *Industrial Fluctuations*, pp. 381–2.
[2] *Review of 1874*, p. 27.   [3] Ibid., p. 14.
[4] *Review of 1875*, pp. 1–2. The tone in which business was carried on is illustrated by this rather unhappy report from the cotton industry (p. 23): 'A protracted series of internal misfortunes, brought about by over-production, aggravated by adverse external influences in the shape of bad trade and financial crisis in every centre throughout the world, have so demoralised the business community that pessimism is everywhere rampant.... Look which way we will there is not visible a single gleam of hearty hopefulness, and a thoroughgoing optimist is quite a curiosity.'
[5] Pigou, op. cit., pp. 381–2. See also *Review of 1875*, pp. 26–7.

both by men and masters'.[1] By 1875 reaction from each of these 'excesses' was under way, even the latter. Economies were scrupulously applied, wages reduced wherever possible.

Figures of unemployment, production, and foreign trade, however, do not justify the gloom of 1875. The production of cotton goods fell off slightly, but goods traffic (in tons) and pig-iron production increased, as did the value of foreign trade, despite a falling price level (1900=100):

	Pig-iron	Cotton yarn	Coal	Goods traffic
1873	74·1	76·7	56·7	44·9
1874	67·4	78·0	55·6	44·5
1875	70·8	75·8	58·2	47·1

The Hoffmann index of consumers goods production declines slightly in 1875. The heavy weight given textiles probably accounts for this.[2] Consumption, except for beer,[3] rises; Wood's general *per capita* index of consumption and real wages move as follows:[4]

	Consumption	Real wages
1873	77·0	70·9
1874	76·7	73·2
1875	78·2	73·7

In 1875 the secular industrial pattern of the Great Depression became more clear: a falling interest-rate, falling prices, increased output and consumption, and bitter complaints from operators in heavy industry.

3. To contemporary chroniclers 1876 was 'a third year in the cycle of reaction and readjustment, marked by dull and limited trade, restricted confidence, the rigorous application of reduction and economies, lessened wages, and the failure of numberless commercial and manufacturing concerns unable to bear the pressure of adverse times'.[5] Similar condi-

[1] *Review of 1875*, pp. 1–2. The lessons of depression were a recurrent subject of homily through the seventies and eighties.

[2] Op. cit., pp. 392–3.

[3] Beer consumption reached an all-time peak in 1874 with 34·0 gallons consumed per head in U.K.

[4] Consumption index, Pigou, op. cit., pp. 387–8: real wages, allowing for unemployment, Layton, Crowther, op. cit., pp. 265–6.

[5] *Review of 1876*, p. 1.

tions prevailed in the U.S., Germany, Austria, Russia, and Belgium. France, busy paying her war indemnity in 1871–3, suffered only a 'mild set-back'.[1] Easy money in 1876 did, however, stimulate some revival in Britain. Consumers of pig-iron, for example, replenished depleted stocks in the interim of cheap loans.[2]

Despite the generally unhappy atmosphere in which trade was conducted, the production of iron, steel, coal, and textiles rose, while building still boomed. In commenting on the prosperous condition of the timber trade, a report states: 'The greatly increased demand seems to be owing chiefly to the low price of money and to the inclination on the part of capitalists to prefer investments in substantial property in England to foreign stocks.'[3]

In the iron industry the foreign purchases of rails were less than half of what they were in 1872, but home consumption by ship-builders and engineers was well maintained.[4] Two revolutions in the metal trades affected the production of iron in these years; steel rails were substituted for iron; and in the ship-building industry, iron superseded wood. Steel production rose as follows (1900 = 100):

1870 .	. 5·1	1877 .	. 18·3
1875 .	. 14·7	1878 .	. 22·8
1876 .	. 17·3	1879 .	. 21·0

At the same time the number of collieries had enormously increased. Under the stimulus of the coal famine (1871–3) capital had been directed on a large scale into coal-mining projects, involving a considerable period of gestation. Of the 3,933 pits open in 1875, 1,048 had been sunk since 1871.[5]

In textiles, as sales to industrial areas declined or stag-

---

[1] *Review of 1876*, pp. 1 and 4. Also A. Monroe, 'The French Indemnity', *Review of Economic Statistics*, preliminary vol. i, 1920.

[2] Ibid., p. 21. A similar movement in textiles, p. 25. A pick-up at the end of the year is noted also in the general description of trade, p. 1.

[3] Ibid., p. 19. Unemployment of carpenters and joiners in 1876 was 0·8 per cent., compared to a general average of 3·4 per cent. For same explanation of building prosperity see report from *Leeds Mercury*, p. 2.

[4] Ibid., pp. 21–2.

[5] Ibid., pp. 21–2.

nated, exports were supported by increased purchases in the East:[1]

	Cotton piece goods exports (in million yards)	
	1875	1876
Germany and Holland . . .	116	103
Turkey, Syria, and South Africa . .	282	323
America and the West Indies . .	556	563
British East Indies and Egypt . .	1340	1400
China and Hong Kong . . .	436	597

As noted above, total textile production rose slightly.

The value of exports, however, fell off, and the total excess (value) of imports over exports continued the increase begun in 1873 (1900 = 100):

1872 .	. 21·3
1873 .	. 35·2
1874 .	. 43·2
1875 .	. 53·0
1876 .	. 68·1

4. With the Bank-rate still at 2 per cent. in January 1877 and some slight recovery evident the conviction was general that the bottom of depression had been reached. Thomas's quarterly figures reveal the basis for this hope and the disappointment to which it was doomed:

1876	I	+0·35	1877	I	−0·31
	II	−0·33		II	−0·76
	III	−0·69		III	−0·92
	IV	−0·61		IV	−1·05

For two quarters, coinciding roughly with the period of cheap money, the progress of depression was halted, only to accelerate in the following two years. The situation was aggravated by a disastrous harvest in 1877 (all indexes, 1900 = 100):[2]

	British harvest index	Price of British wheat	Retail prices
1873	84	218	137·1
1876	100	172	123·6
1877	78	211	127·0

[1] *Review of 1876*, p. 26.
[2] Harvest Index from Sauerbeck, annually in *Journal of Royal Statistical Society*.

Imports continued to rise and exports to fall off in value. In this cycle the import surplus, as well as capital imports, was at its peak in 1877. The temporary unbalancing of Britain's lender position led to elaborate controversy over the sense in which Great Britain was consuming its capital in goods imports.[1]

Internally the iron industry continued the revolution created by the Bessemer process. The adjustment, coming in a time of depressed exports and falling profits, was painful,[2] although relatively full activity in ship-building helped support the home market.[3] By the end of 1877 contracts for private and public building gave out, in some sections: 'At the opening of 1877 most of the masters had contracts yet to complete which promised to occupy them well into the new year. . . . As contracts undertaken in the previous years were completed there was absolutely nothing to go on with . . . it would seem as if the town (Leeds) were overbuilt.'[4] Unemployment figures also place 1877 as the last year of great prosperity in building (per cent.):

1876	.	.	0·8
1877	.	.	1·2
1878	.	.	3·5
1879	.	.	8·2

Among the other of Britain's basic industries, only textiles showed a net fall in output: cotton yarn produced (1900 = 100) moving from 78·5 to 76·2. Iron, coal, and steel produced in slightly higher amounts, although heavy unemployment in many districts attests to a growing productivity.[5]

[1] *Review of 1877*, pp. 9–10. [2] Ibid., p. 24.

[3] Index of new vessels built (tonnage) (1900 = 100):

1872	.	50·3
1876	.	40·0
1877	.	47·8

Index of new merchant vessels built for home and colonies (tonnage) (1900 = 100):

1872	.	53·3
1876	.	48·8
1877	.	58·9

see also *Review of 1877*, p. 31.

[4] Ibid., p. 35.

[5] Ibid., pp. 37–8. See especially reports from Rotherham, Sheffield, and Durham.

By the end of 1877 the depression assumed a new and aggravated character. Activity declined in all branches of trade. In December iron-producers in Birmingham were reported working at less than half time, producing chiefly for stock.[1]

5. 1878 was a thorough-going year of depression. The condition of slowly rising production gave way to heavy unemployment and generally decreased output. Every index of trade, employment, and consumption presents a relative deterioration, except that for the steel industry which was operating under secular influences so strong that full cyclical depression failed to force a reduction in output.[2] The shift in the rate of decline that came in 1878 appears in these quarterly statistics of unemployment among iron-founders (per cent.):[3]

1876	I	4·9	1877	I	7·4	1878	I	13·9	1879	I	23·9
	II	5·1		II	7·6		II	14·4		II	23·7
	III	6·0		III	8·3		III	13·4		III	22·2
	IV	7·6		IV	13·2		IV	16·9		IV	18·6

To contemporaries the chief complaint remained the necessity of cutting prices and profit margins to meet a declining demand. The problem of 'over production' was extensively explored. Price movements from 1873 were as follows[4] (1900 = 100):

	Minerals	Textiles	Food
1873	130·5	156·1	155·1
1874	107·4	139·4	150·7
1875	92·5	133·3	144·9
1876	83·3	128·8	143·5
1877	77·7	128·8	146·4
1878	68·5	118·2	139·2
1879	67·6	112·1	130·4

The relatively easy fall in the textile index may be accounted for: by the maintained export demand from the East; the failure of cotton prices to rise as high in 1871–3 as those of minerals; and textiles' status as a consumption good.

---

[1] *Economist*, 1877, p. 1535.
[2] *Review of 1878*, pp. 27–9.
[3] Thomas, op. cit., p. 61.
[4] Sauerbeck indexes.

Bad harvests and relatively well-maintained money incomes kept the price of food-stuffs from sinking as rapidly as the other commodity groups. In its relatively temperate fluctuation the food index displays, of course, a conventional cyclical phenomenon.

Iron, coal, and textile production did not decrease heavily in 1878 despite the considerable rise in unemployment (production indexes: 1900 = 100):

	Pig-iron	Coal	Steel	Cotton yarn
1873	74·1	56·4	—	69·8
1877	74·2	60·0	18·3	68·5
1878	71·9	58·7	22·8	62·8
1879	67·4	59·6	21·0	63·6

The building industry was still finding a fair amount of work, although the full activity of 1873–6 had gone.[1] In some districts local government contracts for municipal building and schools constituted a substantial part of new construction.[2]

In value, foreign trade fell off in both imports and exports. Quantities, however, increased in many branches. The value indexes of foreign trade, corrected for price movements, show imports remaining at the same level as the previous year, exports rising slightly.

---

[1] *Review of 1878*, pp. 21 and 33. Although building unemployment rose, the consumption of imported wood in London increased:

	Sawn (in million) pieces	Hewn (in thousand) loads	Building per cent. unemployed
1873	14·3	234	0·9
1874	15·6	328	0·8
1875	17·3	285	0·6
1876	19·8	292	0·7
1877	22·0	253	1·2
1878	25·0	312	3·5

A report from Leeds states: 'Owing to the depression in other trades there is at present a great deal of empty house property in town, many families having, for the sake of economy, left their former dwellings and gone to live with their relatives and friends.'

[2] Ibid., p. 33. Also *Review of 1877*, pp. 35–6.

6. The bottom of depression and the beginning of cyclical revival came in 1879. In August and September a flood of new orders came from the U.S., and despite a disastrous harvest, by October 'a great activity of trade had fairly set in'.[1] Thomas's quarterly index also gives the third quarter of the year as the turning-point:

$$
\begin{array}{rlll}
1879 & \text{I} & . & . & 2\cdot48 \\
& \text{II} & . & . & 2\cdot69 \\
& \text{III} & . & . & 2\cdot52 \\
& \text{IV} & . & . & 1\cdot69 \\
\end{array}
$$

In the U.S., a great harvest, with increased grain shipments to Europe, and a partly consequent revival of railway building stimulated British iron exports. The American demand came unexpectedly and was 'unprecedented' in the size of its orders.[2] They came into Britain's iron districts at a time of extreme depression. Iron-founders' unemployment moved as follows in 1879[3] (per cent):

$$
\begin{array}{rlll}
\text{I} & . & . & 23\cdot9 \\
\text{II} & . & . & 23\cdot7 \\
\text{III} & . & . & 22\cdot2 \\
\text{IV} & . & . & 18\cdot6 \\
\end{array}
$$

Exports of iron, steel, and tin plate illustrate vividly the extent to which the revival stemmed from iron exports to the North American continent[4] (in thousand tons):

	1872	*1878*	*1879*
United States . .	888	157	707
Germany and Holland	816	557	502
India . . .	69	210	195
Australia . . .	94	205	165
Canada . . .	165	101	156
France . . .	108	112	106

The coal and shipping trades reflected the changed out-

---

[1] *Review of 1879*, p. 1. Also *Economist*, 1879, pp. 1121 and 1133. For agricultural position, see *Review of 1879*, pp. 43–5.

[2] Ibid., pp. 20–3.

[3] Thomas, op. cit.

[4] *Review of 1879*, p. 21. Note also in the figures for 1872 and 1878 the manner in which exports to the East bolstered trade in the depression, and the steady level at which French purchases were maintained.

look immediately, and by the end of the year textiles, too, felt a revival.[1] The building trade, on the other hand, lapsed into serious depression with unemployment at 8·2 per cent.[2] Prices and profits completed their downward cycle in the year. The 1879 bulletin of Messrs. Ellison includes a table revealing the narrowing margin between prices and costs in the textile industry through the depression[3] (in £ millions):

	Paid for cotton	Paid for wages	Total	Balance per pound for other expenses (in pence)
1873	44·6	25·9	29·6	6·35
1874	38·7	26·3	30·1	6·28
1875	35·9	26·1	30·6	6·04
1876	32·3	26·9	27·3	5·58
1877	32·8	27·1	26·6	5·40
1878	32·1	25·1	24·5	5·09
1879	32·0	23·2	24·1	5·00

7. By the end of 1879 prospects of trade with the East seemed to improve.[4] In the depressed years those markets seemed at times to support exports in textiles and even in iron. But the depreciation of silver, in addition to famine harvests, cast a chronic shadow over British trade relations with India, China, and Hong Kong. Germany, in shifting to a gold currency, had disgorged an immense quantity of silver; by May 1873 the Scandinavian countries and Holland were off silver; the Latin Union had severely limited the coinage of silver in 1874 to prevent its gold supply from being drained off; the American mines increased their output.[5] By 1873 the price of silver began a sharp continuous downward movement. The consequent depreciation of silver currencies made exports to the East difficult, increased the

---

[1] Ibid., p. 24.

[2] Ibid., p. 28.

[3] Ibid., p. 24. Total balance left for other expenses includes rent, taxes, gas, coal, oils, dyes, repairs, interest on capital, and profits.

[4] *Banker's Magazine*, 1879, pp. 539–41. Also *Economist*, 1880, p. 387.

[5] R. Hawtrey, *Currency and Credit*, pp. 314–15 and 321. W. Bagehot, *The Depreciation of Silver*, pp. 41–57.

burden of fixed remittances on investments and government obligations.[1] The Eastern exchanges on London moved as follows:

	Calcutta per rupee	*Hong Kong per dollar*	*Shanghai per tael*	*Bar silver per oz. d.*
March 1872 .	2/–	4/4¾	6/6¾	61
„ 1875 .	1/10½	4/2½	5/9	57
„ 1876 .	1/8⅞	3/10	5/3¼	53
„ 1877 .	1/9⅜	4/–	5/6¼	55
„ 1878 .	1/9	3/11	5/5	54½
„ 1879 .	1/7⅜	3/7¼	4/11	49
June 1879 .	1/8⅛	3/11	5/3½	52

Increased exports of Chinese silk and Indian cotton, along with a cessation of silver sales from Berlin, seem to account for the improved exchange position in 1879.

8. In the years 1874–9 non-cyclical influences operated to change the capital and price structure of British industry. Quite apart from movements on the side of money, productivity and the competitive character of international markets tended to cause cheaper production and lower profit margins. This phenomenon will be dealt with only briefly here; but it lies at the heart of the Great Depression.[2]

The coal, iron, and ship-building industries underwent virtual revolution. In the two years after the coal famine of 1872–3 potential output in the mines was increased by the opening of 1,408 new collieries in Great Britain; in the decade preceding 1879, 150,000 employees were added to the trade.[3] The transition to steel dominated iron, along with the introduction of new cost-saving processes which reduced by almost 30 per cent. the amount of coal necessary to produce iron. At about 1879 the basic process, a refinement of the Bessemer method, was introduced, permitting Cleveland iron to be used in steel manufacture, and eliminating the necessity of hematite imports on the former large scale. In the following five years the basic process came to dominate

[1] *Economist*, 1873, p. 1395. See also the *Indian Budget*, pp. 1019–21.

[2] This question is more fully discussed in Chapter III.

[3] *Banker's Magazine*, 1879, p. 458, and *Review of 1874*, p. 26. Also *Review of 1878*, p. 27.

the steel industry.[1] The use of iron, and even steel, in ship-building kept British yards from serious inactivity at any time during this cycle.[2] It supported as well an iron industry grown dependent on railway orders. The desire to escape the tyranny of falling prices caused rigid economies to be applied. New cost-reducing machinery appeared in every trade, machine and tool makers were well employed until 1878.[3]

In the minds of many business men foreign competition was a prime 'cause' of depression. Reports are full of its menace.[4] There is no question that Belgium, France, Germany, and the U.S. were capable of enormously greater capital goods output in 1879 than in 1873; moreover, depression produced a spawn of subsidies and tariffs that made competition more difficult.[5] The pre-1873 British iron goods' monopoly had vanished; and the next coal 'famine' did not come until 1899.[6]

---

[1] L. Bell, *The Iron Trade of U.K.*, pp. 24 ff.

[2] *Review of 1879*, p. 23: 'A few contracts were for vessels constructed of steel, but these are as yet exceptional.' Also *Review of 1877*, pp. 31–2. For a recent excellent account of the iron and steel trades in these years see D. L. Burn, *The Economic History of Steelmaking, 1867–1939*, chaps. ii, iii, and iv. For the course of output and the nature of the demand for iron and steel in the depression of the seventies, see especially pp. 26–32.

[3] For example see *Review of 1875*, p. 25. Before Committee on Depression and Trade (2689) L. Bell stated, 'the growing depression has stimulated invention in labour-saving devices'.

[4] Ibid., pp. 16, 22, 27. *Review of 1876*, pp. 4 and 24. *Review of 1877*, p. 29.

[5] *Review of 1879*, p. 3. Only after the last quarter revival of 1879 could the *Economist* proclaim: 'the obscure and contemptible movement (so to call it) in this country in favour of revived Protection in the form of Reciprocity has died out.' The threat to free trade was only temporarily diverted, recurring chronically over the subsequent three decades, especially in years of cyclical depression, until broken by the defeat of Joseph Chamberlain in 1906.

[6] According to L. Bell's statistics, Britain was manufacturing 53·2 per cent. of the world's iron in 1871, 42·7 per cent. in 1879.

V. LABOUR

	Business cycle index	Unemployment per cent.	Index of consumption	Indoor pauperism	Money wages	Real wages	T.U.C. membership (unions only, in 000's)
1873	+1·32	1·2	77·0	94·8	88·6	70·9	509
1874	+0·94	1·6	76·7	93·2	87·2	73·2	594
1875	+0·51	2·2	78·2	90·7	86·0	73·7	414
1876	−0·42	3·4	78·9	91·5	84·9	73·2	455
1877	−0·76	4·4	77·7	95·8	84·4	70·9	565
1878	−1·50	6·3	76·4	100·1	82·7	68·7	486
1879	−2·35	10·7	74·3	107·0	81·6	67·6	412

1. The sharpest movement among the major variables from 1873 to 1874 was a rapid fall of prices, especially in coal, iron, and related capital goods. This process created strong pressure for an adjustment of wage rates in the affected industries. Where they existed the trades unions, swollen with power acquired during the boom, in many cases opposed such wage reductions with strikes; and occasionally workers found themselves locked out when agreement could not be reached. Although average unemployment did not rise over 4 per cent. until 1877, labour felt the pinch of narrowing profit margins in harder bargains and increased attention to labour efficiency.[1] With the peculiar moral aura with which this era surrounded economic problems, the *Economist* points the lesson:[2]

The almost universal excitement of 1871–2 had thoroughly disorganized both labour and commerce. The working people became intoxicated and unmanageable under rapid advance of wages, and rapid diminution of the hours of work; and the excessive profits of the coal, iron, shipping, and some other trades introduced into ordinary business a degree of recklessness which

---

[1] *Review of 1874*, pp. 1–2.

[2] Ibid., p. 2. Also ibid., pp. 18–19, in reference to the Sheffield iron and steel trades: 'The depression has obliged the employers to take further steps towards reducing the cost of production . . . it has been decided to reduce the wages of blast furnacemen . . . men at the works of Messrs. Cammell and Co., were asked to accept labourers' wages, a reduction of 9*s.* a week, whilst the machinery was idle. The men refused and the works were closed . . . the places of the men who turned out in opposition to the proposed extension of their time to 59 hours per week, have been filled up with difficulty.'

can only end in mischief. The reduced demand for labour has not only brought down wages, but it has also put an end to many of the rules adopted, under pressure from the trades' unions since 1871, directed to limitation of hours of work, abolition of piece work, restriction of the number of apprentices, &c. In many trades these prohibitions, if persisted in, would have been fatal. The working classes are now learning by the sharpest and rudest experience that combinations among themselves are powerless to control the markets for the products of labour; and, therefore, powerless to maintain wages and rules which the market price of commodities will not afford. And the lesson has not come too soon.

All general indexes, however, show a net improvement in labour's position in 1874. Wood's consumption index alone falls off for the year, but continues in 1875 its upward movement. The *per capita* consumption of beer reached an all-time peak for the United Kingdom in 1874.[1]

2. The same kind of pressure for adjustment of wages to decreasing profits occupied the labour market in 1875:[2] 'Nothing is more certain than that there cannot be any extensive revival of industry over the world until prices and wages of every kind have thoroughly adjusted themselves to a level consistent with profitable returns to capital embarked in the various large fields of production.' The economic theory assumed in this quotation is obscure; but it is clear that entrepreneurs felt themselves ground between prices which fell easily and labour costs which could be reduced only with difficulty.

A turn towards depression appeared in labour statistics: unemployment rose, average money wages fell, the rate of increase of real wages decreased. Consumption, however, increased, the fall in retail prices aiding those with relatively fixed incomes:[3]

1873	.	. 137·1
1874	.	. 131·5
1875	.	. 127·0

---

[1] Pigou, op. cit., pp. 387–8—*per capita* beer consumption (gals.):

1870	. 30·2	1874	. 34·0	1890	. 30·0	1912	. 26·7
1873	. 33·5	1883	. 27·2	1900	. 31·6		

The secular decline from 1874 reflects, of course, the rise of the Temperance Movement as well as the fall in real wages after 1900.

[2] *Review of 1875*, p. 5.   [3] Layton and Crowther, op. cit., pp. 265–6.

Although strikes in opposition to wage decreases were common, and generally lost by the men,[1] the position of the working class was certainly not critical in Great Britain at this time. Nor was it as serious as in the United States or Germany, where the government was petitioned to 'take such measures as the budget allows for promoting a demand for labour'.[2]

British labour won a great legal triumph in 1875 with the repeal of the Criminal Law Amendment Act and the passage of the Employers' and Workmen's Act. At the same time limitation on hours of work and the employment of children in the mines (Act of 1872) were on a scale sufficient for owners to claim that costs had been raised 15 to 20 per cent.[3] In 1876 the minimum age of textile workers was raised to ten, and hours limited to fifty-seven per week.[4] These were concrete evidence of the long-run gains labour had made in the course of the previous boom.

3. The difficult downward adjustment of money wages continued in 1876. In coal, particularly, owners succeeded in forcing rates lower. The sinking of new shafts and various fuel-saving devices in iron had created 'over production':[5] collieries operated four days a week in the Leeds area, and in various districts wages were estimated at from 35 per cent. to 75 per cent. lower than in 1873.[6] But at the same time the Coal Mines Regulation Act was limiting the extent to which costs might be reduced,[7] so that 'colliery owners remember 1876 as profitless and unsatisfactory . . . one of three things is likely to happen—either wages must come down, coal must go up, or ruin and bankruptcy must overtake many coal-mining concerns'.[8]

---

[1] For example, see *Economist*, 1875, pp. 34–5. Also *Review of 1875*, pp. 1, 17.

[2] Ibid., p. 2. The German government decided to continue the state railway system in the face of falling revenues—'hope was expressed that the simultaneous commencement of these works would enable the iron and other manufacturing interests to take on their full sets of workmen'—an interesting early case of a public works programme designed to relieve unemployment.

[3] Idem.

[4] G. D. H. Cole, *A Short History of the Working-class Movement*, vol. ii, pp. 126–8.

[5] *Review of 1876*, p. 29.   [6] Ibid., p. 3.

[7] Ibid., pp. 48–9 for analysis of effects of Coal Mines Act.

[8] Ibid., p. 29. See also pp. 30–1.

In South Yorkshire 20,000 miners struck, causing estimated losses of £500,000 to the owners, £230,000 to the men, £120,000 to the railways. Strikes and wage cuts from 7 to 15 per cent. were reported from every district connected with the coal and iron industries.[1]

The *Review of 1876* reports also the failure of an attempt by the South Yorkshire Miners' Association to practise co-operative mining in Derbyshire.[2] The difficult environment for new enterprise proved too powerful, and the miners' association lost £31,000.

Although they commanded much attention and added measurably to the difficulty of adjustment, the strikes and drastic wage reductions were localized in the two basic capital trades. The general position of labour deteriorated slowly. Indoor pauperism rose slightly and unemployment increased; average money wages fell, and real wages (including unemployment) fell to the level of 1874. But the *per capita* indexes of general consumption and beer consumption both rose slightly.[3]

4. Strikes were considered 'one of the chief difficulties of 1877'.[4] One hundred and twenty-one strikes occurred: 70 in building (where activity was still great but orders falling), 21 in coal-mining, 23 in iron, 22 in wire and store work, 18 in textiles, and the remainder in 9 other trades.[5] Most of the strikes were begun with the tendering of notices to the men of wage decreases, although some of the building strikes took place on the men's demand for higher wages.[6]

---

[1] Idem, for Barnsley, Rotherham, Sheffield, and Cleveland. In the latter district the owners asked for a 15 per cent. wage reduction, arbitrators granted 7½ per cent. There was also a strike between Messrs. Doulton and the Bricklayers' Union (*Economist*, 1876, p. 1226). This strike, however, concerned not wages, but the use of higher-paid artisans to adorn buildings with terra-cotta decorations. This task required special talents. But the labourers objected, insisting that bricklayers were adequate for the task. The company pleaded that under the circumstances 'the public would be denied the advantage of having their buildings artistically embellished'. The *Economist* insisted that 'public interests are in the end best served by leaving buyer and seller to fight out their own battles'. It may be regarded as regrettable that posterity was not afforded a voice in this decision.   [2] *Review of 1876*, p. 3.

[3] See above, statistics at head of section.   [4] *Review of 1877*, p. 8.
[5] Idem, from *The Times* (4 January 1878), article by G. P. Bevan.
[6] Idem.

In Cornwall a bitter dispute arose when the china-clay industry, like various of the newspapers, refused to employ union members. 2,000 trades' unionists were discharged and riots produced a 'reign of terror'. The men, under advice from their secretary, finally admitted defeat and returned to their work as non-unionists. In this and other strikes black-legs—non-unionist and foreigners—were involved in the effort to break the hold of the unions.

In some cases arbitrators were called in and their decisions accepted. The machinery of collective bargaining was developing rapidly—arbitration, conciliation, and sliding scales.[1] The acceptance of collective bargaining, the fact that money wage reductions could be made without serious reduction in real wages, and the impartiality of arbitrators as evidenced in compromise decisions (and, even in depression, occasional decisions for the workers)—these were important background to the Lib.–Lab. attitude which was to dominate labour over the next decade.

The consistent viewpoint of the liberal *Economist* in these disputes is illuminating. Of the instruments of conciliation it wrote: 'all these devices to secure agreement between masters and men are laudable and often useful, but they are palliatives, and no more. Masters cannot give and men cannot obtain as wages more than the means of consumers voluntarily will afford'.[2] The commentator's earnest desire for the working classes to understand the mystic process of the market is further revealed in these observations on the South Wales area:[3]

One chief cause of the badness of trade there is the Great Strike of three months duration in the early part of 1873; resulting in most exhausting losses both to masters and men. That strike was considered to be one of the great achievements of trades' union leaders, as represented on the spot by Mr. Halliday. The present distress must be relieved within reason, but it will be a serious dereliction of duty on the part of the local clergy and gentry if the working people are not very distinctly instructed in the relation of cause and effect between the refusal to work for good wages in 1873 and the impossibility of obtaining any wages at all in 1877.

[1] *Review of 1877*, p. 8.   [2] Idem.   [3] Ibid., p. 9.

5. The general position of labour became seriously worse in 1878. Average unemployment, rising through the year, announced the final phase of the depression. Pauperism moved decisively upward, consumption of food and beer slumped. The only movement favourable to labour was a fall in retail prices, which, in the previous year, had been affected by particularly bad British harvests:[1]

1876	.	. 123·1
1877	.	. 127·0
1878	.	. 123·0
1879	.	. 115·7

'Of strikes in all trades and of all sizes, there have been incessant examples, with the almost uniform results of the defeat of the strikers.'[2] Chief among these was the dispute in North Lancashire, where in April 30,000 weavers were locked out upon refusing to accept a ten per cent. wage reduction. The men put forward the theory that trade was dull because the operators were producing too much, that short-time, restricted production, higher prices, and maintained wage rates were the proper remedy. They finally accepted defeat in late June after riots and bloodshed, disagreement among the strikers and operators themselves, and disgust among the general public.[3]

In coal-mining wage reductions had ceased at a point where 'miners are not now earning much more than half what they did in 1872–3'.[4] Employment continued irregular for those who worked, and non-existent for many: 'short hours of working which were formerly their own deliberate choice (1871–3), has become the miners' stern necessity . . . the labour market is sadly over-stocked.'[5]

---

[1] Layton and Crowther, op. cit., pp. 265–6. For detailed pauperism estimates showing its focus in the mining and manufacturing districts of the North, see *Economist*, 1878, p. 1348. In Caird's estimates (*Review of 1878*, p. 2) British harvests were badly defective in 1875–6–7, the latter year marking a low point in yield per acre, equalled only once previously from 1849.

[2] *Review of 1878*, p. 1.

[3] *Economist*, 1878, pp. 485–6, 490, 543–5, 639–40.

[4] *Review of 1878*, p. 28.

[5] Ibid., 1876, p. 27. The ready-made clothing trade complains of fallen sales due to diminished purchasing power caused by unemployment and the 'pinching effects of short time' (ibid., p. 34).

In iron, steel, and manufacturing districts, where a process of 'weeding out' had operated during the depression,[1] wages were lowered in many cases without opposition: 'the men were convinced that to hold out against a proposed reduction in the face of bad trade would be sheer madness, and have resumed their work with a reduction of wages.'[2]

6. The percentage unemployed among iron-founders moved as follows in 1879[3] (quarters):

I	.	23·9
II	.	23·7
III	.	22·2
IV	.	18·6

Iron-founders were the first labour group to feel the benefits of revival. By the end of 1879 other indexes of employment showed improvement, but average figures for the year reveal a sharp drop in employment, wages, and consumption. The consumption of beer (1900 = 100), which had fallen from 106·6 in 1873 to 101·9 in 1878, went to 88·6 in the following year.[4]

A fall in wages and employment during most of the year and a pick-up in the last quarter appears in the local reports as well. In the iron and leather goods' industries at Leeds 'advances were conceded the men'.[5] In the coal trade 'for the first nine months the men worked four days a week, but during the last three months the average has been from five to six days per week'.[6] In the carpet factories of Halifax work was at full time and Christmas holidays curtailed.[7] Wakefield reported, 'prices of manufacturing goods advanced, the demand for labour increased, and at the present time many of the local manufacturers, merchants, and tradesmen have some good orders on their books'.[8] The 'overflow' of orders from America immediately stimulated employment in

---

[1] *Review of 1878*, p. 35. [2] *Review of 1876*, p. 31.
[3] Thomas, op. cit. [4] Pigou, op. cit.
[5] *Review of 1879*, p. 27. The case of the Durham iron-workers illustrates clearly the pick-up. In January a 5 per cent. reduction was given the men after arbitration by Mr. Shaw-Lefevre; by the end of the year the company had voluntarily raised wages 12½ per cent. until the sliding scale came into operation in May 1880.
[6] Ibid., pp. 27–8.
[7] Ibid., p. 28. [8] Ibid., p. 29.

the iron industry, and by the turn of the year, in finished iron, cutlery, machinery, coal, and textiles as well.[1]

Workers in the building trade enjoyed no such revival. They underwent the kind of adjustment that their fellows in other industries experienced in the preceding years. Wages were lowered, trades' union regulations broken:[2] 'the operators are better to deal with and are willing to discard some of the regulations of their unions and to take employment which they formerly refused. The wages of operatives have been reduced. . . . Masons used to commence work at nine o'clock on Monday morning, but they now start at seven o'clock.'

---

[1] Ibid., pp. 28–9. See Sheffield report giving the order of response among industries to the revival stimulated by exports to America.

[2] Ibid., p. 28.

NOTE

THE PRINCIPAL STATISTICAL INDEXES

(All figures 1900 = 100, unless otherwise indicated)

1. The average Bank Rate. A. Sauerbeck, in the statistical summaries appearing annually in the *Journal of the Royal Statistical Society*, from 1886 on.

2. The average proportion of Bank reserves to liabilities, A. C. Pigou, *Industrial Fluctuations*, p. 397 (100 = 43 per cent.).

3. Rate on good three-months' bankers' bills in London. Pigou, op. cit., p. 399. From T. T. Williams, *J.R.S.S.*, 1912, pp. 382–4 ('The Rate of Discount and the Price of Consols').

4. The average Bank Reserve. *The Bankers' Almanac*, 1930–1, p. 2413 (100 = £21·45 million).

5. Net foreign gold movements (until 1881). *The Statistical Abstract for the United Kingdom*, 1881.

6. Net foreign and internal gold and Bank of England note movements. From W. Beach's quarterly statistics, *British International Gold Movements and Banking Policy, 1881–1913*, pp. 46–7, 62–3, derived from the *Economist* Annual Reviews.

7. Business Cycle Index. From D. Thomas's quarterly figures, *Journal of the American Statistical Association*, 1926, Table II, facing p. 61. The index is the standard deviation from a secular trend, with seasonal fluctuations eliminated. Items included from 1868 to 1881 are the value of exports and per cent. unemployed iron-founders. From 1881 railway freight receipts are included; from 1885 Sauerbeck's price index for 'All Materials'.

8. Yield on Consols. Calculated from average prices given in W. Page, *Commerce and Industry*, vol. ii, pp. 224–5.

9. Enterprise Index. A seven-year moving average of new joint-stock companies registered, D. H. Macgregor, *Enterprise, Purpose, and Profit*, p. 195 (100 = 109). From Company Statistics.

10. Number of new joint-stock companies registered and total new nominal share capital. Stat. Abst. for U.K., 1896 and 1881 (number new joint-stock companies, 100 = 4,966; new capital, 100 = £221·8 million).

10 a. Nominal capital per head of new joint-stock companies registered. W. Beveridge, *Unemployment*, pp. 42–3 (100 = £5·4 millions).

10 b. Capital issued and money calls. In England, England

and elsewhere, Total. *Economist* annual reviews and *Investor's Manual*. The category 'In England' refers to issues which were floated entirely in Britain. The category 'England and Elsewhere' refers to issues which were floated in part within Britain, in part on the Continent, in the U.S., or elsewhere.

11. New capital issues in the United Kingdom and capital exports. C. K. Hobson, *The Export of Capital*, p. 223 (new capital issues in U.K., 100 = £100·1 million; capital export, 100 = £31·2 million). Issues in the U.K. are from the *Economist*. The figure for 1900 is swollen by the government Boer War loans. Capital export is estimated by subtracting from a residual item in the balance of payments—capital and interest transactions— an estimate of income from abroad.

12. Industrial and fixed interest security prices. From K. C. Smith and G. F. Horne, London and Cambridge Economic Service, Memorandum no. 47, 'An Index Number of Securities, 1867–1914', pp. 4 and 5 for annual averages. In the annual figures, given at the head of Section 2, the base has been shifted from 1890 to 1900. When monthly averages are given in the text, the original figures are used. The industrial index contains securities' prices representing the following industries: coal, iron and steel, engineering, electrical equipment, textiles, food, drink, building and contracting materials, lighting and power, chemicals, stores, transport and communications, and a miscellaneous item (containing from 1867 Martin Hall, silversmiths; from 1875, Milner's Safes). The fixed interest index is based upon a simple arithmetic average of separate indexes for the following securities: Consolidated 3 per cent., $2\frac{3}{4}$ per cent., $2\frac{1}{2}$ per cent. Local Loans 3 per cent. Metropolitan Board of Works, $3\frac{1}{2}$ per cent. Consolidated. Birmingham 4 per cent. Debs. Gas and Water Annuities, $3\frac{1}{2}$ per cent. Stock. Manchester 4 per cent. Debs. L.N.W. Railway 4 per cent., 3 per cent. Debs.

13. Capital goods' and consumers' goods' production. W. Hoffmann *Weltwirtschaftliches Archiv*, Sept. 1934, pp. 383–98, 'Ein Index der industriellen Produktion für Grossbritannien seit dem 18. Jahrhundert'. Base year shifted from 1913 to 1900. The indexes are weighted averages of output in various branches of production. Textiles are included among consumers' goods, making the index abnormally sensitive to exports in that line.

14. Average unemployment. W. Beveridge, *Unemployment*, pp. 42–3, col. 3. A weighted average of trades' union unemployment in the following industries: building, woodworking and

furnishing, coal-mining, engineering, ship-building, other metal trades, printing and bookbinding, textiles, and miscellaneous. From the Second Series of Memoranda on British and Foreign Trade and Industry, p. 98.

15. Average unemployment of engineers, ship-builders, and metal-workers; of carpenters and joiners; of woodworkers; of printers and book-binders, Pigou, op. cit., pp. 381–2. From *Seventeenth Abstract of Labour Statistics and British Foreign Trade and Industry* (2nd series), pp. 89–92.

16. Exports of coal. Page, op. cit., p. 154 (100 = 46·1 million tons).

Exports of iron and steel. Idem. (100 = 3·45 million tons).

Exports of cotton piece goods. Ibid., p. 150 (100 = 5·03 bill. yds.).

Exports of machinery, mill-work, and motors. Ibid., pp. 137 and 139 (100 = £22·1 million), from *Stat. Abst. for U.K.*

17. Value of imports and exports. Page, op. cit., pp. 70–3 (imports 100 = £523 million; exports 100 = £354 million). From *Stat. Abst. for U.K.*

18. General prices (Sauerbeck Grand Total). Beveridge, op. cit., p. 456, col. 5. For construction of this index see W. Layton and G. Crowther, op. cit., Appendix A, pp. 225–35, or more completely, 'The Prices of Commodities and the Precious Metals', A. Sauerbeck, *J.R.S.S.*, Sept. 1886.

19. Textile, mineral, sundry material, and food wholesale prices. Sauerbeck annually in the *J.R.S.S.* from 1886. Base year shifted from 1866–7 to 1900.

20. Retail prices. Layton and Crowther, op. cit., pp. 265–6. From G. H. Wood, 'Some Statistics relating to Working-Class Progress since 1860', *J.R.S.S.*, Dec. 1899, pp. 655–6. For description of index see Layton and Crowther, op. cit., p. 232. Base year shifted from 1850 to 1900.

21. Production of pig iron. Page, op. cit., p. 180 (100 = 8·9 mill. tons).

Production of steel. Ibid., p. 181 (100 = 4·9 mill. tons).

Production of coal. Ibid., p. 180 (100 = 225 mill. tons).

From *Stat. Abst. for U.K.*

Net tonnage of new ships. *British Trade and Industry*, 1903, Table xxix, p. 379 (100 = 944 thousand tons).

Production of cotton yarn, G. T. Jones, *Increasing Returns*, pp. 275–6 (100 = 1·5 billion lb.).

22. Goods' traffic on British railways. Page, op. cit., p. 170 (100 = 425 million tons). From *Stat. Abst. for U.K.*

23. British harvest index, Sauerbeck annually in the *J.R.S.S.* from 1886. Base year shifted from 1866–7 to 1900.

24. General *per capita* consumption. Pigou, op. cit., pp. 387–8. From G. H. Wood, loc. cit., pp. 655–6 (100 = 100·8). The commodities included are wheat, cocoa, coffee, cotton, currants and raisins, meat, rice, sugar, tea, tobacco, wool, wine, spirits, and beer.

25. Beer consumed per head. Idem. (100 = 31·6 gallons.) From Beveridge (1909 ed.) op. cit., p. 42 until 1880; subsequently from (Cd. 2145), p. 15 and from the Seventeenth Abstract of Labour Statistics, p. 15.

26. Money wages, real wages (full work), and real wages, allowing for unemployment. Layton and Crowther, op. cit., pp. 265–6. From G. H. Wood, *J.R.S.S.*, 1909, 'Real Wages and the Standard of Comfort since 1850', pp. 91–103. Money wages are given for workmen of unchanged grade. No account is taken of the shift in the average towards higher grades. Real wages constitutes money wages corrected for retail price movements, including rent. The allowance for unemployment is made by subtracting the average per cent. unemployed from the index for real wages, full work (1850 = 100). The base year has been shifted from 1850 to 1900.

27. Wages bill allowing for unemployment. Pigou, op. cit., pp. 383–4. From A. Bowley, *E.J.*, Sept. 1904, 'Tests of National Progress', p. 459 (100 = £710 million). For description of index see p. 458.

28. Indoor pauperism per 1,000 population. *Stat. Abst. for U.K.* (100 = 23·8).

29. Trade-Unions Membership. Cole, G. D. H., *A Short History of the British Working-class Movement*, Appendix, vol. ii.

APPENDIX

MR. KALECKI ON THE DISTRIBUTION OF INCOME
1880–1913[1]

IN the course of a new formulation of the theory of distribution Mr. Kalecki has commented on income distribution in Great Britain, over the period 1880–1913, in terms very different from those used in Chapter IV, above.[2] He holds that the shape of the curve of short-period marginal costs is normally horizontal and equal to average variable costs, for firms, and, on average, for the economy as a whole; and that this fact 'eliminates factors other than the degree of monopoly from the mechanism of distribution'.[3] This analysis groups, on the one hand, payments for labour and raw materials, and on the other, payments in the form of depreciation, salaries, interest, and profits. Prices are assumed to be set with reference to short-period marginal costs. Since the latter are assumed constant, the elasticity of the demand curve facing the firm determines the portion of total income going to depreciation, salaries, interest, and profits. The 'degree of monopoly' is measured by the relation: price minus short-period marginal costs divided by price. The 'degree of monopoly', for a firm, over the whole relevant range of output, may be said to be constant, then, when average variable costs are constant and equal to short-period marginal costs; when prices are assumed to be determined uniquely with reference to short-period marginal costs; and when the demand curve it faces is of constant elasticity.

Against this theoretical background the period 1880–1913 is viewed as follows:[4]

'... the relative share of manual labour in the national income in Great Britain did not change appreciably between 1880 and 1913. It can be shown that the relation of the prices of "basic raw materials" to wage costs also did not alter in this period.

[1] *Essays in the Theory of Economic Fluctuations*, chap. i. For discussion of Kalecki's view of income distribution see J. M. Keynes, 'Relative Movements of Real Wages and Output', *Economic Journal*, Mar. 1939; P. T. Bauer, 'A Note on Monopoly', *Economica*, May 1941; R. H. Whitman, 'A Note on the Concept of "Degree of Monopoly"', *Economic Journal*, Sept. 1941, and Kalecki's *Comment*, April 1942; J. T. Dunlop, *Wage Determination under Trade Unions*, chap. viii, especially pp. 174 ff.   [2] Op. cit., p. 24.

[3] The author is indebted, in this Appendix, to helpful suggestions from Mr. W. M. Allen, Mr. J. R. Hicks, and Mr. C. J. Hitch.

[4] Ibid., pp. 32–3.

For this purpose we shall compare Sauerbeck's index of wholesale prices with Mr. Clark's index for the deflation of national
income [*National Income and Outlay*, p. 231]. It is clear that the
influence of raw material prices as compared with that of wage
costs is much greater upon the first index than upon the second.
Now between 1880 and 1913 both of these indices changed in
the same proportion (increased by 6 per cent.),[1] so that we can
conclude that the prices of "basic raw materials" relative to
wage-cost did not change. Obviously, then, the degree of
monopoly could not have undergone a substantial change
between 1880 and 1913 since with raw material prices unaltered
as compared with wage costs such a change would have been
reflected in the relative share of manual labour in the national
income.'

This quotation appears to imply a constant relation among the
variables determining the distribution of income over the period
1880–1913. In fact, the course of events yielded, almost certainly,
a modest favourable shift in the distribution of income for labour
until about 1900; and an unfavourable shift from that time to
1913.[2] The roughly similar relationships in income distribution
for the years 1880 and 1913 are the result of an historical accident
rather than of long-period stability. Before exploring further
Kalecki's historical judgement, however, it may be useful to
examine the theoretical framework which informs it.

[1] Clark's general price index, constructed for the purpose of calculating the
real national income from money income statistics, is not given, on the indicated
page (p. 231), for 1880, but for the average period 1877–85. The figures
apparently relevant to Kalecki's exposition are 97·8 for 1877–85; 100·0 for 1913,
a rise of about 2 per cent. rather than of 6 per cent. Sauerbeck's index of raw
material prices plus food prices also rises about 2 per cent. from the period
1877–85 to 1913; but raw material prices rise from 87 to 100, and food prices
fall from 116 to 100, within Sauerbeck's general index. See below, p. 230.

[2] It may, perhaps, be objected that the changes indicated in Bowley's income
distribution figures are too small to be regarded as 'significant'. This is, clearly,
a matter for judgement, although relatively small percentage changes in the
distribution of income can involve very substantial shifts in the sense of relative
well-being among the classes affected (see Dunlop, op. cit., p. 151, on the
'propensity to be surprised'). It should be noted, further, that the movements
of income distribution from 1880 to 1913 are not random, but exhibit a rising
trend for 'labour' to 1900, a falling trend to 1913 ('Wages and Income', tab. xiii,
p. 92). Especially if the initial date is moved back to 1873 the whole analysis
of these two trend periods attests to the existence of very strong divergent
pressures in each, operating on real wages and profit margins. These need
not have yielded, of course, changes in the distribution of shares in the national
income; although the sense of the full historical evidence is, strongly, that
they did.

II

The 'degree of monopoly' has been applied to both short-run and long-run problems of income distribution. The comments here are confined to its long-run applications.

The following observations can be made:

1. The empirical basis for the assumption that constant short-period marginal costs (equal to average variable costs) over relevant ranges of output is either normal for all units, or average behaviour for the economic system as a whole has not been established.[1]

2. The assumption that short-period marginal costs are alone relevant to price formation ignores the role of user cost, and the general importance of quasi-long-period and long-period considerations in the process of price formation.[2]

3. The meaning is ambiguous and the legitimacy doubtful of the summing-up process; that is, adding and averaging the 'degrees of monopoly' for firms to derive an average for the whole economy.[3]

4. The 'degree of monopoly', merging as it does a wide variety of economic phenomena, especially when applied to the economic system as a whole, and embracing factors which bear little relation to monopolistic practices, as commonly understood, is under suspicion of concealing more than it illuminates, and of constituting a misnomer.[4]

---

[1] Keynes, loc. cit., pp. 44–5; Bauer, op. cit., p. 201. On the evidence of British cyclical history it seems particularly doubtful that conditions of constant marginal cost obtained in the latter stages of major cycle expansions and the early stages of major cycle contractions. See above, Chapter II, especially pp. 52–3.

[2] Keynes, loc. cit., pp. 46–7; Bauer, op. cit., p. 198. See also R. L. Hall and C. J. Hitch, 'Price Theory and Business Behaviour', *Oxford Economic Papers*, May 1939.

[3] Bauer, op. cit., pp. 194–8. Bauer notes that agriculture operated under conditions of virtually perfect competition and that certain important forms of monopolistic arrangement cannot be effectively measured in terms of the elasticity of the demand curve facing the firm; e.g. conditions of competition in selling costs, where prices are fixed, and situations where the demand curve facing the firm is horizontal, and then vertically downward sloping, within the framework of a cartel agreement. Keynes, loc. cit., p. 43, points out that the concept is compromised because it does not include prices set outside the given economy. In the case of Britain, over the period 1880–1913, the movements of agricultural prices, with their major effects on real wages and on the yield from the significant proportion of British capital invested in agricultural land, make this objection particularly germane.

[4] In its portmanteau quality Bauer, op. cit., pp. 199 and 201, regards the

The weight of the objections to the 'degree of monopoly', as a sovereign concept in the analysis of trends in distribution, and especially to the assumptions which underly it, appears sufficient to justify maintaining the more conventional structure of analysis used above, in Chapter I. Kalecki's formulation does suggest, however, that interest may attach to a brief review of the factors affecting distribution, from 1873 to 1914, under two headings:

> first, relative movements of money wages, as against the prices of raw materials and foodstuffs; for the relationships among them remain, *deus ex machina*, an element in Kalecki's theory of distribution; and
>
> second, apparent changes in the competitive conditions confronting British industries and firms, over these years; this being quite distinct from the 'degree of monopoly', since the assumption of constant short-period marginal costs and of their unique relevance to price formation are not accepted.

III

Kalecki's analysis allows for changes in the proportion of total income going to wages either through changes in the 'degree of monopoly' or through changes in the prices of 'basic raw materials' in relation to 'wage costs'. 'Basic raw materials' include 'the products of agriculture and mining'. The long-term approximate stability of the proportion of the national income going to wages is attributed to fortuitous balancing movements in opposite directions of these two factors.[1]

In the period 1873–1900 analysed above (Chapter IV), the

'degree of monopoly' as akin to the Velocity of Circulation, in the Quantity Theory of Money. It is, perhaps, more directly related to 'surplus value', as used by Marx; see especially, 'Capital', vol. iii, chap. xiii, which is devoted to explaining how 'surplus value' may grow, for the economy as a whole, in the face of a falling rate of profit. An aspect of 4, above, is the view that the 'degree of monopoly' would rise automatically, with the increased capitalization of a firm, irrespective of the elasticity of the demand curve facing it (Bauer, op. cit., pp. 197–8; and especially Whitman, op. cit., pp. 263–4). If one is prepared to accept the concept of a fixed 'degree of monopoly' attaching to a firm—that is, a demand curve of constant elasticity, over its whole relevant portion—then the level of marginal costs, so long as they are constant and equal to average variable costs, and the degree of capitalization become irrelevant to the 'degree of monopoly'. Whitman does not make the assumption of a constant 'degree of monopoly' in exploring the effects of different degrees of capitalization, and for that reason his argument and Kalecki's do not meet.

[1] Kalecki, loc. cit., pp. 29–32.

rise in real wages is traced, proximately, to a lesser fall in money wages than in retail prices, from 1870–5 to 1880–5;[1] and from that time to 1900 money wages, in net, rose, while the downward trend in retail prices persisted.[2] These movements were certainly the operative means by which the share of labour in a rapidly rising real national income was maintained and even somewhat increased. The following table presents the evidence on price-wage rate movements, in relation to Clark's general price index, for deflation of national income figures, which Kalecki takes as standard:

Prices and Wages, 1870–1913

(1913 = 100)

	General prices (Clark)	General prices (Sauerbeck)	Food prices (S'r'k.)	Raw mat. prices (S'r'k'.)	Retail prices (Wood)	Money wages (Wood)	Real wages (Wood)	Net barter terms of trade (Taussig)
1870–6 .	118	119	130	112	112	78	74	—
1877–85 .	98	98	116	87	102	79	80	116 (1880–2)
1894–1903	92	78	86	73	85	90	103	97 (1899–1901)
1913 .	100	100	100	100	100	100	100	100 (1911–13)

The following emerges from an examination of these data:

1. The similar percentage movements of Sauerbeck's general price index and Clark's, as between 1877–85 and 1913, do not represent parallel movements over the whole period; Kalecki would, presumably, judge that either a decrease in the 'degree of monopoly' occurred, from 1877–85 to 1894–1903, and/or that the distribution of income must have shifted favourably to labour; and that an obverse movement or combination of movements must have occurred from that time until 1913.

2. The movements of food prices and of raw material prices, combined without discrimination in Kalecki's formulation, were in opposite directions, from 1877–85 to 1913; and moved at different rates, but in the same directions from 1877–85 to 1894–1903, and from 1894–1903 to 1913.

3. The movements of the net barter terms of trade were favourable to Britain to the turn of the century, slightly unfavourable thereafter.

In Kalecki's formulation the relative movements of money wages and prices must be given, from outside his analytic system. The conventional treatment of distribution, however, is designed

---

[1] See above, table, p. 90. [2] See below.

to include that relationship within the orbit of analysis. As indicated above,[1] an increase in the amount of capital used in conjunction with a given amount of labour would show itself, through changes in productivity, in a decline of prices in relation to money wage rates. A great deal of British investment, at home and abroad (e.g. in steamships and in American railways), was calculated to produce precisely the fall in food and raw material prices in Britain which in fact resulted. To the extent that changes in the relation between the price of 'basic raw materials' and wage rates are introduced, then, productivity remains an element in the analysis. Kalecki is pointing to the market mechanism by which changes in distribution are assumed to be achieved, in the conventional analysis.

Whether a relative change in prices and money wages results in a shift in the distribution of income, in the conventional analysis, depends, under rigid assumptions, on the elasticity of substitution, between labour and capital, a concept which measures the relative productivity of the changes in the amount of capital used in conjunction with labour. This consideration, too, appears to be implicit in Kalecki's formulation.

Over the period 1880–1913 he takes two facts to have been proved:

1. The distribution of the national income, as between manual labour and other recipients, was virtually constant;[2]
2. A price index containing a higher proportion of wage payments (Clark's) moves in parallel with one containing a lower proportion of wage payments (Sauerbeck's).

From these two facts, acceptable as between the two years 1880 and 1913, the conclusion is drawn that 'the degree of monopoly could not have undergone a substantial change between 1880 and 1913'.

The conventional theory of distribution, under the assumption of perfect competition, would account for the similar complex of relationships in 1880 and 1913 by assuming: (*a*) that the increase in the productivity of labour with respect to capital (i.e. economies in the use of labour per unit output) balanced out the rise in money wage rates relative to raw material prices; and (*b*), that

---

[1] Chap. III, especially p. 90.

[2] Kalecki, loc. cit., p. 14, excludes from the calculations on Britain the proportion of income derived from overseas, which rose considerably from 1880 to 1913 (see above, p. 104). Strictly speaking, he is concerned with the proportion of home-produced income going to 'manual labour', a difficult category to identify from available statistics.

the increase in the amount of capital was either proportional to the increase in real national income, with average yield on capital constant; or that the average yield on capital moved in such a way as to balance a disproportionate movement in the amount of capital, in relation to the real national income.

In his elliptical comments on the relative movements of Clark's and Sauerbeck's indexes Kalecki employs a conception much as in (*a*), above. The conclusion that 'the prices of "basic raw materials" relative to wage cost did not change', implies that if profits are a constant element in Clark's index of national output as a whole, and if the physical amounts of raw materials required to produce a given output are constant, then changes in the price of labour were exactly balanced by economies in the use of labour. This is, basically, a judgement about the productivity of investment over the period. It would appear that, having exorcised the conventional theory of distribution,[1] Kalecki re-invokes its concepts implicitly, in his analysis of the relation between the prices of raw materials and labour, and of the relative amounts of raw materials and labour required to produce a given output.

IV

It would, nevertheless, be agreed that conditions of perfect competition did not obtain universally in the British economy over the past century and a half, in markets for both commodities and for labour. Outside agriculture one form or another of market imperfection was, in fact, normal; and, moreover, the degree of monopoly as reflected in (but not uniquely measured by) earnings over and above average variable costs, varied over time. A legitimate question is, clearly, raised by relaxing the assumption of perfect competition often employed in formulations of the theory of distribution.

Chapters III, IV, and IX have referred extensively to the change in the demand conditions facing British industry after 1873. It was concluded that the severity of competition in many important branches of British industry increased; and that, with limited exceptions, such efforts as were made to lessen competition for the individual firm, by institutional monopoly arrangements, were, by and large, unsuccessful in their main aim. These efforts were regarded as symptomatic of the forces operating to depress

---

[1] Loc. cit., p. 24: 'Contrary to the usual view neither inventions nor the elasticity of substitution between capital and labour have any influence on the distribution of income.'

the level of profits rather than as a decisive factor in limiting the fall in prices, restricting output, and checking the mild inroads on the proportionate distribution of income to 'property', which was under way. Analytically, then, a decrease in the degree of monopoly, in the simple sense of increasingly severe competitive conditions, has already been adduced in the analysis of the Great Depression, as a factor producing the fall in prices and profit margins, and the tendency to introduce labour-saving machinery which characterize these years.

The changed competitive conditions after 1873 were related mainly to three large factors which, by changing the conditions of supply within industries, affected the earning power of individual firms:

(a) the rapid development outside Britain of capital industries, notably in the United States and Germany, and a loss of Britain's semi-monopolistic position with respect to railway iron and other capital goods;[1]

(b) decisions to expand industrial plant and other capacity (notably, coal-mines) during the upswing from 1868 to 1873 which, when fulfilled, left margins of unemployed plant, even at high levels of labour employment, and induced price-cutting competition;

(c) a continued high level of home investment, applying new techniques and processes (e.g. machine-tools, steel, electricity, steamships) which, while it helped sustain the level of employment, and increased productivity, made competition severe for those firms attached to the older techniques.

The analysis presented here would recognize that both cost and demand conditions for the individual firm tended to alter, over the Great Depression period; but would emphasize the extent to which phenomena on both sides of individual markets (i.e. costs and demand) were related to the character of previous and current investment outlays. As a factor affecting the demand situation confronting individual firms this view would attach a low relative importance to the institutional devices of monopoly which grew, to some extent, over these years; and, taking British

[1] A special case of (a) above, is the development of the farm lands, opened up in the years before 1873 in the U.S. Here the changed position for Britain appeared simply as a lower wheat price in British markets, rather than a demand curve of increased elasticity, since the world wheat price was set on the basis of virtually perfect competition.

industry in its full international setting, it would attach very considerable importance to changes in the number, capacity, and efficiency of firms within industries.

In the general reversal of the pattern of the British economy, from about 1900, it is likely that the demand situation confronting many British industries—especially in their export branches—notably improved. Although the number of formal monopolistic arrangements made in Britain increased, between 1900 and 1914, and although the fall in the average number of firms in industries continued, again the main impact of the changed position on demand probably arose from other factors.[1] The most important of these was the special ties that developed between Britain and the countries which borrowed British capital, including important areas within the Empire. There is no doubt that the complex of associations that accompanied the increased lending of capital abroad in this period gave a preferred position to the export industries of the lending countries, which modern theory would account an imperfection of competition, and which might be expressed as a demand curve for British exporters, less elastic than it would have been in the absence of British loans abroad.

In addition, it is possible that the relative falling off in domestic investment, over these years, may have removed or lessened the influence of (c), above, as a factor affecting the competitive position within Britain.[2]

V

The following conclusions, then, have been drawn:

1. Applied to available evidence on the period 1880–1913, serious doubt attaches to the applicability of Kalecki's three basic assumptions: namely, that short-period marginal costs can usefully be assumed constant and equal to average variable costs; that such costs are uniquely relevant to price formation; and that the position in individual firms can be

[1] For the limited state of development, powers, and efficiency of the principal cartels operating in Britain in this period see H. Levy, *Monopolies, Cartels, and Trusts in British Industry*, chaps. ix and x. The growing scope and power of trade unions was probably the most significant new monopoly element in the British economy over these years; and coupled with the new influence of labour in politics, which had consequences for the structure of taxation and income distribution, it is quite possible that this development prevented the shift in the distribution of income against labour from proceeding as far as, otherwise, it might have gone, from 1900 to 1914.

[2] See Chapter I, pp. 26–8, for a more general discussion of the course of the economy over the period 1900–14.

summed into a generalized 'degree of monopoly' concept for the economic system as a whole.

2. Kalecki's analysis of the relation between raw material prices and wage costs introduces considerations common to conventional distribution theory, including the relative productivity of investment.

3. Changes in the competitive position confronting British industries were a part of the process of price-wage-profit adjustment over the years 1880–1913; and in general, the severity of competition probably increased between 1873 and 1900, and probably decreased between 1900 and 1914.

4. Such changes were not primarily accomplished by alterations in institutional monopoly arrangements, which operated in a direction counter to the trend, from 1873 to 1900, and which perhaps somewhat reinforced the trend, from 1900 to 1914, although their impact on distribution, as between labour and capital, was not wholly in favour of the latter. The principal changes, except in the labour market, were accomplished by changes in the demand position of individual firms which stemmed from the supply position of industries, in their domestic and international settings, and from the consequences of British loans abroad.

The separation and measurement of the related forces which produced changes in the relations among prices, wages, and the yield on capital into elements affecting costs and elements affecting demand appears outside the scope of present data on the period. Kalecki's formulation, however, in no way proves that the nature and productivity of investment are irrelevant to the problem of income distribution over the period 1880–1913. On the contrary, the evidence available would suggest that changes in the severity of competition as well as in relative costs may have had a common basis in the character of investment outlays, over the period 1880–1913.

INDEX